Working with NHibernate 3.0

Benjamin Perkins

John Wiley & Sons, Inc.

Working with NHibernate 3.0

Published by
John Wiley & Sons, Inc.
10475 Crosspoint Boulevard
Indianapolis, IN 46256
www.wiley.com

Copyright © 2011 by John Wiley & Sons, Inc., Indianapolis, Indiana

ISBN: 978-1-118-11257-1

Associate Publisher	**Copy Editor**	**Vice President and Executive Publisher**
Jim Minatel	Luann Rouff	Neil Edde
Senior Project Editor	**Editorial Manager**	**Proofreader**
Ami Frank Sullivan	Mary Beth Wakefield	Nancy Carrasco
Technical Editor	**Production Manager**	**Indexer**
Stephen Bolen	Tim Tate	Robert Swanson
Production Editor	**Vice President and Executive Group Publisher**	
Daniel Scribner	Richard Swadley	

ABOUT THE AUTHOR

 **Benjamin Delcamp Perkins** is currently employed at ISOware, GmbH in Munich, Germany and has been working professionally in the IT industry for more than 16 years. He started computer programming with QBasic at the age of 11 on an Atari 1200XL desktop computer. He takes pleasure in the challenges trouble shooting technical issues offer and values the merit of a well written program. After successfully completing his military service and serving in the Gulf War of 1990, he received a Bachelor of Business Administration in Management Information Systems from Texas A&M University.

His roles in the IT industry have spanned the entire spectrum from programmer, to system architect, technical support engineer, to team leader and management. While employed at Hewlett-Packard, he received numerous awards, degrees, and certifications. He has a passion for technology and customer service. Benjamin enjoys sharing his C# and other programming experiences and has created many free training videos which are available on YouTube. He also has an active blog found at: www.thebestcsharpprogrammerintheworld.com.

"My approach is to write code with support in mind, and to write it once correctly and completely so we do not have to come back to it again, except to enhance it."

CONTENTS

Getting Started with NHibernate 3

My first experiences programming data-driven computer systems required registering COM objects with the `regsrv32.exe`, invoking the `Server.CreateObject` method to create an `ADODB.Connection` and `ADODB.Recordset`, and then using the `MoveFirst()`, `MoveLast()`, `MoveNext()`, and `MovePrevious()` methods that navigate, forward only, through the result set. At the time, the practice was groundbreaking technology. The ADO data access technique laid the foundation for the next advancement, which Microsoft released in late 2005, ADO .NET. In late 2005, Microsoft released the .NET Framework version 2.0. Programmers said goodbye to `regsrv32.exe`, COM, and a whole lot of other unwanted features of a nonmanaged code way of life.

ADO.NET provided programmers with an object-oriented, or component-oriented, approach to creating data-driven computer systems. Programmers were able to isolate the SQL queries from the database connection, and the business logic from the data implementation logic. This multi-layered capability greatly reduced the complexity and the unwanted side effects caused by changes, while increasing the speed with which new or enhanced features are introduced.

However, despite the many new features and advancements provided by ADO.NET, programmers still faced difficulties developing data-driven software applications, including the following:

➤ Using multiple database management systems (DB2, Oracle, SQL Server, etc.)

➤ Easily responding and adapting to changes in data structures

➤ Managing the connection between computer system and database

➤ SQL injection

> ➤ Database concurrency

> ➤ Performing complex SQL operations without specialized technical skills

The next generation of data-driven software solutions is upon us. This next generation is called *object-relational mapping,* or *ORM.* Programmers can now say goodbye to the data access layer and numerous SQL queries, to the methods returning data reader objects, and the writing of complex SQL queries. For programmers with many years of experience with large enterprise systems, moving from ADO to ORM is the equivalent of moving from COM to ADO.

NHibernate is a C# .NET port of the very popular Hibernate project for Java, which came into existence in 2001. For a number of years, both NHibernate and Hibernate were supported and managed by the same company, JBoss, Inc. (now part of Red Hat); however, as of 2006, NHibernate is totally managed by the user community.

Numerous ORMs are available. However, NHibernate is one of the most, if not the most, mature .NET open-source libraries available. It has a very active user community that drives new feature development and allows newcomers a place to ask technical or best practice questions.

The following sections cover how this new approach to data access resolves many of the challenges programmers and IT organizations face today. After a short introduction to ORM, you will learn:

> ➤ How to configure NHibernate

> ➤ The benefits of lazy loading

> ➤ How to configure `log4net`

> ➤ How to serialize NHibernate's startup

> ➤ Many other features and tips about NHibernate

WHAT IS AN ORM?

Object-relational mapping (ORM) is one of many techniques used to retrieve and modify data stored in a database. An ORM approach to a data solution requires that you view your data more as a group of objects than as a relationship between data tables. Take, for example, the SQL query shown in Listing 1-1, which joins two tables to get a `Guitar` type and model.

LISTING 1-1: A basic relational SQL query

```
SELECT
      g.TYPE, i.MODEL
FROM
      GUITAR g, INVENTORY i
WHERE
      g.ID = i.TYPEID
ORDEY BY
      g.TYPE;
```

This returns a list of `Guitar` types and their models to a result set that could then be displayed in a GUI. It's assumed that the two tables have a foreign key relationship between the `ID` on the `GUITAR` table and the `TYPEID` on the `Inventory` table. This is a standard relational database configuration.

If you wanted to implement a similar query using the `IQuery` (HQL) interface of NHibernate, it would look something like what is shown in the following code snippet:

```
Select g.Type, g.Inventory.Model from Guitar g order by g.Type
```

Notice how HQL enables programmers to state their queries in terms of objects in the same way SQL enables them to state queries in terms of relational data.

Again, the preceding query returns a list of `Guitar` types and their models to a result set that could then be displayed in a GUI. An assumption that the two tables have a relationship defined on the database may or may not be correct. However, it is certain that the relationship has been defined in the program and that the `Guitar` class contains an instance of the `Inventory` class.

As the preceding query shows, an ORM like NHibernate provides the capability to navigate a data structure using dot notation instead of complicated `join` or embedded SQL clauses. Once the object relational model has been designed and built, or the mapping of an existing relational database to objects completed, you can say farewell to SQL. As a result of using an ORM, a C# programmer no longer needs to write SQL and can focus on writing reusable and maintainable code.

It is a mistake to believe that by implementing an ORM solution you no longer need qualified database administrators. It could result, however, in needing fewer of them or less of their time. This reduction of technical resources is a direct result of adding an additional layer of abstraction, NHibernate, between a skilled programmer and the database. NHibernate enables developers to work in the area of system development for which they are most skilled, while delegating the details of query construction to the ORM, rather than co-opting developers into writing complex queries in SQL for which they aren't adequately trained and skilled. By reducing the technical skill set required to create a program, an additional reduction in the amount of time required to build, modify, and maintain it is realized.

CREATING A SAMPLE PROJECT: THE GUITARSTORE

A good way to learn a new technology is to create something with it. This chapter walks through the creation of a small program based on Windows Presentation Foundation (WPF). This program enables the user to insert, update, select, search, and delete guitar inventory. Figure 1-1 and Figure 1-2 show the final `GuitarStore` WPF windows.

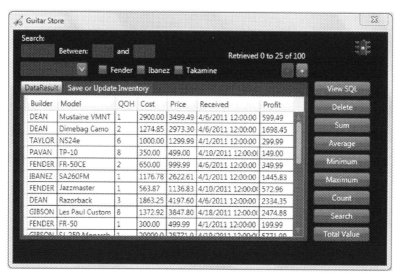

FIGURE 1-1

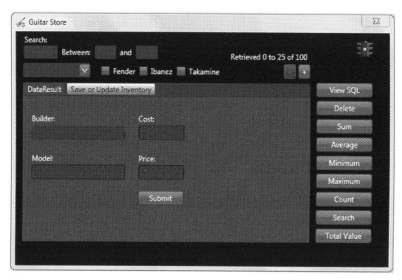

FIGURE 1-2

Project Requirements

In our example scenario, imagine you have been contacted by a small music store that specializes in selling guitars. The owner has requested that you create a system that enables them to track their guitar inventory. The requirements for the database include the following:

➤   Retrieve a list of all guitars ordered by the builder.

➤   Retrieve the total value of merchandise by guitar type.

> Search for guitar models.

> Retrieve 25 records per query and allow paging.

> Store an audit of inventory deletions.

> View details of each guitar in inventory.

> Insert new guitars into the database.

These requirements are used throughout this book to show many of NHibernate's capabilities.

Creating the GuitarStore Solution

The example Visual Studio solution will contain three C# projects:

> A WPF project that presents the data to the user

> A class library that uses NHibernate to interact with the database

> A console application for testing

Creating the GuitarStore WPF Project and Solution

Using Visual C# 2010 Express, create and save a new project called `GuitarStore`. Add an `app.config` file, which is used to store NHibernate and `log4net` configurations. Figure 1-3, shows the `GuitarStore` solution.

FIGURE 1-3

 NOTE *This WPF program uses the* `ExpressionDark.xaml` *theme. It can be downloaded from SourceForge at this address:* `http://wpf.codeplex.com/wikipage?title=WPF Themes`.

Creating the NHibernate.GuitarStore Class Library

Add a class library to project to the solution by following these steps:

1. Right-click on the `GuitarStore` solution and add a new class library project called `NHibernate.GuitarStore`.

2. Delete the auto-generated `Class1.cs` file, as it is not used.

3. Add three directories to the class library project named `Common`, `Mapping`, and `DataAccess`.

These directories are used to group the class, mapping, and data access files together, respectively. The grouping of like files into directories simplifies and sustains the ongoing development and support of a program. As the program grows in size and complexity, having a logical structure that team members can quickly understand and use is a necessity. Figure 1-4 shows the modified `GuitarStore` solution.

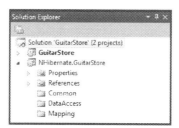

FIGURE 1-4

Note the following main points:

➤   The \\`Common` directory contains all the class files used to store the data retrieved from the database.

➤   The \\`DataAccess` directory contains all the methods that interact with the NHibernate methods and your classes.

➤   The \\`Mapping` directory contains the NHibernate XML mapping files.

Creating the Console Application

The console application provides a quick and easy way to test the NHibernate interface methods contained within the `NHibernate.GuitarStore` class library. Right-clicking on the `GuitarStore` solution and adding a new console application project named `NHibernate.GuitarStore.Console` results in the solution shown in Figure 1-5, which shows the three projects contained within `GuitarStore`.

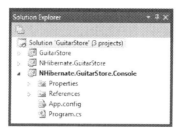

FIGURE 1-5

Add an `app.config` file to the console project to store NHibernate and log4net configurations. More details are provided in the sections titled "Using an app/web.config File" and "Creating a Console Application for Testing" later in this chapter.

Creating the Database

A database is used to store the guitar inventory used by the program created in this book. In this section, you will perform two actions:

1. Create the SQL Server 2008 database.

2. Create the Guitar and Inventory tables.

Creating a SQL Server 2008 Database

Open and connect to SQL Server Management Studio. Right-click the Database folder, select New Database . . ., and create a database named **myGuitarStore**. Figure 1-6 shows the newly created database.

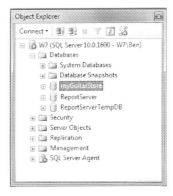

FIGURE 1-6

Creating the Guitar and Inventory Tables

Expand the myGuitarStore database, right-click the Tables directory, select New Table..., and create the Guitar and Inventory tables, as shown in Figure 1-7.

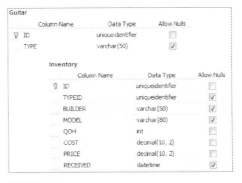

FIGURE 1-7

While in design mode of the `Inventory` table, add the foreign key relationship between the `Guitar` and `Inventory` tables by selecting Table Designer menu item ⮕ Relationships. Figure 1-8 shows the windows required to add the foreign key.

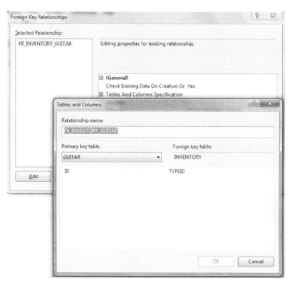

FIGURE 1-8

Understanding the Guitar and Inventory Tables

NHibernate makes it unnecessary for developers to create a data access layer (DAL) containing large numbers of SQL queries. Nor must developers write database SQL queries. From this point on, data can be retrieved from the `Guitar` and `Inventory` tables, shown in Figure 1-9, after implementing one of the many NHibernate interfaces.

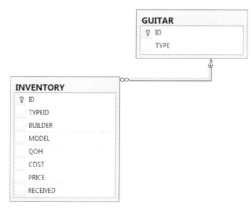

FIGURE 1-9

Table 1-1 describes the `Guitar` and `Inventory` tables that exist in the myGuitarStore database, and Table 1-2 provides the definition.

TABLE 1-1: Database Tables

TABLE NAME	DESCRIPTION
GUITAR	The type of guitar (electric, acoustic, etc.)
INVENTORY	Quantity of each guitar type in stock, plus other details

TABLE 1-2: Guitar Table Definition

COLUMN	TYPE	NULLABLE	DESCRIPTION
ID	uniqueidentifier	False	Primary key, GUID
TYPE	varchar(50)	False	Type of guitar (electric, acoustic, bass, etc.)

`Guids` are used as the primary keys for the tables; and as previously mentioned, the foreign key relationship is between the `Guitar.ID` and the `Inventory.TYPEID`. You can use almost any database to create these tables. You need only to confirm that NHibernate contains the driver for it. You can do this by looking within the `NHibernate.Driver` namespace source code. All the standard DMBSs are supported, including Oracle, SQL Server, MySQL, DB2, ODP.NET, SQLite, and so on. Even ODBC and OLEDB connections are supported.

Table 1-3 describes the column data types, and indicates whether a null value is allowed.

TABLE 1-3: Inventory Table Definition

COLUMN	TYPE	NULLABLE	DESCRIPTION
ID	uniqueidentifier	False	Primary key, GUID TYPEID
TYPEID	uniqueidentifier	False	Foreign key to Guitar table
BUILDER	varchar(50)	True	Manufacturer of the guitar (Fender, Gibson, Taylor, etc.)
MODEL	varchar(80)	True	Model of the guitar
QOH	int	False	Quantity on hand
COST	decimal(10,2)	False	Price paid for the guitar
PRICE	decimal(10,2)	False	Price to sell guitar to customer
RECEIVED	datetime	True	Date the guitar is received for resale

> **WARNING** *There is some debate about using GUIDs as the primary keys on tables. The argument is related to two main issues. The first is the size of the GUID and the space it occupies on the hard drive, which is 36 bytes, or 32 digits with 4 dashes. Therefore, a table with 100,000 rows requires 3.6MB of space just for the primary key. The second issue is index fragmentation. However, NHibernate provides a sequential GUID (*`guid.comb`*) id generator that prevents this fragmentation.*

CONFIGURING NHIBERNATE

Configuring NHibernate requires a number of actions:

- ≫ Download and install NHibernate.
- ≫ Create the class files.
- ≫ Create the mapping files.
- ≫ Create an `NHibernateBase` class, to centralize data access. (This is recommended but not required.)
- ≫ Configure the `SessionFactory`.

Downloading and Installing NHibernate

Start by downloading the current version of NHibernate. The `GuitarStore` program uses version `NHibernate-3.X.X.GA-bin`, which is downloadable from `http://nhforge.org`.

Figure 1-10 shows the extracted list of the NHibernate binary files from the downloaded zip file. The files are copied into a single directory on a development computer. If you are part of a development team or the lead developer, it is a good idea to place the NHibernate files your team references in a specific location. Everyone should use the same group of files. Instead of hosting the entire NHibernate download, supply only the binaries you or the team needs to successfully utilize the NHibernate interface.

Name	Date modified	Size	Type
NHibernate.dll	4/17/2011 9:07 AM	3,766 KB	Application extension
log4net.dll	3/20/2011 5:05 PM	264 KB	Application extension
Iesi.Collections.dll	4/17/2011 9:07 AM	32 KB	Application extension

FIGURE 1-10

You need to add the preceding NHibernate binaries to all three projects in the `GuitarStore` solution by right-clicking the `References` folder and selecting Add Reference. Then select the Browse tab, navigate to where the binary files are stored, select them, and press OK.

Creating the Class Files

Now that the database and the `GuitarStore` solution are created, it's time to create the classes that store the data. The first step in the process is to create a class file (.cs) for each table in the domain.

> **NOTE** *There are tools that can automate the mapping of your database entities. In this example, you perform the mapping manually, but if your database has a large number of tables and relationships, you should consider using an automated approach. Fluent NHibernate is one such tool, which is found here:* `http://fluentnhibernate.org`.

Building the Common/class.cs Files

The first class you need to create is the `Inventory.cs` class. Within the `NHibernate.GuitarStore` project, right-click the `Common` directory, then select Add ➪ Class . . ., enter **Inventory.cs** ➪ Add.

Listing 1-2 shows the code for the `Inventory` class. Notice that all properties are preceded by a virtual declaration. This is required in order to use the lazy loading feature of NHibernate. As you can see, NHibernate does not require inheritance from a base class or implementation of any interfaces to utilize its features. Instead, NHibernate creates a *proxy* of the class. In this context, an NHibernate proxy is an inherited type of the `Inventory` class (sometimes referred to as an *entity*). The `Inventory` class is considered the base class to NHibernate's proxies. At application startup, NHibernate inherits and overrides the class, adding the required logic to support lazy loading. Lazy loading is covered in more detail later in this chapter.

LISTING 1-2: Inventory.cs

```
namespace NHibernate.GuitarStore.Common
{
    public class Inventory
    {
        public Inventory() { }

        public virtual Guid Id { get; set; }
        public virtual Guid TypeId { get; set; }
        public virtual string Builder { get; set; }
        public virtual string Model { get; set; }
        public virtual int? QOH { get; set; }
        public virtual decimal? Cost { get; set; }
        public virtual decimal? Price { get; set; }
        public virtual DateTime? Received { get; set; }
    }
}
```

Notice that a nullable `DateTime?` value is used to define the `Received` property. This is because in .NET, the `System.DateTime` is a value type and therefore cannot be null. However, a `DateTime` value within a database table can be null. If `Received` is not defined as nullable, attempting to load a null into that property results in a `PropertyValueException`, which needs to be handled appropriately.

The differences between value types and reference types are not covered here, but this aspect of NHibernate makes it important that a programmer understand them.

All value types should be implemented as nullable or you need to ensure that the values on the database do not allow nulls. Table 1-4 lists the common .NET value types to which you should pay attention.

TABLE 1-4: Nullable .NET Value Types

TYPE	DECLARATION
System.DateTime	DateTime?
System.Int32	int?
System.Double	double?
System.Boolean	bool?
System.Char	char?
System.Decimal	decimal?

Note the use of the auto-implemented property declaration, which was new in C# 3.0. This isn't required for NHibernate, but it is a good coding practice. Using the `{ get; set; }` format makes the code more legible. This is important because these classes and mapping files (mapping files will be created in the next section) do not change often, nor do developers need to access them very often. After the mapping has been completed, accessing them again is unlikely—only if the data structure changes or a new persistent object is required, as in the `Guitar` class covered next. Hence, making them compact and clear ensures they are quickly and clearly understood when a modification needs to be made later.

 WARNING *When using NHibernate's property-level accessor mappings, using the underlying private field value (instead of going through the `{get; set;}` property) will circumvent lazy loading and produce unexpected results. Consider this another reason to use auto-implemented or automatic properties.*

At this point, create the `Guitar.cs` class in the same way the `Inventory.cs` class was created. Name the new class `Guitar.cs`. The `Guitar` class, shown in Listing 1-3, contains an enumerable list of the `Inventory` class called `Inventory`. Access to this list returns the inventory data for the specific Guitar type. It is important to set lazy loading to true; otherwise, when loading the data into the Guitar class, the Inventory is loaded, too, even if it is not needed.

LISTING 1-3: Guitar.cs

```
namespace NHibernate.GuitarStore.Common
{
    public class Guitar
    {
        public virtual Guid Id { get; set; }
        public virtual string Type { get; set; }

        IList<Inventory> Inventory { get; set; }
    }
}
```

Creating the Mapping Files

So far, the database has been created, you have built a solution with three projects, and you have programmed your class files. Now it is time to create the mapping files.

Mapping files (*.hbm.xml) are used by NHibernate to correlate the classes and properties in the persistent objects with the tables and fields in the relational database. This information is then used by NHibernate to generate the SQL needed to perform Select, Insert, Update, and Delete operations for the computer program.

Installing the NHibernate XML Schema Templates

The release of NHibernate 3.0 includes two XML schema files. These files enable you to use IntelliSense during the creation of the mapping files, which allows the Visual Studio XML editor to display syntax errors as you work in the mapping files. These files, in combination with IntelliSense, provide a list of allowable NHibernate mapping elements and attributes, as shown in Figure 1-11, which you may find extremely useful.

FIGURE 1-11

Installing the NHibernate XML schema templates requires Visual Studio Professional or higher. The Schemas menu item is found within the XML menu. Selecting Schemas opens the XML Schemas window shown in Figure 1-12.

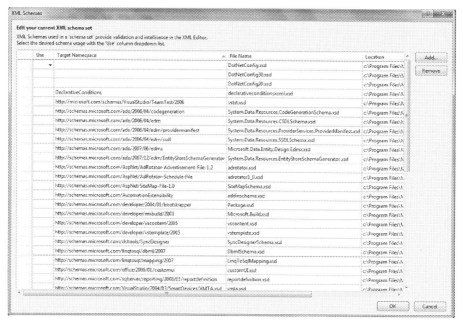

FIGURE 1-12

Selecting the Add button opens a browse window that you can use to navigate to the two NHibernate XML schema templates (.xsd) shown in Figure 1-13. Select the templates and then click OK.

nhibernate-mapping	4/13/2011 2:16 PM	66 KB	XML Schema File
nhibernate-configuration	3/24/2011 7:17 PM	10 KB	XML Schema File

FIGURE 1-13

Building the Mapping/class.hbm.xml Files

NHibernate uses the mapping files to gather the required information to create a SQL query. The mapping file contains the class and assembly where the data is stored once retrieved from the database.

To create a mapping file, right-click on the Common directory within the NHibernate.GuitarStore project ⇨ Add ⇨ New Item. Scroll down to the bottom of the window and select XML File, enter **Inventory.hbm.xml** ⇨ Add. Lastly, add the mapping configuration, as shown in Listing 1-4.

LISTING 1-4: Inventory.hbm.xml

```
<?xml version="1.0" encoding="utf-8" ?>
<hibernate-mapping xmlns="urn:nhibernate-mapping-2.2"
                   assembly="NHibernate.GuitarStore">
  <class name="NHibernate.GuitarStore.Common.Inventory,
```

```
                                                     NHibernate.GuitarStore"
          table="INVENTORY">
     <id        name="Id"       column="ID"       type="System.Guid" />
     <property name="TypeId"    column="TYPEID"   type="System.Guid" />
     <property name="Builder"   column="BUILDER"  type="System.String" />
     <property name="Model"     column="MODEL"    type="System.String" />
     <property name="QOH"       column="QOH"      type="System.Int32" />
     <property name="Cost"      column="COST"     type="System.Decimal" />
     <property name="Price"     column="PRICE"    type="System.Decimal" />
     <property name="Received" column="RECEIVED" type="System.DateTime" />
  </class>
</hibernate-mapping>
```

The assembly is defined within the `hibernate-mapping` element using the `assembly` attribute. Within the `class` element, you need to provide the fully-namespaced type-name for the class (optionally, include its containing assembly name) and the database table from which the data is persisted. The `id` element contains the primary key of the table that is identified by the `table` attribute of the `class` element.

 NOTE *If you provide an assembly attribute value for the* `<hibernate-mapping>` *element, you only need to provide the namespace in the* `<class>` *element and not its assembly.*

Both the `id` and `property` elements contain a `name`, `column`, and `type` attribute. When using the default mapping strategy, as is being done in the `GuitarStore` example, the value provided for the `name` attribute must match the `property` name defined within your class, as shown in Listing 1-5.

LISTING 1-5: Matching C# code with the XML mapping

```
     <property name="Received" column="RECEIVED" type="System.DateTime" />
public virtual DateTime? Received { get; set; }
```

The `name` attribute is case-sensitive. If you try to run your program with misspelled or wrongly cased properties in your mapping file, you will receive an exception. The most common of these is `PropertyNotFoundException`, shown in Figure 1-14. If you receive this exception, check your spelling.

> ⚠ **PropertyNotFoundException was unhandled**
>
> Could not find a getter for property 'ReceiveD' in class 'GuitarStore.Common.Inventory'

FIGURE 1-14

The `column` attribute defines the name of the database column to which this property is associated. This valuable feature enables you to have a property name in your code that is different from the name of the column. For example, perhaps in some situations you need to reference the BUILDER database column as Manufacturer, as shown in Listing 1-6. In this case, you can achieve that by simply setting the name attribute to Manufacturer and the column attribute to BUILDER. Then, when the class is populated with data, the BUILDER database column value can be referenced via a property named Manufacturer.

LISTING 1-6: Matching column and name properties in the mapping XML file

```
<property name="Manufacturer"  column="BUILDER"  type="System.String" />

list.Add(item.Manufacturer);
```

Note that by default the mapping files assume that the table name is the same as the class name and the fields are the same name as their properties. You only need to provide the optional values for table or column if the names are something other than what exists in the database.

The last attribute discussed here is the type attribute. NHibernate provides an interface to create custom types, such as the currency type, which is covered in Chapter 5, "Managing State and Saving Data." The type attribute is not required because NHibernate uses *reflection*, which enables the reading of metadata at runtime, to determine the type into which it needs to convert the database data value. However, it is a good practice to use it. The more information you provide, the better; and if you need to implement a custom type, then it easily falls into place with your other mapped properties.

Now that the Inventory mapping is complete, the Guitar mapping file, shown in Listing 1-7, must be created by the programmer. Perform the same actions you took to create the Inventory.hbm.xml file. The Guitar table is referenced and uses the Guitar.cs file to store the retrieved data. Recall within the Guitar class definition where an IList<Inventory> collection was added to store the Inventory per Guitar type. A <bag> element is used to store the Inventory collection.

LISTING 1-7: Guitar.hbm.xml

```
<?xml version="1.0" encoding="utf-8" ?>
<hibernate-mapping xmlns="urn:nhibernate-mapping-2.2"
assembly="NHibernate.GuitarStore">
  <class name="NHibernate.GuitarStore.Common.Guitar, NHibernate.GuitarStore"
            table="GUITAR">
    <id name="Id"          column="ID"        type="System.Guid" />
    <property name="Type"        column="TYPE"      type="System.String" />
    <bag name="Inventory"   table="INVENTORY" lazy="true">
      <key column="TYPEID" />
      <one-to-many class="NHibernate.GuitarStore.Common.Inventory" />
    </bag>
  </class>
</hibernate-mapping>
```

Several different methods for storing a collection using NHibernate are available, as described in Table 1-5.

TABLE 1-5: NHibernate Collection Options

STORAGE TYPE	DESCRIPTION
`<set>`	Unordered and unique
`<bag>`	Unordered and non-unique; for example, books in a library
`<list>`	Positioned and non-unique; for use when order has meaning
`<map>`	Unordered and key/value pairs
`<idbag>`	Not recommended for use

The `NHibernate.GuitarStore` class library should now contain two classes and two mapping files. The project should now resemble what is shown in Figure 1-15.

FIGURE 1-15

Deploying the Mapping Files

There are two ways to deploy the XML files:

➤ As an embedded resource

➤ As separate XML files

Deploying the mapping files as embedded resources requires setting the Build Action file property to Embedded Resource, as shown in Figure 1-16. By doing this, the mapping files are packaged with the assembly, which prevents programmers and system administrators from tampering with them. It also reduces the complexity of deployment because you have fewer files to install.

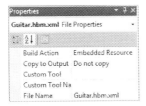

FIGURE 1-16

It is also possible to deploy the mapping files as separate files alongside the assembly. This method facilitates being able to adjust your mapping as needed after the program has been compiled. Both approaches are common as they serve different use cases. For simplicity, the GuitarStore program uses the embedded approach to deploying the mapping files.

Mapping by Code

With the release of NHibernate 3.2 comes the concept of mapping by code. The concept relies on the ClassMapping class found within the NHibernate.Mapping.ByCode.Conformist namespace. If you choose to map your database using this method, you do not need to manually create hbm.xml files. As well, you have the flexibility to decide for yourself how to organize the mappings — for example within the same class file (class-by-class).

To map the Inventory class using the class-by-class approach, open the Inventory.cs file found within the Common directory of the NHibernate.GuitarStore project and modify it, as shown in Listing 1-8.

LISTING 1-8: Mapping the Inventory class by code

```
using NHibernate.Mapping.ByCode.Conformist;

namespace NHibernate.GuitarStore.Common
{
  public class Inventory
  {
    public Inventory() { }

    public virtual Guid Id { get; set; }
    public virtual Guid TypeId { get; set; }
    public virtual string Builder { get; set; }
    public virtual string Model { get; set; }
    public virtual int? QOH { get; set; }
    public virtual decimal? Cost { get; set; }
    public virtual decimal? Price { get; set; }
    public virtual DateTime? Received { get; set; }
  }

  public class InventoryMap : ClassMapping<Inventory>
  {
    public InventoryMap()
    {
      Id<Guid>(x => x.Id, map =>
      {
        map.Column("ID");
      });
      Property<Guid>(x => x.TypeId, map => map.Column("TYPEID"));
      Property<string>(x => x.Builder, map => map.Column("BUILDER"));
      Property<string>(x => x.Model, map => map.Column("MODEL"));
      Property<int?>(x => x.QOH, map => map.Column("QOH"));
```

```
            Property<decimal?>(x => x.Cost,  map => map.Column("COST"));
            Property<decimal?>(x => x.Price, map => map.Column("PRICE"));
            Property<DateTime?>(x => x.Received, map => map.Column("RECEIVED"));
        }
    }
}
```

The implementation of this method is covered in the "Using a Strongly Typed Configuration" section.

Understanding the property-ref Attribute

The property-ref attribute, shown in Listing 1-9, is worth a mention. In some legacy databases, relationships have been built between tables without using a foreign key. That means the connection between the tables is not built on a primary-key-based relationship. Recall the creation of the bag element in the Guitar.hbm.xml file, as shown previously in Listing 1-7.

The Inventory.TYPEID is the foreign key link to the ID on the Guitar table. This relationship is defined via the column attribute value within the key element. However, if you were required to connect your tables using a column value that is not the primary one, your mapping bag element may resemble something like what is shown in Listing 1-9.

LISTING 1-9: Mapping a property-ref attribute

```
<bag name="Inventory"  table="INVENTORY" lazy="true">
  <key column="ID"          property-ref="OID" />
  <one-to-many class="GuitarStore.Common.Inventory" />
</bag>
```

This configuration represents an ID on the Inventory table as the pseudo-foreign key with the OID on the Guitar table. The OID is not the primary key on the Guitar table. Nonetheless, when the bag is persisted, the Inventory.ID value is used as the foreign key link to the Guitar.OID column.

Configuration Techniques

One of NHibernate's best characteristics is the many different types of database management systems (DBMSs) it can support. DBMSs such as Oracle, Microsoft SQL Server, Sybase, MySQL, and so on, are quickly up and running by simply using the correct NHibernate dialect and driver. If your program interacts with different database management systems, then it is good practice to configure your installation in an app.config or web.config file. Conversely, if your program employs a single database management system, then you will be interested in a cool new feature in version 3 of NHibernate: support for a *strongly typed configuration*, which uses a number of hard-coded values.

In addition to an overview of the Configuration and SessionFactory classes, this section describes two types of NHibernate configuration techniques: one approach that is easily changed, and another hard-coded approach that uses the strongly typed dialect and driver within the code base.

TIP *Because it is possible to mix and match both code-based configuration and configuration files, you can add configuration values that change to the configuration file, and the values that will not change can be hard-coded.*

Understanding Configuration and the SessionFactory

The `NHibernate.Cfg.Configuration` class is an initialize-time object that is used to store properties and map documents for use by the `NHibernate.ISessionFactory` interface. The minimum properties required to build a `SessionFactory` are defined in Table 1-6. In most cases, a program creates a single `Configuration`, builds a single `SessionFactory`, and then instantiates `Sessions` that manage the client requests.

TABLE 1-6: SessionFactory Required Properties

NAME	EXAMPLE VALUE
Dialect	NHibernate.Dialect.MsSql2008Dialect
DriverClass	NHibernate.Driver.SqlClientDriver
ConnectionString	Database-specific connection information
ConnectionProvider	NHibernate.Connection.DriverConnectionProvider
ProxyFactory	NHibernate.ByteCode.Castle.ProxyFactoryFactory

NOTE *With the release of NHibernate 3.2, the* `ProxyFactory` *is no longer a required property, as there is now a default proxy. However, versions prior to 3.2 require this property.*

Within the `NHibernate.Cfg.Environment.cs` file you can find all the properties that can be set via the `Configuration` class. The following list defines and explains each of these required properties:

➤ **Dialect** — Each DBMS has its own dialect, which means that although the majority of the language is the same across databases, it contains some unique terms. For example, Oracle has a keyword `rownum`, but there is no direct equivalent in Microsoft SQL Server, even though the latter DBMS also provides a way to achieve the same effect using a different method. There are also differences between versions of the same DBMS. Choosing the correct dialect for the driver helps to manage these differences within the specific DBMS only.

➤ **DriverClass** — This specifies the driver that is used to connect and interact with a specific database. These classes are responsible for interacting on behalf of NHibernate with each of the ADO.NET drivers that are often provided by the individual database vendors — for example, `SqlClientDriver` for SQL Server or `OracleDataClientDriver` for ODP.NET.

➤ **ConnectionString** — This defines the data source. It generally includes the server name; the initial catalog, which is the name of the database on the server; and the user id and password. Examples for Oracle and SQL Server are shown in Table 1-7.

➤ **ConnectionProvider** — The `DriverConnectionProvider` is an interface that manages the opening and closing of database connections. If the requirements state that connections to the database must be audited, it is possible to implement an application-specific `ConnectionProvider` and override the methods within the interface to perform the logic. This is similar to Interceptors, which are discussed later in this chapter.

➤ **ProxyFactory** — This is the proxy class used for lazy loading. In the `GuitarStore` program, the `Castel` proxy is implemented. Three different proxies are provided and required only with NHibernate 3.1 and earlier:

  ➤ `NHibernate.ByteCode.Castle.ProxyFactory`

  ➤ `NHibernate.ByteCode.LinFu.ProxyFactory`

  ➤ `NHibernate.ByteCode.Spring.ProxyFactory`

TABLE 1-7: ConnectionString Examples

DBMS	Connection String
MS SQL Server 2008	"Data Source=PC-W7;Initial Catalog=myGuitarStore;Integrated Security=True"
Oracle 11g	"user id=*****;password=*****;data source=(DESCRIPTION =(ADDRESS=(PROTOCOL=tcp)(HOST=192.168.1.1)(PORT=1521)) (CONNECT_DATA=(SERVICE_NAME=ora11g)))"

Since the release of NHibernate 3.2, the proxy components are no longer distributed nor required. Instead, a `DefaultProxyFactory` class is utilized, which is found in the `NHibernate.Proxy` namespace.

Creating an NHibernate Base Class

Add a new class file to the `DataAccess` directory within the `NHibernate.GuitarStore` project named `NHibernateBase.cs`. The `NHibernateBase` class contains the logic to initialize the `Configuration`, `SessionFactory`, and `Session` classes.

This base class also provides a nice "library-like" code base, similar to that of a pre-ORM data access repository. This means that you can consolidate all your querying logic in whatever manner you like — for example, by business function or domain.

Now add the following code in Listing 1-10:

LISTING 1-10: NHibernateBase class

```
using NHibernate;
using NHibernate.Cfg;

namespace NHibernate.GuitarStore.DataAccess
{
  public class NHibernateBase
  {
    private static Configuration Configuration { get; set; }
    protected static ISessionFactory SessionFactory { get; set; }
    private static ISession session = null;
    private static IStatelessSession statelessSession = null;

    public static Configuration ConfigureNHibernate(string assembly)
    {
      Configuration = new Configuration();
      Configuration.AddAssembly(assembly);

      return Configuration;
    }

    public void Initialize(string assembly)
    {
      Configuration = ConfigureNHibernate(assembly);
      SessionFactory = Configuration.BuildSessionFactory();
    }

    public static ISession Session
    {
      get
      {
        if (session == null)
        {
            session = SessionFactory.OpenSession();
        }
        return session;
      }
    }

    public static IStatelessSession StatelessSession
    {
      get
      {
        if (statelessSession == null)
        {
            statelessSession = SessionFactory.OpenStatelessSession();
        }
        return statelessSession;
      }
    }
  }
}
```

The `Initialize()` method is the entry point for the `GuitarStore` NHibernate configuration. This method is called once when the program begins. The `Initialize()` method first calls the `ConfigureNHibernate()` method, which uses the `NHibernate.Cfg.Configuration` class's `AddAssembly()` method to add all of the assembly's mapped resources whose name ends with `.hbm.xml`. The `NHibernate.Cfg.Configuration` object loads and validates the configured driver class, proxy, dialect, mappings, and so on.

Once the assembly and properties have been added and the configuration object instantiated, the `BuildSessionFactory()` method of the `NHibernate.Cfg.Cofiguration` class is used to instantiate a new `NHibernate.SessionFactory` object. The `SessionFactory` property of the `NHibernateBase` class is used to store the object returned from the `BuildSessionFactory()` method. The `SessionFactory` property is also used to call the `OpenSession()` method, which returns a `Session` object for executing queries via the NHibernate library.

The NHibernate `Session` gives you access to a rich collection of querying APIs needed to save, update, and delete data from your database, plus a whole lot more. `ICriteria`, `IQuery` (HQL), `IMultiQuery`, `IMultiCritiera`, and `IQueryOver` are all accessible from the `Session` object. The `Session` is the main entry point to your application's interaction with NHibernate, and its implementation is a very important design decision.

The decision regarding how to manage the `Session` lifetime/lifecycle in a program is a complicated one. It depends very much on the requirements of the specific program. For the `GuitarStore` WPF program created in this book, the session-per-presenter implementation is utilized. The session-per-presenter has the following benefits:

>> Retains access to all benefits NHibernate offers, such as lazy loading and flushing.

>> Easy implementation within a program-specific context. For example, you can create a single `Session` per form and dispose of it when the form is closed, making the `Session` eligible for garbage collection.

>> Optimally manages the opening and closing of the database connection.

>> Better system recovery from a `StaleObjectException` because more than a single `Session` exists.

 TIP *Take a look at the* `NHibernate.ISession.cs` *file for a great description of the* `Session` *and the role it plays. The source code is well documented and you can learn a lot from it. The comments were written by experts and you can find some real gems in there.*

Lastly, create an additional method within the `NHibernatBase` class called `ExecuteICriteria<T>()`. Notice that this method uses generics. By using generics, the `Guitar` class, the `Inventory` class, or any class created in the future can use this method and get the expected results. Add the code in Listing 1-11 to the `NHibernatBase` class.

LISTING 1-11: The ExecuteICriteria<T>() method

```
public IList<T> ExecuteICriteria<T>()
{
  using (ITransaction transaction = Session.BeginTransaction())
  {
    try
    {
      IList<T> result = Session.CreateCriteria(typeof(T)).List<T>();
      transaction.Commit();
      return result;
    }
    catch (Exception ex)
    {
      transaction.Rollback();
      throw;
    }
  }
}
```

The preceding code shows an example of a typical C# NHibernate transaction implementation that uses an explicit transaction. As you learn more about NHibernate, the importance of the transaction becomes clearer. Each time you do something on the database, at minimum a `Session` is required. That `Session` is used to begin a transaction. The specific query and transaction commit should be performed between the beginning and the end of the transaction.

It's a good practice to place the code within a `try ... catch` block, rolling back the transaction if one of the steps fails. This is done by calling the `Rollback()` method of the `NHibernate` `.ITransaction` interface.

 WARNING *NHibernate's second-level cache is updated only after a transaction commit is performed. If changes to the database are made, of any kind, without committing, the integrity of the data stored in the cache is compromised.*

Now that it is clear which properties are required to create the `Configuration` class so a `SessionFactory` can be successfully built, and how to initialize them, the following sections describe implementation of the two different configuration techniques.

Using an app/web.config File

This configuration method is best for programs that use a single database but could be deployed to different users who want different database management systems. For example, suppose your company offers a software package for which the licensed customers have the option to use a different database management system. Having an NHibernate configuration that supports a simple conversion between databases can increase your customer reach and reduce the technical development and implementation costs.

Listing 1-12 is an example of how NHibernate is implemented into the `app.config` file of a WPF or console application. To use another database management system, you only need to change three values: `Dialect`, `Driver_Class`, and `ConnectionString`.

LISTING 1-12: app.config NHibernate configuration

```xml
<?xml version="1.0"?>
<configuration>
  <configSections>
    <section name="hibernate-configuration"
             type="NHibernate.Cfg.ConfigurationSectionHandler, NHibernate"/>
  </configSections>
  <hibernate-configuration xmlns="urn:nhibernate-configuration-2.2">
    <session-factory>
      <property name="dialect">NHibernate.Dialect.MsSql2008Dialect</property>
      <property name="connection.driver_class">
      NHibernate.Driver.SqlClientDriver</property>
      <property name="connection.connection_string_name">GuitarStore
      </property>
      <property name="connection.provider">
      NHibernate.Connection.DriverConnectionProvider</property>
    </session-factory>
  </hibernate-configuration>
  <connectionStrings>
    <add name="GuitarStore"
         connectionString="Data Source=PERKINS-W7;Initial
      Catalog=myGuitarStore;Integrated Security=True"/>
  </connectionStrings>
</configuration>
```

 NOTE The `<configSections>` element, where the `name="hibernate-configuration"` attribute is defined, must be placed directly after the initial `<configuration>` element.

Add Listing 1-12 to the `app.config` file located within the `NHibernate.GuitarStore.Console` project and then open the `Program.cs` file. To test that the class files, mapping files, and `app.config` settings are correctly configured, add Listing 1-13 to the `Main()` method of the `Program` class.

LISTING 1-13: Console code for configuration testing

```csharp
using NHibernate.Cfg;
using NHibernate.GuitarStore.DataAccess;

try
{
```

continues

LISTING 1-13 *(continued)*

```
    NHibernateBase NHB = new NHibernateBase();
    NHB.Initialize("NHibernate.GuitarStore");
    System.Console.WriteLine("NHibernate.GuitarStore assembly initialized.");

    System.Console.ReadLine();
}
catch (Exception ex)
{
    string Message = ex.Message;
    if (ex.InnerException != null)
    {
      Message += " - InnerExcepetion: " + ex.InnerException.Message;
    }
    System.Console.WriteLine();
    System.Console.WriteLine("***** ERROR *****");
    System.Console.WriteLine(Message);
    System.Console.WriteLine();
    System.Console.ReadLine();
}
```

Run the `NHibernate.GuitarStore.Console` application by pressing the F5 button. When the message in the console window states that the assembly has been initialized, the `app.config`-based configuration is successful. For more details about creating the console application, see the section "Creating a Console Application for Testing" later in this chapter.

Using a Strongly Typed Configuration

This configuration method is useful with an internal program that uses a single database management system and is unlikely to change, such as the `GuitarStore` program or a system that has implemented DBMS-specific technology.

I like this method because a strongly typed implementation provides very good IntelliSense and access to all the methods and properties, unlike using the `app.config` file to create the configuration, whereby the programmer has to know which elements, attributes, and properties are required. In addition, the strongly typed implementation clearly indicates your options; simply place the . (dot) after the object to see them displayed using IntelliSense.

As shown in Listing 1-14, a strongly typed configuration uses many of the NHibernate classes. These classes enable you to choose the dialect, connection driver, and so on needed for your program.

LISTING 1-14: Additional directives for a strongly typed configuration

```
using System.Data;
using NHibernate.ByteCode.Castle; //For NHibernate 3.1 and before
using NHibernate.Cfg.Loquacious;
using NHibernate.Connection;
using NHibernate.Dialect;
using NHibernate.Driver;
```

Implementing or migrating to a strongly typed configuration is not difficult. No configuration values are needed in the app.config file; however, the connection string, such as in the GuitarStore example, continues to be configured and retrieved from it. This is because, for example, if the password for the database is changed, only the app.config file needs to be changed. However, if the connection string is hard-coded in the program, a new executable needs to be distributed. The code shown in Listing 1-15 can replace the current ConfigureNHibernate() method that exists in the NHibernateBase.cs class file.

LISTING 1-15: Strongly typed NHibernate configuration

```
public static Configuration ConfigureNHibernate(string assembly)
{
    Configuration = new Configuration();

    Configuration.DataBaseIntegration(dbi =>
    {
        dbi.Dialect<MsSql2008Dialect>();
        dbi.Driver<SqlClientDriver>();
        dbi.ConnectionProvider<DriverConnectionProvider>();
        dbi.IsolationLevel = IsolationLevel.ReadCommitted;
        dbi.Timeout = 15;
    });

    Configuration.AddAssembly(assembly);

    return Configuration;
}
```

Once the preceding code has replaced the existing method in the NHibernateBase class, press F5 to run the console application and confirm that the initialization was successful.

The most important point to understand here is that the type of configuration is determined based on the program's requirements. The crux of this determination is whether the configuration settings change often. If they are unlikely to change, then the strongly typed configuration is a good alternative, regardless of the fact that some configurations are hard-coded.

If you have chosen to implement the class-by-class mapping by code concept, additional code needs to be added to the ConfigureNHibernate() method shown previously in Listing 1-15. When mapping by code and using the ConfigureNHibernate() method, you are required to add the mapping to the Configuration prior to adding the assembly, as shown in Listing 1-16.

LISTING 1-16: Implementing mapping by code

```
using NHibernate.Mapping.ByCode;
using NHibernate.Cfg.MappingSchema;
using NHibernate.GuitarStore.Common;

public static Configuration ConfigureNHibernate(string assembly)
```

continues

LISTING 1-16 *(continued)*

```
{
  Configuration = new Configuration();

  Configuration.DataBaseIntegration(dbi =>
  {
    dbi.Dialect<MsSql2008Dialect>();
    dbi.Driver<SqlClientDriver>();
    dbi.ConnectionProvider<DriverConnectionProvider>();
    dbi.IsolationLevel = IsolationLevel.ReadUncommitted;
    dbi.Timeout = 15;
  });
  ModelMapper mapper = new ModelMapper();
  mapper.AddMapping<InventoryMap>();
  HbmMapping mapping = mapper.CompileMappingFor(new[] { typeof(Inventory) });
  Configuration.AddDeserializedMapping(mapping, "GuitarStore");

  Configuration.AddAssembly(assembly);

  return Configuration;
}
```

Creating a Console Application for Testing

The initial mapping of a database can take significant time and effort if done manually. A single spelling, typo, or case mistake can sometimes take an hour or more to sort out and resolve. An example of a case typo and a spelling mistake is shown in Listing 1-17.

LISTING 1-17: Invalid class and mapping example

```
public virtual string Type { get; set; }
  <property name="type" column="TYPE" type="System.String" />

public virtual DateTime? Received { get; set; }
  <property name="Received" column="RECEIVED" type="System.DateTime" />
```

When the AddAssembly("NHibernate.GuitarStore") method of the Configuration class is called from the NHibernateBase class, the mapping documents (.hbm.xml) are validated. If there are spelling, type, or case errors, you will likely get the error shown in Figure 1-17.

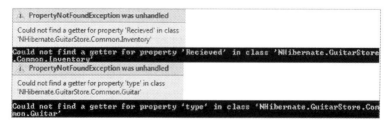

FIGURE 1-17

If you try to make the changes to the class library, and implement and then test them directly in the GuitarStore WPF program, troubleshooting becomes more complex. This is because the programmer must test not only the configuration, but also the implementation in the WPF program. It is complicated to determine whether a failure is a configuration problem or an implementation problem. Having a simple tool to confirm the configuration before implementation greatly helps in the development process.

 TIP *You can write the NHibernate-generated SQL to the console by adding the* show_sql *property to the NHibernate configuration file:*

```
<property name="show_sql">true</property>
```

To begin, add some general ICriteria, IQuery (HQL), or LINQ to NHibernate queries, as shown in Listing 1-18, to the code previously created in Listing 1-13. The following code is used to confirm that each of the classes and mapping files return expected results:

LISTING 1-18: Console testing examples

```
using NHibernate.GuitarStore.Common;
using NHibernate.Linq;

IList<Inventory> list1 =
NHibernateBase.StatelessSession.CreateQuery("from Inventory").List<Inventory>();

IList<Inventory> list2 =
NHibernateBase.Session.CreateCriteria(typeof(Inventory)).List<Inventory>();

IQueryable<Inventory> linq =
    (from l in NHibernateBase.Session.Query<Inventory>() select l);
```

Executing the console application results in something like what is shown in Figure 1-18.

FIGURE 1-18

Creating a console application to test your class library configuration and modifications saves a lot of time and prevents a lot of headaches. If the queries and assembly validation succeed, then you can be very confident that they function the same way when used in your more complex applications.

 TIP *Add your testing code within a* try ... catch *block and write the error message to the screen. Be sure to include the* InnerException.Message *because it often contains valuable information.*

CONFIGURING THE GUITARSTORE WPF PROGRAM

Now that the projects, the database, the classes, and the mapping files are created, and NHibernate has been configured, the creation of the GuitarStore WPF program can begin. You will perform the following actions in this section:

1. Initialize the NHibernate SessionFactory.

2. Add and populate the DataGrid ordered by Builder.

3. Add and populate a ComboBox.

4. Filter the DataGrid based on ComboBox selection.

Initializing NHibernate

To initialize NHibernate within the GuitarStore WPF program, you need to first open the MainWindow.xaml.cs file. From the MainWindow() constructor, call the Initialize() method found within the NHibernateBase class, as shown in Listing 1-19.

LISTING 1-19: Initializing NHibernate in the WPF program

```
using NHibernate.GuitarStore.DataAccess;
namespace GuitarStore
{
    public partial class MainWindow : Window
    {
        public MainWindow()
        {
            InitializeComponent();
            NHibernateBase nhb = new NHibernateBase();
            nhb.Initialize("NHibernate.GuitarStore");
        }
    }
}
```

Adding and Populating the DataGrid Control

To add and populate the DataGrid, the following actions will be taken:

1. Add the DataGrid control to the MainWindow.

2. Populate the DataGrid.

3. Create a new NHibernateInventory class.

4. Add an orderBy method to the NHibernateInventory class.

Add a DataGrid control to the GuitarStore WPF MainWindow.xaml window by dragging and dropping the control from the Toolbox. Then add a Loaded element to the MainWindow.xaml window with a value of Window_Loaded() method. The MainWindow.xaml code should resemble what is shown in Listing 1-20.

LISTING 1-20: MainWindow.xaml with Loaded element

```
<Window x:Class="GuitarStore.MainWindow"
        xmlns="http://schemas.microsoft.com/winfx/2006/xaml/presentation"
        xmlns:x="http://schemas.microsoft.com/winfx/2006/xaml"
        Title="Guitar Store" Height="400" Width="625"
        WindowStartupLocation="CenterScreen" BorderBrush="Black"
        Background="Black" Icon="Images/Guitar.ico"
        ResizeMode="NoResize" Loaded="Window_Loaded">
    <Grid>
        <DataGrid AutoGenerateColumns="True" HorizontalAlignment="Stretch"
                Margin="12,59,110,52" Name="dataGridInventory"
                VerticalAlignment="Stretch" />
    </Grid>
</Window>
```

Next, open again the `MainWindow.xaml.cs` file and add the following code in Listing 1-21, which populates the `DataGrid`.

LISTING 1-21: Populating the GuitarStore inventory DataGrid

```
using NHibernate.GuitarStore.Common;

namespace GuitarStore
{
    public partial class MainWindow : Window
    {
        private void Window_Loaded(object sender, RoutedEventArgs e)
        {
            NHibernateBase nhb = new NHibernateBase();
            List<Inventory> list =
                (List<Inventory>)nhb.ExecuteICriteria<Inventory>();
            dataGridInventory.ItemsSource = list;

            if (list != null)
            {
                dataGridInventory.Columns[0].Visibility =
                                System.Windows.Visibility.Hidden;
                dataGridInventory.Columns[1].Visibility =
                                System.Windows.Visibility.Hidden;
                dataGridInventory.Columns[8].Visibility =
                                System.Windows.Visibility.Hidden;
            }
        }
    }
}
```

Change the `GuitarStore` project to the startup project by right-clicking it and selecting Set as Startup Project from the context menu. Press F5 to run the `GuitarStore` WPF program. The inventory is retrieved and loaded into the `DataGrid`.

The `ExecuteICriteria<T>()` method in the `NHibernateBase` class does not order the result set by `Builder`, as the requirements dictate. Therefore, create a new class called `NHibernateInventory` that inherits from `NHibernateBase` and resembles the code shown in Listing 1-22. The new class should be added into the `DataAccess` folder of the `NHibernate.GuitarStore` class library.

LISTING 1-22: NHibernateInventory class with OrderBy method

```
using NHibernate.Criterion;
using NHibernate.GuitarStore.Common;

namespace NHibernate.GuitarStore.DataAccess
{
  public class NHibernateInventory : NHibernateBase
  {
    public IList<Inventory> ExecuteICriteriaOrderBy(string orderBy)
    {
      using (ITransaction transaction = Session.BeginTransaction())
      {
        try
        {
          IList<Inventory> result = Session.CreateCriteria(typeof(Inventory))
                                        .AddOrder(Order.Asc(orderBy))
                                        .List<Inventory>();
          transaction.Commit();
          return result;
        }
        catch (Exception ex)
        {
          transaction.Rollback();
          throw;
        }
      }
    }
  }
}
```

The method shown here uses `ICriteria` and its `AddOrder` method to retrieve the data from the database. The projection methods of `ICriteria` are found in the `NHibernate.Criterion` namespace and therefore require the addition of the `NHibernate.Criterion` directive.

Lastly, update the `Window_Loaded()` method to call the `ExecuteICriteriaOrderBy()` method, passing it `"Builder"`, as shown in Listing 1-23. Note that the `NHibernateInventory` class is instantiated, unlike the `NHibernateBase` class.

LISTING 1-23: Implementing the OrderBy ICritera method

```
NHibernateInventory nhi = new NHibernateInventory();
List<Inventory> list = (List<Inventory>)nhi.ExecuteICriteriaOrderBy("Builder");
```

Press F5 to see the results shown in Figure 1-19. This window provides the current Inventory list.

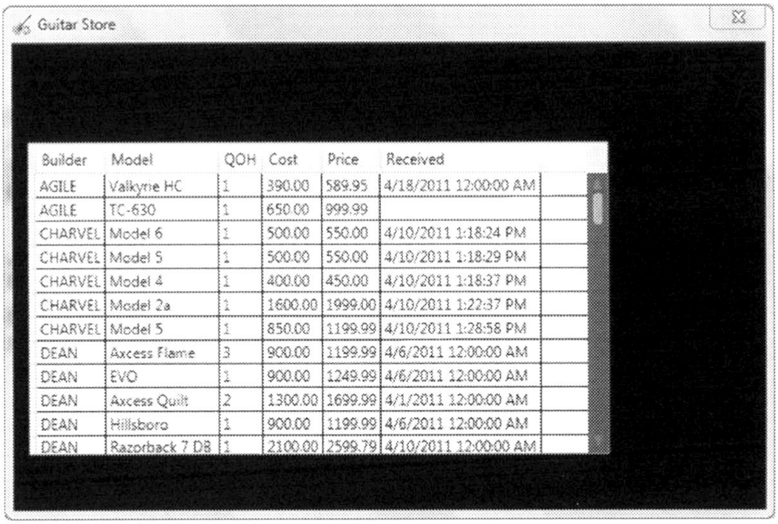

Builder	Model	QOH	Cost	Price	Received
AGILE	Valkyrie HC	1	390.00	589.95	4/18/2011 12:00:00 AM
AGILE	TC-630	1	650.00	999.99	
CHARVEL	Model 6	1	500.00	550.00	4/10/2011 1:18:24 PM
CHARVEL	Model 5	1	500.00	550.00	4/10/2011 1:18:29 PM
CHARVEL	Model 4	1	400.00	450.00	4/10/2011 1:18:37 PM
CHARVEL	Model 2a	1	1600.00	1999.00	4/10/2011 1:22:37 PM
CHARVEL	Model 5	1	850.00	1199.99	4/10/2011 1:28:58 PM
DEAN	Axcess Flame	3	900.00	1199.99	4/6/2011 12:00:00 AM
DEAN	EVO	1	900.00	1249.99	4/6/2011 12:00:00 AM
DEAN	Axcess Quilt	2	1300.00	1699.99	4/1/2011 12:00:00 AM
DEAN	Hillsboro	1	900.00	1199.99	4/6/2011 12:00:00 AM
DEAN	Razorback 7 DB	1	2100.00	2599.79	4/10/2011 12:00:00 AM

FIGURE 1-19

Adding and Populating a ComboBox

Drag and drop a ComboBox control from the Toolbox and add it to the MainWindow.xaml window. In the MainWindow.xaml.cs file, add a new method called PopulateComboBox(), adding the code shown in Listing 1-24.

LISTING 1-24: PopulateComboBox() method

```
private void PopulateComboBox()
{
  NHibernateBase nhb = new NHibernateBase();
  IList<Guitar> GuitarTypes = nhb.ExecuteICriteria<Guitar>();
  foreach (var item in GuitarTypes)
  {
    Guitar guitar = new Guitar(item.Id, item.Type);
    comboBoxGuitarTypes.DisplayMemberPath = "Type";
    comboBoxGuitarTypes.SelectedValuePath = "Id";
    comboBoxGuitarTypes.Items.Add(guitar);
  }
}
```

Lastly, call the PopulateComboBox() method from the Window_Loaded() method so that the ComboBox is populated with the GuitarTypes result set.

Filtering the DataGrid Based on the ComboBox Selection

To add filtering capabilities to the GuitarStore WPF program, you need to take the following actions:

1. Add a SelectionChanged event and method.

2. Create a method that returns a result set based on Guitar type.

3. Modify the SelectionChanged() method to capture the selection and repopulate the DataGrid.

In the MainWindow.xaml file, add a SelectionChanged event within the ComboBox control, as shown in Listing 1-25.

LISTING 1-25: comboBoxGuitarTypes ComboBox

```
<ComboBox Height="23" SelectionChanged="comboBoxGuitarTypes_SelectionChanged"
          HorizontalAlignment="Left" Margin="12,50,0,0" Name="comboBoxGuitarTypes"
          VerticalAlignment="Top" Width="195" />
```

Next, create a method within the NHibernateInventory class that accepts a Guid as parameter and returns the matching Inventory data, as shown in Listing 1-26.

LISTING 1-26: Guitar type filter method

```
public IList<Inventory> ExecuteICriteria(Guid Id)
{
  using (ITransaction transaction = Session.BeginTransaction())
  {
    try
    {
      IList<Inventory> result = Session.CreateCriteria(typeof(Inventory))
                                  .Add(Restrictions.Eq("TypeId", Id))
                                  .List<Inventory>();
      transaction.Commit();
      return result;
    }
    catch (Exception ex)
    {
      transaction.Rollback();
      throw;
    }
  }
}
```

The last step is to add the code that clears the existing data in the DataGrid, capture the selected value from the ComboBox, and call the method created in Listing 1-26. The SelectionChanged() method is shown in Listing 1-27.

LISTING 1-27: SelectionChanged() method

```
private void comboBoxGuitarTypes_SelectionChanged(object sender,
                                            SelectionChangedEventArgs e)
{
  try
  {
    dataGridInventory.ItemsSource = null;
    Guitar guitar = (Guitar)comboBoxGuitarTypes.SelectedItem;
    Guid guitarType = new Guid(guitar.Id.ToString());

    NHibernateInventory nhi = new NHibernateInventory();
    List<Inventory> list = (List<Inventory>)nhi.ExecuteICriteria(guitarType);
    dataGridInventory.ItemsSource = list;

    if (list != null)
    {
      dataGridInventory.Columns[0].Visibility = System.Windows.Visibility.Hidden;
      dataGridInventory.Columns[1].Visibility = System.Windows.Visibility.Hidden;
      dataGridInventory.Columns[8].Visibility = System.Windows.Visibility.Hidden;
    }
    PopulateComboBox();
  }
  catch (Exception ex)
  {
    labelMessage.Content = ex.Message;
  }
}
```

Notice that a label has been added to display an error and a message, if one is thrown.

Within this section some basic functionality has been implemented using NHibernate's ICriteria interface. Both the Restrictions and the AddOrder ICriteria methods were used to restrict and format the data. The remaining sections in this chapter discuss other NHibernate capabilities that are important to understand. Further implementation of functionality into the GuitarStore WPF program occurs in the following chapters.

UNDERSTANDING LAZY LOADING

One of NHibernate's strongest features is *lazy loading*, which means that data is not retrieved from the database until it is specifically requested. For example, the mapping shown in Listing 1-28 specifies that when the Guitar class is populated with data from the database using any of the NHibernate querying mechanisms, it is not automatically retrieved. If the Inventory bag is not specifically accessed by the application, the property is not populated.

LISTING 1-28: Mapping lazy loading configuration

```
<bag name="Inventory" table="INVENTORY" lazy="true">
  <key column="TYPEID" />
  <one-to-many class="NHibernate.GuitarStore.Common.Inventory" />
</bag>
```

This makes a lot of sense. Why retrieve data that the user will not use? The code in Listing 1-29 shows an example of retrieving all the Guitar types from the Guitar table and then, at a later point, within the same method, retrieving the Inventory for a single type of Guitar. The first line performs a simple ICriteria select of all Guitar types. The program could then do some processing of the different Guitar types and load the specific Inventory details as required, and only if required.

LISTING 1-29: Lazy loading the inventory for a specific guitar type

```
IList<Guitar> GuitarTypes = session.CreateCriteria(typeof(Guitar))
                                   .List<Guitar>();

//Do something else within the session context logic here

Inventory inventory = GuitarTypes[0].Inventory[0];
```

If lazy loading were set to false, all the guitars and the Inventory are loaded with one large SQL statement. Although this isn't an issue using the current example, imagine a system that has hundreds of thousands of rows. System performance would be severely affected in that case. The recommendation is to leave lazy loading set to true.

Not only is it possible to lazy load a bag, it is also possible to lazy load a specific property. For example, suppose user manuals or images are stored in the database for each guitar in inventory. Clearly, it isn't a good idea to retrieve the user manuals or images when a user only wanted to check the price or quantity of a specific guitar. Images and documents are large and cause unnecessary load on the system if they are unnecessarily retrieved. By turning lazy loading on or off at the property level, as shown in the following code snippet, images, manuals, or large data types are not retrieved unless specifically referenced from the program.

```
<property name="Image" column="IMAGE" lazy="true" />
```

Specifically setting the Image property to lazy load means NHibernate retrieves the image only if it is included in the NHibernate query.

 NOTE *Using the* fetch *attribute affects lazy loading.* Select, *which is the default value, lazy loads the data. If the value is changed to* join, *as shown in Listing 1-30, the data is eagerly loaded, meaning all data is loaded at once. Be aware of this and implement the* fetch *attribute only if dictated by the program's requirements.*

LISTING 1-30: Using fetch with your collection

```
<bag name="Inventory" table="INVENTORY" fetch="join">
  <key column="TYPEID" />
  <one-to-many class="NHibernate.GuitarStore.Common.Inventory"  />
</bag>
```

CONFIGURING LOGGING USING LOG4NET

The `log4net.dll` is found in the `Test` directory contained within the NHibernate download. It is tightly integrated with NHibernate and is used to log NHibernate activities. It can also be used for customized logging within a program.

 TIP *Confirm that your C# project is configured to use a full version of the .NET Framework. If your project is configured to use a Client Profile version of the .NET Framework, you will not be able to add the log4net directive to your solution without error, and therefore will not obtain access to any of its methods.*

Return to the `NHibernateBase` class and add a constructor and the code shown in Listing 1-31.

LISTING 1-31: Enabling the log4net configurator

```
using log4net;

public NHibernateBase()
{
    log4net.Config.XmlConfigurator.Configure();
}
```

To configure log4net, you need to make some modifications to the `app.config` file. The configuration example shown in Listing 1-32 specifies where the log should be placed (console or file), the format of the log, and much more. This listing shows a default configuration for logging to a file.

LISTING 1-32: app.config log4net configuration example

```
<?xml version="1.0" encoding="utf-8" ?>
<configuration>
 <configSections>
   <section name="log4net"
            type="log4net.Config.Log4NetConfigurationSectionHandler, log4net"/>
 </configSections>
 <log4net>
   <appender name="NHLog" type="log4net.Appender.RollingFileAppender, log4net" >
     <param name="File" value="NHLog.txt" />
     <param name="AppendToFile" value="true" />
     <param name="maximumFileSize" value="200KB" />
     <param name="maxSizeRollBackups" value="1" />
     <layout type="log4net.Layout.PatternLayout, log4net">
      <conversionPattern
       value="%date{yyyy.MM.dd hh:mm:ss} %-5level [%thread] - %message%newline" />
```

continues

LISTING 1-32 *(continued)*

```
    </layout>
  </appender>
  <!-- levels: ALL, DEBUG, INFO, WARN, ERROR, FATAL, OFF -->
  <root>
    <level value="INFO" />
    <appender-ref ref="NHLog" />
  </root>
  <logger name="NHBase.SQL">
    <level value="ALL" />
    <appender-ref ref="NHLog" />
  </logger>
 </log4net>
</configuration>
```

The log4net configuration has two parts, the appender and the logger.

The Appender

The appender is used to provide log4net with the information it needs to store or present the generated logs. The preceding configuration in Listing 1-32 instructs log4net to store the log in a text file named `NHLog.txt`. This is done using the `param` tag with the name of `File` and the value of `NHLog.txt`. The `value` attribute that contains `NHLog.txt` can contain an absolute path; if it isn't set, then the log file is stored in the relative working directory.

Some other parameters are `AppendToFile` and `maximumFileSize`. `AppendToFile` simply specifies whether you want to create a new log file each time the NHibernate-based program begins. If it is set to `true`, then each time the program is started it adds log information to the same `NHLog.txt` file. If it is set to `false`, then the file is deleted each time a new `Session` is created. The size of the log file can affect your system's performance, so you should set the maximum size to which the log file can grow. Note that when the maximum file size is exceeded, the log file is automatically deleted and a new one created.

If you want the old one to be backed up before the new one is created, use the `maxSizeRollBackups` parameter, setting the value for the number of files you want before they are removed. I have seen many performance and availability issues caused by large log files and/or the reduction of disk space. Therefore, carefully consider your logging strategy and configuration.

A very nice feature in log4net is the capability to configure the layout of your log. The example configuration results in a row in the text file, as shown in Figure 1-20.

```
2011.04.26 07:53:02 INFO  [9] - NHibernate 3.2.0.1002 (3.2.0.1002)
2011.04.26 07:53:02 INFO  [9] - Using reflection optimizer
2011.04.26 07:53:02 INFO  [9] - Searching for mapped documents in assembly: NHibernate.GuitarStore
2011.04.26 07:53:02 INFO  [9] - Mapping resource: NHibernate.GuitarStore.Mapping.Guitar.hbm.xml
2011.04.26 07:53:02 INFO  [9] - Using dialect: NHibernate.Dialect.MsSql2008Dialect
2011.04.26 07:53:02 INFO  [9] - Mapping class: NHibernate.GuitarStore.Common.Guitar -> GUITAR
2011.04.26 07:53:02 INFO  [9] - Mapping resource: NHibernate.GuitarStore.Mapping.Inventory.hbm.xml
2011.04.26 07:53:02 INFO  [9] - Using dialect: NHibernate.Dialect.MsSql2008Dialect
2011.04.26 07:53:02 INFO  [9] - Mapping class: NHibernate.GuitarStore.Common.Inventory -> INVENTORY
2011.04.26 07:53:02 INFO  [9] - checking mappings queue
2011.04.26 07:53:02 INFO  [9] - processing one-to-many association mappings
2011.04.26 07:53:02 INFO  [9] - mapping collection: NHibernate.GuitarStore.Common.Guitar.Inventory -> INVENTORY
2011.04.26 07:53:02 INFO  [9] - processing one-to-one association property references
2011.04.26 07:53:02 INFO  [9] - processing foreign key constraints
```

FIGURE 1-20

The Logger

The logger is where the source of the logs is determined. The seven values that can be provided to the logger are described in Table 1-8.

TABLE 1-8: log4net Logging Levels

VALUE	LEVEL	DESCRIPTION
OFF	-	No logging
FATAL	1	Logs all configured events, excluding DEBUG, INFO, WARN, and ERROR
ERROR	2	Logs all configured events, excluding DEBUG, INFO, and WARN
WARN	3	Logs all configured events, excluding DEBUG and INFO
INFO	4	Logs all configured events, excluding DEBUG logs
DEBUG	5	Logs all configured events (same as ALL)
ALL	5	Logs all configured events

If you look at the log values hierarchically, you can see, for example, that if level 4 is chosen, configured events with a level lower than or equal to level 4 are logged.

It is possible to configure and use more than one appender within your solution. Each appender is uniquely identified by the name attribute. This name is referenced within the logger, using the ref attribute within the appender-ref tag. If you want to capture different levels of events in different areas of your system, you can configure multiple appenders and configure your loggers to use them. The example shown in Listing 1-33 uses an appender named NHErrorLog and logs only ERROR or FATAL events.

LISTING 1-33: Addition to log4net app.config configuration

```
<logger name="NHSQL">
  <level value="ERROR">
    <appender-ref ref="NHErrorLog" />
  </level>
</logger>
```

The NHErrorLog can also be configured, perhaps to log the error to a different file in a different location.

Configuring Your Program to Use log4net

If you decide to use and configure log4net to log NHibernate events, you should know that you can use the same configuration to log events within your own system. This is an alternative to using the .NET capabilities or another third-party tool. It is done by adding just a few simple lines of code.

Within the class you want to log, add the `log4net` directive and the following code snippet:

```
private static ILog log = LogManager.GetLogger("NHBase.SQL");
```

The value passed to the `GetLogger` method must match a logger name within the log4net configuration section in the `app.config` file. You can see an example toward the bottom of Listing 1-33 and in the previous section. Lastly, you need to tell the `LogManager` when and what level of log you want to record. This is done by using the private static log instance you created within the class and selecting the needed level, as shown in Listing 1-34.

LISTING 1-34: Writing custom messages to the log4net log file

```
log.Debug("Add a message to write to the log file");
log.Info("Add a message to write to the log file");
```

This logs all events at the DEBUG level and below to the logger named `NHBase.SQL`, which has been configured to use the `NHLog` appender.

All error values are accessible from the `LogManager`, excluding ALL. You can, however, use DEBUG for this.

> **TIP** You may need to manually copy the `log4net.dll` into the `/bin/Debug` or `/bin/release` directories. Alternately, you can set the Copy Local property of the log4net.dll to `true`.

SERIALIZING STARTUP

Before a query can be executed via NHibernate, it must validate all the `.hbm.xml` files that exist within the assembly. As mentioned, the example in this book has only two HBM files, so validation is quick. However, if a mapped database has hundreds of tables, and therefore hundreds of `.hbm.xml` files, validation can take some time — often too much time.

The validation happens one time during the life of your program. The performance hit is apparent during the initial query or when the assembly is loaded into the configuration object. All queries after the initial validation are generated using the validated `.hbm.xml` files and therefore run as fast as the normal query would. When the program is stopped and restarted for any reason, the `.hbm.xml` files are revalidated.

> **NOTE** The placement of your NHibernate configuration is important. If the configuration is performed at program startup, then the startup may be perceived as slow. If the configuration is performed prior to the first query, then the first query may be perceived as slow. Consider using a background worker thread to validate the `hbm.xml` files(s) during startup.

For users, this performance issue may not be so bad, meaning a few seconds or more, one or two times per day, is acceptable. Conversely, a programmer who needs to stop and start the program numerous times a day in the process of coding, debugging, and testing the program may find the constant validation unacceptable.

 NOTE *An alternate solution that can be implemented to reduce startup time is to consolidate all your mapping files into a single* .hbm.xml *file. This has been proven to reduce startup times as well.*

Recognizing that other options to improve the validation process exist, the method discussed in detail here is *serialization* of the NHibernate configuration. Serialization is simply the conversion of an object to a stream of bytes, which is then written to a data stream. In this context, the NHibernate configuration instance is the object. When the assembly is loaded into the configuration object, it validates all the .hbm.xml files, which are configured as an embedded resource against the schema. It is then possible to take the NHibernate configuration instance, serialize it, and persist it to disk. If you view the NHibernate.Cfg.Configuration implementation, you see that it implements the ISerializable interface, so serialization can be utilized.

The activities required to serialize, deserialize, and use the serialized configuration are as follows:

1. Serialize the configuration.

2. Check whether the serialized configuration is the most current.

3. Load the configuration from the serialized file.

4. Modify the NHibernateBase.ConfigureNHibernate() method to use the serialized configuration.

Add the code in Listing 1-35 to the NHibernateBase class of the NHibernate.GuitarStore class library. Note that you must add the System.Configuration assembly as a reference and the directive before the C# code in Listing 1-35 works.

LISTING 1-35: Declaring a serialized filename

```
using System.Configuration;

private static string SerializedConfiguration =
                ConfigurationManager.AppSettings["SerializedFilename"];

Add to both  app.config files contained in the solution:
  <appSettings>
    <add key="SerializedFilename"
        value="nhibernate.guitarstore.serialized.cfg"/>
  </appSettings>
```

The SerializedConfiguration property stores the name of the serialized NHibernate configuration. It is good practice to store values in a place where changes to them do not require a recompilation and redeployment of your program. Therefore, the value is captured from the `appSetting` section of the `app.config` file using the `ConfigurationManager`, also shown in Listing 1-35.

Serializing the Configuration

The NHibernate configuration can be serialized regardless of configuration method — app `.config`, strongly typed, or mixed configuration — used. The first step is to modify the existing `ConfigureNHibernate()` found within the `NHibernate.GuitarStore` class library. Listing 1-36 shows the modified method.

LISTING 1-36: Serializing an NHibernate configuration

```
using System.IO;
using System.Runtime.Serialization;
using System.Runtime.Serialization.Formatters.Binary;

public static NHibernate.Cfg.Configuration ConfigureNHibernate(string assembly)
{
  if (Configuration == null)
  {
     Configuration = new NHibernate.Cfg.Configuration();
     Configuration.AddAssembly(assembly);
     FileStream file = File.Open(SerializedConfiguration, FileMode.Create);
     IFormatter bf = new BinaryFormatter();
     bf.Serialize(file, Configuration);
     file.Close();
  }
  return Configuration;
}
```

Notice that after the NHibernate configuration object is created, the assembly is added and then passed to the `Serialize()` method of the `BinaryFormatter` class. The method then writes the serialized file to the file identified in Listing 1-35.

Validating a Serialized Configuration

Reflection is used to validate that the serialized configuration contains the most current NHibernate configuration, as shown in Listing 1-37.

LISTING 1-37: The IsConfigurationFileValid property

```
using System.Reflection;

private static bool IsConfigurationFileValid
{
  get
  {
     try
     {
```

```
        Assembly assembly = Assembly.Load("Nhibernate.GuitarStore");
        FileInfo configInfo = new FileInfo(SerializedConfiguration);
        FileInfo asmInfo = new FileInfo(assembly.Location);

        return configInfo.LastWriteTime >= asmInfo.LastWriteTime;
    }
    catch (Exception ex)
    {
        return false;
    }
  }
}
```

This code compares the modification dates of the assembly against the serialized configuration file. I use the `Assembly` class of `System.Reflection` to get the correct reference to the NHibernate `.GuitarStore.dll` binary file. I use the `FileInfo` class of `System.IO` to provide the specifics about the file. In this example, the code only confirms that the binary file's `LastWriteTime` is less than the `LastWriteTime` of the serialized configuration. If the binary file's modified date is greater than the serialized configuration, then the program will need to reserialize the configuration.

 NOTE *If the binary file changes and the serialized configuration file is not updated, then modifications in the new configuration are not available within the program that implements the changes.*

The logic in Listing 1-37 only checks for a change in the binary file. If a programmer decides to store the dialect, database driver, proxy, and connection string in the `app.config` file, for example, the preceding logic does not recognize the change and does not create a new serialized configuration. Therefore, if the database instance is changed within the `app.config` file, for example, the user needs to either delete the serialized configuration file so that a new configuration is created using the newest modifications or create a method to perform the check and take appropriate action.

 NOTE *This configuration uses the relative path to store, access, and validate the serialized configuration. It is possible to include an absolute path if you want to store the serialized configuration file in a location other than the working directory.*

Loading the Current Serialized Configuration

The next code segment implemented in the serialization of the NHibernate configuration is the method that deserializes an existing configuration. Use the `Deserialize()` method of the `BinaryFormatter` class to perform this. This is done by adding the method in Listing 1-38 to the `NHibernateBase` class.

LISTING 1-38: The LoadConfigurationFromFile() method

```
private static NHibernate.Cfg.Configuration LoadConfigurationFromFile()
{
    if (!IsConfigurationFileValid) return null;

    try
    {
        using (FileStream file =
                File.Open(SerializedConfiguration, FileMode.Open))
        {
            BinaryFormatter bf = new BinaryFormatter();
            return (NHibernate.Cfg.Configuration)bf.Deserialize(file);
        }
    }
    catch (Exception)
    {
        return null;
    }
}
```

Recall that earlier the concept of serialization was described as converting a stream of bytes into a data stream. It makes sense, therefore, that the serialized configuration is loaded into a class named FileStream. This file stream is then used as the parameter for the Deserialize() method within the BinaryFormatter class which is used to return the deserialized file to the ConfigureNHibernate() method.

 NOTE *Serialization and deserialization of the configuration does incur some performance overhead. However, it is much less than the overhead from NHibernate's validation of all .hbm.xml files each time the program begins.*

Using a Serialized Configuration

In the ConfigureNHibernate() method, the serialized configuration needs to be loaded into the NHibernate.Cfg.Configuration object or a new configuration must be created and then serialized. This is achieved by adding the single line of code shown in the following code snippet to the existing ConfigureNHibernate() method:

```
Configuration = LoadConfigurationFromFile();
```

This method attempts to get the configuration from the LoadConfigurationFromFile() method. If the returned Configuration is null, then a new configuration is created; otherwise, the existing serialized configuration is used.

Here the relative path is used to create the serialized configuration in the working directory; and instead of the `Deserialize()` method, the `Serialize()` method of the `BinaryFormatter` class is used.

How much this improves performance depends on the number of .hbm.xml mapping files that need to be validated during program startup. A typical real- world example might be reducing the validation of ~20 .hbm.xml files from ~8 seconds to ~3 seconds.

Prior to serialization of the console application program, the validation took 4.65 seconds. After implementing the serialization, startup took 2.52 seconds. That's almost a 50% improvement. Results from the console test application are shown in Figure 1-21.

```
Loading the configuration took: 04.65
NHibernate.GuitarStore assembly initialized.
ExecuteICriteria<Guitar> executed with 10 results
ExecuteHQL<Inventory> executed with 89 results
ExecuteLINQ<Inventory> executed with 89 results

Loading the configuration took: 02.52
NHibernate.GuitarStore assembly initialized.
ExecuteICriteria<Guitar> executed with 10 results
ExecuteHQL<Inventory> executed with 89 results
ExecuteLINQ<Inventory> executed with 89 results
```

FIGURE 1-21

Timing the Startup

The configuration time was captured using the `Stopwatch` class in the `System.Diagonistics` namespace, as shown in Listing 1-39.

LISTING 1-39: Stopwatch timing of configuration serialization

```
using System.Diagnostics;

Stopwatch stopwatchConfiguration = new Stopwatch();
TimeSpan timespanConfiguration;
stopwatchConfiguration.Start();

NHIC.Initialize("NHibernate.GuitarStore");

stopwatchConfiguration.Stop();
timespanConfiguration = stopwatchConfiguration.Elapsed;
```

The specifications of the machine that that validates and serializes the configuration plays a significant role in startup time performance.

> **NOTE** *Each time the configuration is serialized, there is a performance hit. This hit results from validation of the* .hbm.xml *files, not from the serialization process. Any changes to the* .hbm.xml *file results in reserialization and validation.*

INTERCEPTORS AND EVENTS

NHibernate `Interceptors` and `Events` provide an interface for executing custom logic before a transaction begins, before a transaction completes, or after a transaction completes. With few, if any, exceptions, `Interceptors` and `Events` function the same way within NHibernate. In both cases, an interface with one or more method(s) are provided for implementation or override. The primary differences between them are their implementation and the different capabilities they contain. Some users believe that NHibernate `Events` are the new way and `Interceptors` are the old way. However, I recommend you use the one that best meets the requirements of the program.

Interceptors

To utilize an `Interceptor` in NHibernate you need to implement the `IInterceptor` interface. The `IInterceptor` interface contains methods such as `OnLoad()`, `OnSave()`, `OnDelete()`, and `OnPrepareStatement()`. Each method can be included and overridden in your class that implements the interface. I recommend that the class used to implement an `Interceptor` should also inherit from `Nhibernate.EmptyInterceptor.cs`. This way, you won't need to implement every method found in the interface; instead, you only need to override the methods specifically needed.

Using an `Interceptor`, you can create a very useful tool for troubleshooting, programming, or tuning NHibernate. For example, you might want the capability to quickly view the SQL generated from statements (e.g., `IQuery` (HQL), `ICriteria`, etc). It is possible to use log4net as previously discussed in the section "Configuring Logging Using log4net," but that requires navigating to a directory and opening a log file each time you want to see the SQL. Nor is the format of the query as user friendly.

Capturing NHibernate-Generated SQL in Real time

Capturing the NHibernate-generated SQL in real time requires the following actions:

1. Create a new class to store and format the SQL.

2. Add the `Interceptor` code to the `NHibernateBase` class.

3. Activate the `Interceptor`.

First, in the `NHibernate.GuitarStore` class library, add a new class, `Utils.cs`, to the `DataAccess` directory. Add the code in Listing 1-40 to the class.

LISTING 1-40: The Utils class

```
using NHibernate.AdoNet.Util;

namespace NHibernate.GuitarStore.DataAccess
{
    public class Utils
    {
        public static string NHibernateGeneratedSQL { get; set; }
```

```
        public static int QueryCounter { get; set; }

        public static string FormatSQL()
        {
            BasicFormatter formatter = new BasicFormatter();
            return formatter.Format(NHibernateGeneratedSQL.ToUpper());
        }

    }
}
```

Next, open the NHibernateBase class and create an Interceptor, as shown in Listing 1-41.

LISTING 1-41: Capturing an NHibernate-generated SQL query

```
using NHibernate.SqlCommand;

public class SQLInterceptor : EmptyInterceptor, IInterceptor
{
    SqlString IInterceptor.OnPrepareStatement(NHibernate.SqlCommand.SqlString sql)
    {
        Utils.NHibernateGeneratedSQL = sql.ToString();
        Utils.QueryCounter++;
        return sql;
    }
}
```

The QueryCounter created previously in Listing 1-40 and then implemented here in Listing 1-41, counts the number of times NHibernate generates a SQL query. This property is useful in later chapters when MultiQuery, MultiCriteria, and the Future() method are implemented using IQuery, ICriteria, and LINQ. It demonstrates that batching the queries together is truly working.

 TIP Use the OnPrepareStatement() of the IInterceptor interface, along with the NHibernate.AdoNet.Util.BasicFormatter.Format() method, to format the SQL generated by NHibernate. By default, the SQL is not formatted and therefore not easy to read. The formatter improves the readability of the NHibernate-generated SQL.

Lastly, add the Interceptor to the ConfigureNHibernate() method of the NHibernateBase class. The following line of code adds the Interceptor to the configuration:

```
Configuration.SetInterceptor(new SQLInterceptor());
```

An Interceptor can be applied to either a Session or a Configuration. If the Interceptor is implemented using the SetInterceptor() method of the configuration, the Interceptor is applied to all Sessions opened from the SessionFactory. Think of this as the global implementation.

Conversely, passing the `Interceptor` as a parameter to the `OpenSession()` method of the `SessionFactory` applies the `Interceptor` to that specific `Session` only.

The `Interceptor` class provides some methods that do not exist in the `Event` context. Some interesting ones are `OnPrepareStatement()`, mentioned previously; `AfterTransactionBegin()`; `BeforeTransactionCompletion()`; and `AfterTransactionCompletion()`. That being said, if you need to perform an action before a transaction, before the end of a transaction, or after a transaction, use an `Interceptor`, because `Events` do not have this capability.

Events

NHibernate also contains many event interfaces, found in the `NHibernate.Event` namespace. The event interfaces such as `IPreDeleteEventListener.cs`, `IPostDeleteEventListener.cs`, and `IPreInsertEventListener.cs` typically implement a single method, such as `OnPreDelete()`, `OnPostDelete()`, or `OnPreInsert()`, respectively, which can be modified and enhanced in a custom class.

Creating an Event to Log Deletions

The code required to log an event when a delete occurs is shown in Listing 1-42. Add the code to the `NHibernateBase` class found in the `NHibernate.GuitarStore` class library.

LISTING 1-42: Creating a PostDeleteEvent

```
using NHibernate.Event;

public class AuditDeleteEvent : IPostDeleteEventListener
{
    public void OnPostDelete(PostDeleteEvent @event)
    {
        log.Info(@event.Id.ToString() + " has been deleted.");
    }
}
```

The `OpenSession()` method of the `SessionFactory` does not provide a method that accepts `Events`. Therefore, `Events` must be registered via the `NHibernate.Cfg.Configuration` class, which provides a private `EventListeners` class that allows the inclusion of `Events` into the configuration object. Listing 1-43 shows the line of code that adds an `Event` to the configuration.

LISTING 1-43: Adding an Event to the configuration

```
using NHibernate.Event;

Configuration.EventListeners.PostDeleteEventListeners =
    new IPostDeleteEventListener[] { new AuditDeleteEvent() };
```

Implementing the Interceptor and Event Classes

Now that the `Interceptor` and `Event` classes have been created, the next step is to implement them into the `GuitarStore` WPF program. In this section, you will perform the following tasks:

1. Add a View SQL button to the `GuitarStore` to display the most recently executed SQL query.

2. Add a traffic-light image to display database round-trips.

3. Add a Delete `Button` control to remove an item from inventory, then log the `Event` to a log file.

Viewing NHibernate-Generated SQL in Real Time

Add a button to the `GuitarStore` WPF program by dragging and dropping a `Button` control onto the `MainWindow.xaml` window. Modify the `Content` to "View SQL" and add a `Click` event. The code behind the `Click` event should resemble what is shown in Listing 1-44.

LISTING 1-44: Showing the NHibernate-generated SQL

```
private void buttonViewSQL_Click(object sender, RoutedEventArgs e)
{
   MessageBox.Show(Utils.FormatSQL(), "Most recent NHibernate generated SQL",
            MessageBoxButton.OK, MessageBoxImage.Information);
}
```

Running the `GuitarStore` WPF program and clicking the View SQL button results in the window shown in Figure 1-22.

FIGURE 1-22

Currently, the last query run on the database is the one that populates the `ComboBox` with the `Guitar` types on the `Guitar` table.

Implementing the Database Round-Trip Counter

The round-trip database counter is a cool tool that counts the number of times a unit of work goes back and forth between the program and the database server.

The first action is to add the three traffic-light images (red, yellow, green) to the `GuitarStore` WPF project. Right-click on the `Images` directory ⇨ Add ⇨ Existing Item. Next, drag and drop an `Image` control onto the `MainWindow.xaml` window, add a `Source` element that points to `/Images/green .jpg`, and name the `Image` control `ImageDatabaseCounter`.

Next, in the `MainWindow.xaml` window, add the code shown in Listing 1-45 directly after the `Window` element.

LISTING 1-45: Round-trip counter image settings

```
<Window.Resources>
    <ResourceDictionary>
        <ImageSource x:Key="ImageDatabaseCounterGreen">
                                        Images/green.jpg</ImageSource>
        <ImageSource x:Key="ImageDatabaseCounterYellow">
                                        Images/yellow.jpg</ImageSource>
        <ImageSource x:Key="ImageDatabaseCounterRed">
                                        Images/red.jpg</ImageSource>
    </ResourceDictionary>
</Window.Resources>
```

Next, add Listing 1-46 to `MainWindow.xaml.cs`. The `SetDatabaseRoundTripImage()` method checks the number of times a round-trip to the database has occurred and sets the `Image` control to the proper image.

LISTING 1-46: Setting the image based on the number of database round-trips

```
public void SetDatabaseRoundTripImage()
{
  if (Utils.QueryCounter < 0)
  {
    ImageDatabaseCounter.Source =
                (ImageSource)FindResource("ImageDatabaseCounterRed");
    ImageDatabaseCounter.ToolTip = "Error";
  }
  else if (Utils.QueryCounter == 0)
  {
    //Image is reset when, for example, the Configuration is changed
    ImageDatabaseCounter.Source =
                (ImageSource)FindResource("ImageDatabaseCounterGreen");
    ImageDatabaseCounter.ToolTip = "";
  }
  else if (Utils.QueryCounter == 1)
  {
    ImageDatabaseCounter.Source =
                (ImageSource)FindResource("ImageDatabaseCounterGreen");
    ImageDatabaseCounter.ToolTip = "1 round trip to database";
  }
  else if (Utils.QueryCounter == 2)
  {
    ImageDatabaseCounter.Source =
```

```
                         (ImageSource)FindResource("ImageDatabaseCounterYellow");
    ImageDatabaseCounter.ToolTip = "2 round trip to database";
  }
  else if (Utils.QueryCounter > 2)
  {
    ImageDatabaseCounter.Source =
                    (ImageSource)FindResource("ImageDatabaseCounterRed");
    ImageDatabaseCounter.ToolTip =
                    Utils.QueryCounter.ToString() + " round trip to database";
  }
  //reset the value each time this method is called.
  Utils.QueryCounter = 0;
}
```

Calling the preceding method at the end of the Window_Loaded() method results in a yellow image, as two database round-trips were performed. The first query populates the DataGrid and the second populates the ComboBox.

Using the Event to Write to a Log

One of the requirements listed for the GuitarStore WPF program is to log when an Inventory item is deleted from the database. An NHibernate Event is used to write to a log.

The first action to take is to write the query to delete the Inventory item. Open the NHibernateInventory.cs file and add the IQuery method shown in Listing 1-47.

LISTING 1-47: Deleting an Inventory item using HQL

```
public bool DeleteInventoryItem(Guid Id)
{
  using (ITransaction transaction = Session.BeginTransaction())
  {
    try
    {
      IQuery query = Session.CreateQuery("from Inventory where Id = :Id")
                            .SetGuid("Id", Id);
      Inventory inventory = query.List<Inventory>()[0];
      Session.Delete(inventory);
      transaction.Commit();
      return true;
    }
    catch (Exception ex)
    {
      transaction.Rollback();
      return false;
    }
  }
}
```

Now add a button to the GuitarStore WPF program by again dragging and dropping a Button control onto the MainWindow.xaml window. Rename the button content to Delete. Add a Click event, which calls the preceding listing. The following code in Listing 1-48 shows the contents of the `Click` event found in the `MainWindow.xaml.cs` file:

LISTING 1-48: Deleting an Inventory item from the GuitarStore WPF program

```
private void buttonDelete_Click(object sender, RoutedEventArgs e)
{
    Inventory inventoryItem = (Inventory)dataGridInventory.SelectedItem;
    Guid item = new Guid(inventoryItem.Id.ToString());

    NHibernateInventory nhi = new NHibernateInventory();
    if (nhi.DeleteInventoryItem(item))
    {
        dataGridInventory.ItemsSource = null;
        PopulateDataGrid();
        labelMessage.Content = "Item deleted.";
    }
    else
    {
        labelMessage.Content = "Item deletion failed.";
    }
}
```

When a row from the `Inventory` is selected and the Delete button is clicked, the row is deleted from the database and a log is written to the file. Writing to the log file takes place in the `AuditDeleteEvent()` method using the previously configured log4net feature. The entry in the log file resembles what is shown in Figure 1-23.

```
2011-03-09 10:25:30 INFO  [10] ~ 9c68aaea-4a93-11e0-9f1c-cb52dfd72085 has been deleted.
```

FIGURE 1-23

SUMMARY

A lot has been covered in this chapter, from the creation of the Visual Studio solution to the implementation of some of NHibernate's sophisticated features, such as `Interceptors`, serialization, and lazy loading. You learned that using serialization significantly reduces the time required to build the `SessionFactory` because the mapping files are validated and serialized once, and then future startups do not require validation again. Additionally, you learned that with the release of NHibernate 3.2 there now exists a default proxy, which means its manual configuration is no longer required and that instead of using `.hbm.xml` files to map your entities, you can map your entities by code. In the following chapters, detailed instruction and implementation of the different data manipulation interfaces that NHibernate exposes, such as `IQuery`, LINQ, `ICriteria`, and `QueryOver`, are discussed.

2

Using HQL

In the previous chapter, you learned about a few of NHibernate's capabilities, such as lazy loading, `Interceptors`, logging, and `Events`. Most important, you learned how to install and configure NHibernate so that it can be used to retrieve data from a database. This chapter addresses using *Hibernate Query Language (HQL)*, which is a fully object-oriented query language similar in appearance to SQL. This chapter covers the following topics:

> ➤   `CreateQuery`, `CreateMultiQuery`, `GetNamedQuery`, `DetachedQuery`, `DetachedNamedQuery`, and Futures

> ➤   Implementing paging

> ➤   Creating a round-trip database counter

INTRODUCTION

The `IQuery` API is used for executing HQL queries on a database. HQL is my personal preference when I don't have or need a specific class to store the results of a query. As shown later in this chapter, some NHibernate methods require using a strongly typed class to retrieve data from the database.

Many HQL methods are made available via the `Session` interface to execute a query against the database. Figure 2-1 shows a graphical representation of the methods, such as `CreateQuery` and `CreateNamedQuery`, and their corresponding execution methods, such as `List<T>()` or `List()`, for using the `IQuery` API. This chapter describes each of the methods and provides examples demonstrating how they can be used to fulfill most of the `GuitarStore` project requirements defined in Chapter 1.

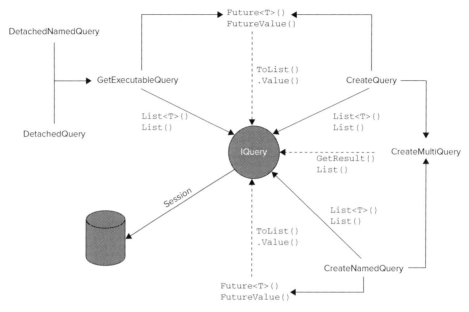

FIGURE 2-1

Figure 2-2 shows the IQuery, AbstractQueryImpl, and QueryImpl class diagram. IQuery is the interface that is used to implement and create your query objects. When you call the Session.CreateQuery() method, for example, it returns an IQuery. The methods used to execute HQL queries are found in the NHibernate.Impl namespace. An implementation of the IQuery interface is found in the QueryImpl class, which inherits from the abstract AbstractQueryImpl class. Figure 2-2 also shows a few of the methods found in both the QueryImpl and the AbstractQueryImpl classes. Download the NHibernate source code from http://nhforge.org to see them all and how they work.

FIGURE 2-2

The example project used in this book does not require the creation of complex SQL queries, because only two tables exist. As shown in following code snippet, it is possible to create joins between tables using dot (.) notation:

```
Select g.Type, g.Inventory.Model from Guitar g order by g.Type
```

This is a powerful technique, and one that makes data access intuitive from a programmer's perspective.

Users new to NHibernate frequently ask which query API should be used, as there are several of them. In most cases it is just a matter of preference. I have seen no proof of one API being faster than another in terms of the performance of generated SQL. In many cases the SQL generated using IQuery is identical to ICriteria. Take, for example, a query used to search for models on the GUITAR table. Listing 2-1 compares the SQL query generated using IQuery and ICriteria.

LISTING 2-1: SQL generated using IQuery and ICriteria

```
IQuery:
select inventory0_.MODEL as col_0_0_
from INVENTORY inventory0_
where inventory0_.MODEL like @p0

ICriteria:
SELECT this_.MODEL as MODEL1_0_
FROM INVENTORY this_
WHERE this_.MODEL like @p0
```

Other than the naming and case, the NHibernate-generated SQL queries shown here are identical. Nonetheless, there are some things about the IQuery (HQL) API that I personally like and can recommend:

> ➤ You can use it when a query has a WHERE clause that is known at design time.

> ➤ Data can be retrieved dynamically or strongly typed.

> ➤ You can use it when a query has a significant number of joins.

> ➤ You can use it when the entire query is known at runtime.

> ➤ You can view and modify the HQL query because it is a string.

> ➤ IQuery considers everything lazy by default.

> ➤ You can define parameters explicitly using a method or add them directly to the string.

It is common for programs to execute queries with static WHERE clauses. Take the program created in this book, for example. The query used to retrieve the data based on a user's selection of guitar type uses the foreign key relationship between the GUITAR and INVENTORY tables, as shown in the following code snippet.

```
from Inventory where TypeId = :TypeId order by Builder
```

The `Id` of the type selected from the `ComboBox` is passed to the preceding HQL query, which retrieves the inventory of those types of guitars. Figure 2-3 shows how the `GuitarStore` Windows Presentation Foundation (WPF) program looks with a filtered `DataGrid`.

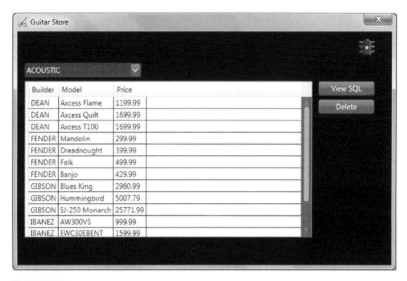

FIGURE 2-3

Until now, only strongly typed data retrieval with NHibernate has been discussed. What if the requirements don't call for retrieving all the columns or properties within the class? True, it is possible to lazy load some of the properties, but that wouldn't be the best solution in this scenario because of the limited amount of data being retrieved. What is needed is projection, an example of which is shown in the following code snippet.

```
select Model, QOH, Price from Inventory where TypeId = :TypeId
```

This HQL query returns only the `Model`, `QOH`, and `Price` for a given guitar type. However, you cannot return it as an `Inventory` class. It is executed using the `List()` execution method, rather than the `List<T>()`, as shown in Listing 2-2.

LISTING 2-2: Returning a dynamic HQL result set

```
public IList GetProjectedInventory()
{
    using (ITransaction transaction = Session.BeginTransaction())
    {
        IQuery query = Session.CreateQuery
            ("select Model, QOH, Price from Inventory order by Builder");
        return query.List();
    }
```

```
}

Generated SQL:

select inventory0_.MODEL as col_0_0_,
       inventory0_.QOH as col_1_0_,
       inventory0_.PRICE as col_2_0_
from INVENTORY inventory0_
order by inventory0_.BUILDER
```

When the result from an NHibernate query is not strongly typed, using that data becomes a little more complex. This is because with a strongly typed result, it is possible to access the data by property name. Conversely, when a result is not strongly typed, the data is accessible by index only. Figure 2-4 shows the difference between a strongly typed result (on the left) and a dynamic one (on the right).

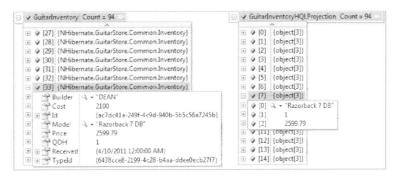

FIGURE 2-4

You can see a significant difference when you want to bind the dynamic result to a `DataGrid`. To bind a strongly typed result, you simply set the `AutoGenerateColumns` attribute of the `GuitarStore` WPF application to `true`, and the data is shown as retrieved. This is not the case with a dynamic result set. To display a dynamic result set, you need to build a `DataTable`, add the columns and rows to it, and then bind the `DataTable` to the `DataGrid`. The value of the `AutoGenerateColumns` attribute of the `DataGrid` should be set to `false`.

WORKING WITH CREATEQUERY()

The `CreateQuery()` method is the most commonly used method in the `IQuery` API. Implementing the `CreateQuery()` method in the `NHibernate.GuitarStore` class library and the `GuitarStore` WPF program requires the following actions:

1. Program a `CreateQuery()` method that returns a dynamic list of all inventory.

2. Create a `BuildDataTable()` method that converts the dynamic list to a `DataTable`.

3. Bind the result from the `BuildDataTable()` to a `DataGrid`.

4. Program a `CreateQuery()` method that accepts and uses a guitar type as parameter to constrain the result set.

First, open the `GuitarStore` solution if it's not already open. Within the `NHibernate.GuitarStore` project, double-click the `NHibernateInventory.cs` file. Add the method in Listing 2-3, which returns an `Inventory` result set containing only `Model`, `QOH`, and `Price`.

LISTING 2-3: CreateQuery() method returning projected inventory

```
public IList GetDynamicInventory()
{
  using (ITransaction transaction = Session.BeginTransaction())
  {
    IQuery query = Session.CreateQuery
      ("select Builder, Model, Price, Id from Inventory order by Builder");
    return query.List();
  }
}
```

Generated SQL:

```
select inventory0_.BUILDER as col_0_0_,
inventory0_.MODEL as col_1_0_, inventory0_.PRICE as col_2_0_,
inventory0_.ID as col_3_0_
from INVENTORY inventory0_
order by inventory0_.BUILDER
```

Next, from the `GuitarStore` WPF project, open the `MainWindow.xaml.cs` file and add the method shown in Listing 2-4. The `BuildDataTable()` method converts a list of column names and an `IList` containing an NHibernate dynamic result set into a `DataTable`.

LISTING 2-4: Creating a DataTable using an IList containing a dynamic result

```
public DataTable BuildDataTable(List<string> columns, IList results)
{
  DataTable dataTable = new DataTable();
  foreach (string column in columns)
  {
    dataTable.Columns.Add(column, typeof(string));
  }

  if (columns.Count > 1)
  {
    foreach (object[] row in results)
    {
      dataTable.Rows.Add(row);
    }
  }
  return dataTable;
}
```

To retrieve the dynamic `Inventory` result set, use the method created previously in Listing 2-3, then bind the result of the `BuildDataTable()` method to the `DataGrid`, as shown in Listing 2-5.

```
using System.Collections;
using System.Data;
using NHibernate.GuitarStore.DataAccess;

private void Window_Loaded(object sender, RoutedEventArgs e)
{
    NHibernateInventory nhi = new NHibernateInventory();
    List<string> fields = new List<string>
    {
        "Builder", "Model", "Price", "Id"
    };

    IList GuitarInventory = nhi.GetDynamicInventory();
    dataGridInventory.ItemsSource =
            BuildDataTable(fields, GuitarInventory).DefaultView;

    if (GuitarInventory != null)
    {
        dataGridInventory.Columns[3].Visibility = System.Windows.Visibility.Hidden;
    }
}
```

Finally, add a new method to the NHibernateInventory class that accepts a guitar type as a parameter and then constrains the result based on that value, and then modify the comboBoxGuitarTypes_SelectionChanged() method within the MainWindow.xaml.cs file of the GuitarStore WPF project to use the newly added method. Listing 2-6 shows the code for the new method added to the NHibernateInventory class that accepts and uses a guitar type.

LISTING 2-6: CreateQuery() method returning inventory by guitar type

```
public IList GetDynamicInventory(Guid TypeId)
{
    using (ITransaction transaction = Session.BeginTransaction())
    {
        string hqlQuery = "select Builder, Model, Price, Id " +
                          "from Inventory " +
                          "where TypeId = :TypeId order by Builder";
        IQuery query = Session.CreateQuery(hqlQuery).SetGuid("TypeId", TypeId);

        return query.List();
    }
}

Generated SQL:

select inventory0_.BUILDER as col_0_0_,
       inventory0_.MODEL as col_1_0_,
       inventory0_.PRICE as col_2_0_,
       inventory0_.ID as col_3_0_
from INVENTORY inventory0_
```

continues

LISTING 2-6 *(continued)*

```
where inventory0_.TYPEID=@p0
order by inventory0_.BUILDER;
@p0 = 471c5b3f-19da-4fcb-8e9f-48dd17a00a3d [Type: Guid (0)]
```

Before implementing the preceding code in the `GuitarStore` WPF program, add it to the `Main()` method of the `NHibernate.GuitarStore.Console` application and test to ensure that it returns the expected results. Listing 2-7, shows how to do this.

LISTING 2-7: Testing CreateQuery() in the console application

```
Guid guitarType = new Guid("471c5b3f-19da-4fcb-8e9f-48dd17a00a3d");
IList list11 = nhi.GetDynamicInventory(guitarType);
Console.WriteLine("GetDynamicInventory(guitarType): " +
                  list11.Count.ToString() + " results");
```

Testing the method in the console application also gives you an opportunity to view the SQL generated by NHibernate.

Lastly, the `comboBoxGuitarTypes_SelectionChanged()` method should be updated to resemble the code in Listing 2-8.

LISTING 2-8: CreateQuery() method from a SelectionChanged() method

```
private void comboBoxGuitarTypes_SelectionChanged
                          (object sender, SelectionChangedEventArgs e)
{
  try
  {
    dataGridInventory.ItemsSource = null;
    Guitar guitar = (Guitar)comboBoxGuitarTypes.SelectedItem;
    Guid guitarType = new Guid(guitar.Id.ToString());

    NHibernateInventory nhi = new NHibernateInventory();
    IList GuitarInventory = nhi.GetDynamicInventory(guitarType);
    List<string> fields = new List<string>
    {
        "Builder", "Model", "Price", "Id"
    };
    dataGridInventory.ItemsSource =
                    BuildDataTable(fields, GuitarInventory).DefaultView;

    if (GuitarInventory != null)
    {
      dataGridInventory.Columns[3].Visibility =
                      System.Windows.Visibility.Hidden;
    }
  }
  catch (Exception ex)
```

```
    {
      labelMessage.Content = ex.Message;
    }
  }
```

The preceding method captures the selected guitar type from the ComboBox, passes its Id to the GetDynamicInventory() method, builds the DataTable, and binds it to the DataGrid.

Implementing Paging

It is always a good idea to restrict the number of rows returned with a query. Currently, this implementation returns all the rows in the INVENTORY table. It works well enough now because the table contains fewer than 100 rows. If this were implemented in a scenario in which the result set were in the thousands or hundreds of thousands, it would not perform as well.

The IQuery API provides two methods for implementing paging: SetMaxResults() and SetFirstResult(). The SetMaxResults() method accepts an integer as a parameter that defines the maximum number of rows that should be returned for the query. This is often referred to as *Top N*.

 NOTE *You don't need to worry about implementing paging differently between, for example, Microsoft SQL Server and Oracle. SQL Server uses Top N, whereas Oracle uses* rownum *to restrict results. Code it once using NHibernate and it works without modification whether the database is changed from SQL Server to Oracle or vice versa.*

The SetFirstResult() method also accepts an integer as a parameter. As the name of the method implies, it sets the first row returned from the database. Therefore, for the first query, the value should be 0, with future queries being *n* plus the value sent to the SetMaxResults() method.

 NOTE *When using* IQuery *for paging, the first value passed to the* SetFirstResult() *should be 0. However, the* ICriteria SetFirstResult() *method expects a 1.*

The steps required to add paging functionality to the GuitarStore WPF program are as follows:

1. Create a method that accepts both a max result and a first result as parameters and uses them to return the expected result.

2. Program a method to retrieve the total number of rows on the INVENTORY table.

3. Create and use a PopulateDataGrid() method to populate the DataGrid, rather than using the Window_Loaded() method.

4. Add paging buttons and logic to the GuitarStore WPF program.

The first action taken to implement paging in the GuitarStore WPF program is to create a new GetPagedInventory() method. This method should accept a max result and a first result as parameters. Add the code shown in Listing 2-9 to the NHibernateInventory class.

LISTING 2-9: HQL paging method

```
public IList GetPagedInventory(int MaxResult, int FirstResult)
{
  string hqlQuery = "select Builder, Model, Price, Id " +
                    "from Inventory order by Builder";
  using (ITransaction transaction = Session.BeginTransaction())
  {
    IQuery query = Session.CreateQuery(hqlQuery)
                          .SetMaxResults(MaxResult)
                          .SetFirstResult(FirstResult);
    return query.List();
  }
}

Generated SQL (where max=25 and first=0):

select TOP (@p0)
       inventory0_.BUILDER as col_0_0_,
       inventory0_.MODEL as col_1_0_,
       inventory0_.PRICE as col_2_0_,
       inventory0_.ID as col_3_0_
from INVENTORY inventory0_
order by inventory0_.BUILDER;
@p0 = 25 [Type: Int32 (0)]

Generated SQL (where max=25 and first=26):

SELECT TOP (@p0)
       col_0_0_,
       col_1_0_,
       col_2_0_,
       col_3_0_
FROM (select inventory0_.BUILDER as col_0_0_,
             inventory0_.MODEL as col_1_0_,
             inventory0_.PRICE as col_2_0_,
             inventory0_.ID as col_3_0_,
             ROW_NUMBER()
             OVER(ORDER BY inventory0_.BUILDER) as __hibernate_sort_row
      from INVENTORY inventory0_) as query
WHERE query.__hibernate_sort_row > @p1
ORDER BY query.__hibernate_sort_row;
@p0 = 25 [Type: Int32 (0)],
@p1 = 26 [Type: Int32 (0)]
```

Note that two generated SQL queries are shown. The first displays the NHibernate-generated SQL query created when the SetMaxResults() method is 25 and the SetFirstResult() method is 0. When the first result is 0, it generally means that it is the first page being selected. The second

NHibernate-generated SQL query results from `SetMaxResults()` being 25 and `SetFirstResult()` being 26. The second SQL query returns rows 26 through 50.

When implementing paging, it is common practice to provide information about the current page and the overall result set to the user. That means the `GuitarStore` WPF program should populate a label with information about where the paged result set is in relation to the entire number of selectable rows on the table — for example, "Records 0 to 25 of 196 displayed." To do this, add a `GetInventoryCount()` method to the `NHibernateInventory` class that returns the total number of records on the `INVENTORY` table. This method is shown in Listing 2-10.

LISTING 2-10: HQL method to retrieve total record count of the **INVENTORY** table

```
public int GetInventoryCount()
{
    using (ITransaction transaction = Session.BeginTransaction())
    {
      IQuery query = Session.CreateQuery("select count(*) from Inventory");
      return Convert.ToInt32(query.UniqueResult());
    }
}

Generated SQL:

select count(*) as col_0_0_
from INVENTORY inventory0_
```

Up until now, the binding of the `CreateQuery` result set has been performed within the `Window_Loaded()` method of the `MainWindow.xaml.cs` file found in the `GuitarStore` WPF project. Instead of the using the `Window_Loaded()` method, a new method called `PopulateDataGrid()` is created in Listing 2-11. This new method is needed to provide paging buttons with a method for triggering the retrieval of a paged result set.

LISTING 2-11: PopulateDataGrid() using HQL paging functionality

```
public int FirstResult = 0;
public int MaxResult = 25;
public int totalCount = 0;

private void PopulateDataGrid()
{
    NHibernateInventory nhi = new NHibernateInventory();
    List<string> fields = new List<string>
    {
      "Builder", "Model", "Price", "Id"
    };
    IList GuitarInventory = nhi.GetPagedInventory(MaxResult, FirstResult);
    int inventoryCount = nhi.GetInventoryCount();
    dataGridInventory.ItemsSource =
```

continues

LISTING 2-11 *(continued)*

```
                BuildDataTable(fields, GuitarInventory).DefaultView;

    if (GuitarInventory != null)
    {
      dataGridInventory.Columns[3].Visibility = System.Windows.Visibility.Hidden;
    }

    labelPaging.Content = "Retrieved " + FirstResult.ToString() +
                    " to " + (FirstResult + GuitarInventory.Count).ToString() +
                    " of " + inventoryCount.ToString();
    totalCount = inventoryCount;
}
```

The preceding listing uses the GetDynamicInventory() method created in Listing 2-6 and the GetInventoryCount() method shown in Listing 2-10. The final step is to add paging buttons to the GuitarStore WPF program that call the PopulateDataGrid() method, which sets the FirstResult and the MaxResult class variables.

Add two buttons by dragging and dropping two Button controls from the Toolbox onto the GuitarStore WPF window. The XAML code should resemble Listing 2-12.

LISTING 2-12: Adding Button controls to the GuitarStore WPF program

```
<Button Content="-" IsEnabled="False" Click="buttonPrevious_Click" Height="23"
        HorizontalAlignment="Left" Margin="445,50,0,0" Name="buttonPrevious"
        VerticalAlignment="Top" Width="20" />
<Button Content="+" Click="buttonNext_Click" Height="23"
        HorizontalAlignment="Left" Margin="469,50,0,0" Name="buttonNext"
        VerticalAlignment="Top" Width="20" />
```

Lastly, add the code for both the buttonPrevious_Click() method and the buttonNext_Click() method, shown in Listing 2-13, to the MainWindow.xaml.cs file.

LISTING 2-13: buttonPrevious_Click() and buttonNext_Click() paging logic

```
private void buttonPrevious_Click(object sender, RoutedEventArgs e)
{
  if (FirstResult > 0)
  {
    FirstResult = FirstResult - MaxResult;
    if (FirstResult < 0) FirstResult = 0;
  }
  else
  {
    buttonPrevious.IsEnabled = false;
  }

  PopulateDataGrid();

  if (FirstResult.Equals(0))
```

```
    {
      buttonPrevious.IsEnabled = false;
    }
  }

  private void buttonNext_Click(object sender, RoutedEventArgs e)
  {
      buttonPrevious.IsEnabled = true;
      FirstResult = FirstResult + MaxResult;

      PopulateDataGrid();

      if (FirstResult > 0)
      {
        buttonPrevious.IsEnabled = true;
      }

      if (FirstResult + MaxResult >= totalCount)
      {
        buttonNext.IsEnabled = false;
      }
  }
```

The result of adding the paging buttons and label for tracking to the GuitarStore WPF program resembles Figure 2-5.

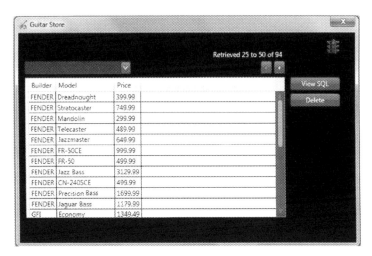

FIGURE 2-5

Using the Database Round-Trip Counter

Recall from Chapter 1 that an Interceptor named SQLInterceptor was implemented that captured the NHibernate-generated SQL query. The same Interceptor included a static integer named QueryCounter that is incremented each time a SQL query is created by NHibernate.

The stoplight image that was added to the GuitarStore WPF program is used to graphically represent the value contained within the QueryCounter property.

Referring to Figures 2-3 and 2-5, you can see the lights are yellow and red, respectively. The `GuitarStore` WPF program required two round-trips to the database to complete the `DataGrid` population and retrieve the total number of rows on the `INVENTORY` table in Figure 2-3. In Figure 2-5, the stoplight is red because three queries are performed when the program begins: selection of the `DataGrid` data, the `ComboBox` data, and the total count of rows on the `INVENTORY` table. Each selection uses a round-trip to the database.

It is not a bad thing to have multiple database round-trips when running a program. The stoplight thresholds used in this example are completely arbitrary and apply only to the `GuitarStore` WPF program. If this capability is implemented into your program, you need to decide which thresholds best apply to your program.

Calling the `SetDatabaseRoundTripImage()` method at the end of the `PopulateDataGrid()` method sets the stoplight image to yellow, which means it took two database round-trips to execute that method. It is important to do this here, because in the next section you will use the `CreateMultiQuery` method to combine the two round-trips into one.

 NOTE One of the most expensive pieces of a database transaction is the time spent sending requests between servers. Reducing the number of requests can improve performance.

Working with Calculated Fields

A calculated field derives its value from a calculation of other fields. One example is profit, which is a product of sale price minus cost. It is possible to use calculated fields with NHibernate. To add calculated fields to the `GuitarStore` solution, you perform the following steps:

1. Add a property to the `Inventory.cs` file to store the field called `Profit`.

2. Add a `Profit` property to the corresponding `Inventory.hbm.xml` mapping file, and include the formula that calculates the value.

3. Add a `Profit` column to the HQL query.

4. Add a `Profit` column to `DataTable` and display it in `DataGrid`.

First, open the `Inventory.cs` file found in the `Common` directory of the `NHibernate.GuitarStore` project. Add a new property named `Profit` so that the class file now resembles Listing 2-14.

LISTING 2-14: Inventory class with additional calculated field property

```
namespace NHibernate.GuitarStore.Common
{
    public class Inventory
    {
```

```
        public Inventory() { }

        public virtual Guid Id { get; set; }
        public virtual Guid TypeId { get; set; }
        public virtual string Builder { get; set; }
        public virtual string Model { get; set; }
        public virtual int? QOH { get; set; }
        public virtual decimal? Cost { get; set; }
        public virtual decimal? Price { get; set; }
        public virtual DateTime? Received { get; set; }
        public virtual decimal? Profit { get; set; }
    }
}
```

Next, open the `Inventory.hbm.xml` file in the `Mapping` directory of the `NHibernate.GuitarStore` project. Add a new property so that the mapping file now resembles Listing 2-15.

LISTING 2-15: Inventory mapping file with additional calculated field property

```xml
<?xml version="1.0" encoding="utf-8" ?>
<hibernate-mapping xmlns="urn:nhibernate-mapping-2.2"
                   assembly="NHibernate.GuitarStore">
  <class name="NHibernate.GuitarStore.Common.Inventory, NHibernate.GuitarStore"
         table="INVENTORY">
    <property name="TypeId"    column="TYPEID"    type="System.Guid"
    <property name="Builder"   column="BUILDER"   type="System.String" />
    <property name="Model"     column="MODEL"     type="System.String" />
    <property name="QOH"       column="QOH"       type="System.Int32" />
    <property name="Cost"      column="COST"      type="System.Decimal" />
    <property name="Price"     column="PRICE"     type="System.Decimal" />
    <property name="Received"  column="RECEIVED"  type="System.DateTime" />
    <property name="Profit"    formula="ROUND((Price-Cost), 2)" type="decimal"  />
  </class>
</hibernate-mapping>
```

Notice that the `formula` attribute is used. This attribute supports the insertion of SQL to calculate a property. Executing an HQL query that includes the `Profit` property results in the NHibernate-generated SQL shown in Listing 2-16. This approach calculates the `Profit` value on the database.

LISTING 2-16: NHibernate-generated SQL using the formula attribute

```sql
select inventory0_.BUILDER as col_0_0_,
       inventory0_.MODEL as col_1_0_,
       inventory0_.PRICE as col_2_0_,
       ROUND((inventory0_.Price-inventory0_.Cost), 2) as col_3_0_,
       inventory0_.ID as col_4_0_
from INVENTORY inventory0_
order by inventory0_.BUILDER
```

You can implement a calculated field without using the `formula` attribute. Instead of adding the code previously shown in Listing 2-15 and 2-16, add the code in Listing 2-17 to the `Inventory.cs` file located in the `Common` directory of the `NHibernate.GuitarStore` project. Because the `Price` and `Cost` already exist in this `Inventory` class, `Profit` can be defined as a normal property and is calculated using local memory.

LISTING 2-17: Inventory class calculated field property

```
public virtual decimal? Profit
{
  get { return ((decimal)Price - (decimal)Cost); }
}
```

No addition to the `Inventory.hbm.xml` mapping file is required if the code in Listing 2-17 is used. Next, add a general-purpose method to the `NHibernateInventory` class called `ExecuteHQL<T>()` that returns a strongly typed result set, as shown in Listing 2-18.

LISTING 2-18: General-purpose HQL query method

```
public IList<T> ExecuteHQL<T>(string hqlQuery)
{
  using (ITransaction transaction = Session.BeginTransaction())
  {
    IQuery query = Session.CreateQuery(hqlQuery);
    return query.List<T>();
  }
}

Generated SQL:

select inventory0_.ID as ID1_,
       inventory0_.TYPEID as TYPEID1_,
       inventory0_.BUILDER as BUILDER1_,
       inventory0_.MODEL as MODEL1_,
       inventory0_.QOH as QOH1_,
       inventory0_.COST as COST1_,
       inventory0_.PRICE as PRICE1_,
       inventory0_.RECEIVED as RECEIVED1_
from INVENTORY inventory0_
order by inventory0_.BUILDER
```

Notice that the SQL NHibernate generates for the `Inventory` class no longer contains the injected SQL formula, as in Listing 2-18. Modify the `PopulateDataGrid()` method located in the `MainWindow.xaml.cs` file within the `GuitarStore` WPF project, as shown in Listing 2-19.

LISTING 2-19: PopulateDataGrid() with strongly typed result set

```
private void PopulateDataGrid()
{
    NHibernateInventory nhi = new NHibernateInventory();
    IList<Inventory> GuitarInventory =
            nhi.ExecuteHQL<Inventory>("from Inventory order by Builder");
    dataGridInventory.ItemsSource = GuitarInventory;

    if (GuitarInventory != null)
    {
        dataGridInventory.Columns[0].Visibility = System.Windows.Visibility.Hidden;
        dataGridInventory.Columns[1].Visibility = System.Windows.Visibility.Hidden;
        dataGridInventory.Columns[9].Visibility = System.Windows.Visibility.Hidden;
    }
    SetDatabaseRoundTripImage();
}
```

The Profit property is now visible within the GuitarStore WPF window, as shown in Figure 2-6.

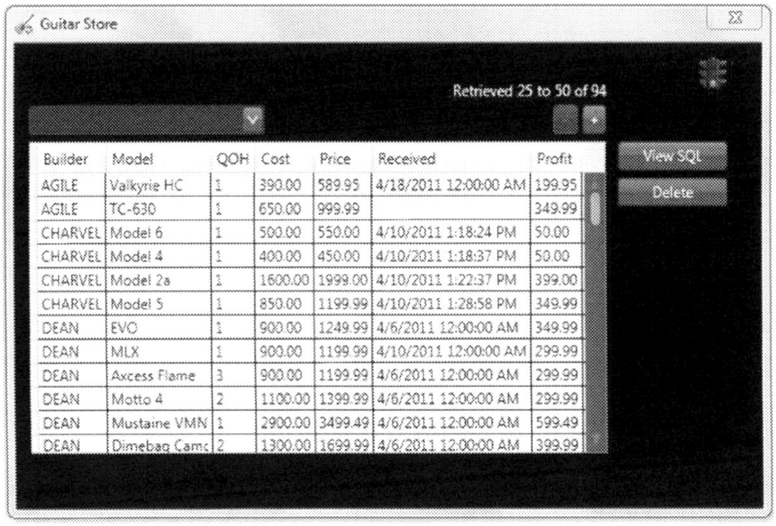

FIGURE 2-6

IMPLEMENTING CREATEMULTIQUERY()

One of the powerful features NHibernate supports is the batching of queries. This means it is possible to execute two or more queries on the database with a single trip. Two steps are needed to combine the query that populates the DataGrid and the query that selects the total row count of the INVENTORY table into one:

1. Create a method that uses CreateMultiQuery().

2. Modify the GuitarStore WPF PopulateDataGrid() method to use the multi-query method.

The first step is to create a new method named GetInventoryPaging() in the NHibernateInventory class to use CreateMultiQuery() and attach both the query that populates the DataGrid and the query that retrieves the total row count on the INVENTORY table. Listing 2-20 shows how it's done.

LISTING 2-20: Example of the CreateMultiQuery() method

```
public int GetInventoryPaging(int MaxResult, int FirstResult, out IList resultSet)
{
  using (ITransaction transaction = Session.BeginTransaction())
  {
    string hqlQuery = "select Builder, Model, Price, Id " +
                      "from Inventory order by Builder";
    IQuery query = Session.CreateQuery(hqlQuery)
                         .SetMaxResults(MaxResult)
                         .SetFirstResult(FirstResult);
    IQuery count = Session.CreateQuery("select count(*) from Inventory");

    IMultiQuery mQuery = Session.CreateMultiQuery()
                             .Add("result", query)
                             .Add<long>("RowCount", count);
    resultSet = (IList)mQuery.GetResult("result");
    int totalCount = (int)((IList<long>)mQuery.GetResult("RowCount")).Single();
    return totalCount;
  }
}

Generated SQL:

select TOP (@p0)
       inventory0_.BUILDER as col_0_0_,
       inventory0_.MODEL as col_1_0_,
       inventory0_.PRICE as col_2_0_,
       inventory0_.ID as col_3_0_
from INVENTORY inventory0_
order by inventory0_.BUILDER;
;@p0 = 25 [Type: Int32 (0)]
from INVENTORY inventory0_;
```

The GetInventoryPaging() method implements two CreateQuery() methods, each one being a different HQL query. Then the CreateMultiQuery() method is used to execute both methods and return the IMultiQuery interface. Notice the Add() method is used to attach the two HQL queries to the CreateMultiQuery() method. The strings ("result", "RowCount") are the values used in the GetResult() method of the IMultiQuery implementation to fetch the results retrieved from the database in a single round-trip.

The final step is to modify the PopulateDataGrid() method within the GuitarStore WPF program to use the method just shown. The PopulateDataGrid() method should resemble the code shown in Listing 2-21.

LISTING 2-21: Implementing CreateMultiQuery() in the GuitarStore WPF program

```
private void PopulateDataGrid()
{
  NHibernateInventory nhi = new NHibernateInventory();
  List<string> fields = new List<string>
  {
    "Builder", "Model", "Price", "Id"
  };
  IList GuitarInventory = null;
  int inventoryCount = nhi.GetInventoryPaging(MaxResult,
                                              FirstResult,
                                              out GuitarInventory);
  dataGridInventory.ItemsSource =
                  BuildDataTable(fields, GuitarInventory).DefaultView;

  if (GuitarInventory != null)
  {
    dataGridInventory.Columns[3].Visibility = System.Windows.Visibility.Hidden;
  }

  labelPaging.Content = "Retrieved " + FirstResult.ToString() +
                        " to " + (FirstResult + GuitarInventory.Count).ToString() +
                        " of " + inventoryCount.ToString();

  totalCount = inventoryCount;

  SetDatabaseRoundTripImage();
}
```

Two different ways to confirm that the count and the DataGrid retrieval occurred via a single round-trip to the database have been implemented. Notice in Figure 2-7 that the stoplight is now green and the tool tip says "1 round-trip to database."

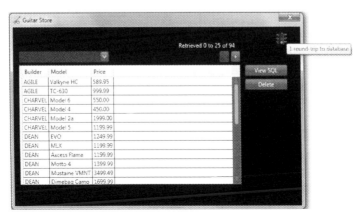

FIGURE 2-7

The second possibility is to select the View SQL button, which displays the most recently executed NHibernate-generated SQL query. As shown in Figure 2-8, the first query is the paging query, which returns the data for the DataGrid, and the second query is the select count(*) query.

FIGURE 2-8

Not all database management systems (DBMSs) support multiple queries. To determine whether the DBMS supports multiple queries, navigate to the namespace NHibernate.Driver.YOURDRIVER.cs and search for an overridden instance of the SupportsMultipleQueries() method. If you find it and it returns true, then you can use multiple queries. The YOURDRIVER.cs class inherits from the NHibernate.Driver.DriverBase class and contains the virtual method SupportsMultipleQueries(), which returns false. Therefore, unless it is overridden in a child class to return true, batching the queries together does not work.

If you are developing a program that may be used with a number of different DBMSs, you need to be careful about using CreateMultiQuery(). Multiple queries work on Microsoft SQL Server; however, if you point it to an Oracle or DB2 database, you will receive an error stating that this DBMS does not support multiple queries. This is demonstrated in Listing 2-22.

LISTING 2-22: MultiQueryImpl method() throwing an exception

```
internal MultiQueryImpl(ImplSession session,
    ISessionFactoryImplementor factory)
{
    IDriver driver = session.Factory.ConnectionProvider.Driver:
    if (!driver.SupportMultipleQueries)
    {
        throw new NotSupportedException(
       string.Format("The driver {0} does not support multiple queries.",
            driver.GetType().FullName);
```

```
    }
    dialect = session.Factory.Dialect;
    this.session = session;
    this.factory = factory;
}
```

> **TIP** *Oracle and many other database management systems do not support multiple queries. Use Futures instead. In this case, the queries won't be batched but they will execute and return results.*

UNDERSTANDING GETNAMEDQUERY()

The `GetNamedQuery()` method enables programmers to store a static HQL or SQL query that can be accessed and executed by passing its name as a parameter. For example, if you know that the query you need to run may change, an alternative to storing the query as a string in the source code is to store the query in an `.hbm.xml` file instead. Similar to a normal HQL query using the `CreateQuery()`, it is possible to send parameters to a named query.

> **NOTE** *When using named queries, the syntax is validated against the mapping files when the* `SessionFactory` *is initially built at runtime. If the HQL query is stored within a function as a string, you will only know if it works when attempting to execute the query.*

To implement `GetNamedQuery`, the following must be performed:

1. Create a `query.hbm.xml` file to contain named queries.
2. Create an HQL query that returns the SUM of each guitar type.
3. Create a general-purpose method that retrieves data using a named query.
4. Add a Sum `Button` to the `GuitarStore` WPF program and display the named query results in the `DataGrid`.

As described in the preceding list, the first action to take is to create a `Query.hbm.xml` file to store the named queries. The file containing the named queries can have any name, but it is good practice to separate the named queries from the class mappings. It is very important, as previously mentioned, that in the properties window you set the Build Action to Embedded Resource or that you add the `.hbm.xml` file to the program's working directory. Otherwise, it is not included in the `Configuration` and an exception is thrown.

The contents of the `Query.hbm.xml` file are shown in Listing 2-23. Queries to calculate the sum of each guitar type have been added using both SQL and HQL.

LISTING 2-23: Named Query.hbm.xml example

```xml
<?xml version="1.0" encoding="utf-8" ?>
<hibernate-mapping xmlns="urn:nhibernate-mapping-2.2">
  <sql-query name="GuitarValueByTypeSQL">
    <![CDATA[
      SELECT G.TYPE, SUM(I.COST)
      FROM GUITAR G, INVENTORY I
      WHERE G.ID = I.TYPEID
      GROUP BY G.TYPE
      ]]>
  </sql-query>
  <query name="GuitarValueByTypeHQL">
    <![CDATA[
      select g.Type, SUM(i.Cost)
      from Guitar g, Inventory i
      where g.Id = i.TypeId
      group by g.Type
      ]]>
  </query>
</hibernate-mapping>
```

Note that using the `sql-query` element notifies NHibernate that the contained query is native SQL. NHibernate utilizes the `SqlQueryImpl` class instead of the `QueryImpl` class to execute the SQL and return the result as an `IQuery` object.

 WARNING *Using native SQL should be avoided because the syntax is completely database specific and nonportable between different databases (so a `sql-query` that runs in SQL Server probably won't run in Oracle or other databases); the example is here only to show that it is possible. HQL is the preferred syntax for use with named queries.*

When an HQL query is provided, the `QueryImpl` class is used. If you want to view the source code for `GetNamedQuery()`, it can be found in the `NHibernate.Impl` namespace within the `AbstractSessionImpl` class. Comparing the `GetNamedQuery()` method source to the `CreateQuery()` method source, located in the same class, would reveal many similarities.

Next, create a general-purpose method that can take the name of the query as an argument and return the results. Listing 2-24 displays this method added to the `NHibernateInventory` class.

LISTING 2-24: Example using the GetNamedQuery() method

```csharp
public IList ExecuteNamedQuery(string QueryName)
{
  using (ITransaction transaction = Session.BeginTransaction())
  {
    IQuery query = Session.GetNamedQuery(QueryName);
    return query.List();
```

```
    }
  }

Generated SQL:

select guitar0_.TYPE as col_0_0_,
       SUM(inventory1_.COST) as col_1_0_
from GUITAR guitar0_,
     INVENTORY inventory1_
where guitar0_.ID=inventory1_.TYPEID
group by guitar0_.TYPE
```

Before implementing the ExecuteNamedQuery() in the GuitarStore WPF program, open the Program.cs file found in the NHibernate.GuitarStore console application project and add the following code in Listing 2-25.

LISTING 2-25: Testing the ExecuteNamedQuery() method from the console

```
IList guitarTypeSUM = nhi.ExecuteNamedQuery("GuitarValueByTypeHQL");
Console.WriteLine("ExecuteNamedQuery(GuitarValueByTypeHQL): " +
                  guitarTypeSUM15.Count.ToString() + " results");
```

Rather than try to implement the previous method directly in the GuitarStore WPF program, test it first to ensure that it works. This way, you are removing the implementation layer from any debugging efforts required if problems occur.

The next step is to drag a Button control from the Toolbox and add it to the GuitarStore WPF window. Listing 2-26 shows the addition of the Button and the Click event, buttonSUM_Click, which is called when the button is selected.

LISTING 2-26: Adding the Sum button, which calls the ExecuteNamedQuery() method

```
<Button Content="Sum" Height="23" HorizontalAlignment="Left"
        Margin="499,137,0,0" Name="buttonSUM" VerticalAlignment="Top"
        Width="92" Click="buttonSUM_Click" />
```

Finally, add the code to the buttonSUM_Click() method created in the MainWindow.xaml.cs file that uses the ExecuteNamedQuery() method and binds the results to the DataGrid. Listing 2-27 shows the contents of the buttonSUM_Click() method.

LISTING 2-27: Using the buttonSUM_Click() method to run the ExecuteNamedQuery() method

```
private void buttonSUM_Click(object sender, RoutedEventArgs e)
{
   NHibernateInventory nhi = new NHibernateInventory();
   List<string> fields = new List<string>
   {
     "Guitar Type", "Total Value"
   };
```

continues

LISTING 2-27 *(continued)*

```
    IList GuitarInventory = nhi.ExecuteNamedQuery("GuitarValueByTypeHQL");
    dataGridInventory.ItemsSource =
                        BuildDataTable(fields, GuitarInventory).DefaultView;

    SetDatabaseRoundTripImage();
}
```

Figure 2-9 is an example of the data returned from the `ExecuteNameQuery()`, which utilizes NHibernate's `GetNamedQuery()` method.

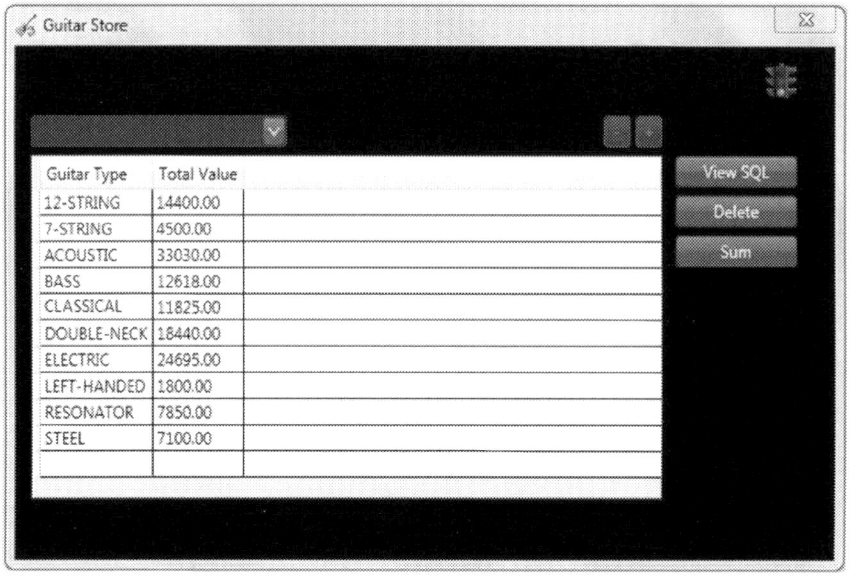

FIGURE 2-9

Implementing Aggregate Database Functions with GetNamedQuery

NHibernate supports the most common aggregate database functions, but not all of them. The following list shows aggregates supported by NHibernate:

➤ AVG

➤ SUM

➤ MIN

➤ MAX

➤ COUNT

In this section, aggregate database functions will be implemented via the `GetNamedQuery()` method. However, it is possible to use them directly within an HQL statement or `ICriteria`, which is discussed in the next chapter. You will perform the following steps in this section:

1. Add AVG, MIN, MAX, and COUNT queries to the `Query.hbm.xml` file.

2. Add AVG, MIN, MAX, and COUNT buttons to the `GuitarStore` WPF program.

3. Reuse the general-purpose method, `ExecuteNamedQuery()`, to execute each of the aggregate database functions.

First, add a few more named queries to the `Query.hbm.xml` file to retrieve the average cost of the guitars by type, the least expensive guitar by type, the most expensive guitar by type, and the quantity on hand by guitar type. The HQL queries that use AVG, MIN, MAX, and COUNT are shown in Listing 2-28.

LISTING 2-28: Example of HQL aggregate functions

```
<query name="GuitarAVGValueByTypeHQL">
  <![CDATA[
    select g.Type, ROUND(AVG(i.Cost), 2)
    from Guitar g, Inventory i
    where g.Id = i.TypeId
    group by g.Type
    ]]>
</query>
<query name="GuitarMINValueByTypeHQL">
  <![CDATA[
    select g.Type, MIN(i.Cost)
    from Guitar g, Inventory i
    where g.Id = i.TypeId
    group by g.Type
    ]]>
</query>
<query name="GuitarMAXValueByTypeHQL">
  <![CDATA[
    select g.Type, MAX(i.Cost)
    from Guitar g, Inventory i
    where g.Id = i.TypeId
    group by g.Type
    ]]>
</query>
<query name="GuitarCOUNTByTypeHQL">
  <![CDATA[
    select g.Type, COUNT(DISTINCT i.Model)
    from Guitar g, Inventory i
    where g.Id = i.TypeId
    group by g.Type
    ]]>
</query>
```

The ExecuteNamedQuery() method is used to execute the previously listed HQL named queries. No additional method needs to be added to the NHibernateInventory class to execute them. The NHibernate-generated SQL for the named HQL queries in Listing 2-28 are shown in Listing 2-29.

LISTING 2-29: NHibernate-generated aggregate database function SQL query

```
Average:

select guitar0_.TYPE as col_0_0_,
       round(AVG(inventory1_.COST), 2) as col_1_0_
from GUITAR guitar0_,
     INVENTORY inventory1_
where guitar0_.ID=inventory1_.TYPEID
group by guitar0_.TYPE

Minimum:

select guitar0_.TYPE as col_0_0_,
       MIN(inventory1_.COST) as col_1_0_
from GUITAR guitar0_,
     INVENTORY inventory1_
where guitar0_.ID=inventory1_.TYPEID
group by guitar0_.TYPE

Maximum:

select guitar0_.TYPE as col_0_0_,
       MAX(inventory1_.COST) as col_1_0_
from GUITAR guitar0_,
     INVENTORY inventory1_
where guitar0_.ID=inventory1_.TYPEID
group by guitar0_.TYPE

Count:

select guitar0_.TYPE as col_0_0_,
       count(distinct inventory1_.MODEL)as col_1_0_
from GUITAR guitar0_,
     INVENTORY inventory1_
where guitar0_.ID=inventory1_.TYPEID
group by guitar0_.TYPE
```

TIP *If you plan to use ODP.NET for your Oracle connection, be aware that there is a problem with the conversion of decimals. This is why I have used the* ROUND *method with the* AVG *function in Listing 2-30.* ROUND *is supported in both Oracle and Microsoft SQL Server.*

Next, add four `Button` controls (Average, Minimum, Maximum, and Count) to the `GuitarStore` WPF program. The XAML is shown in Listing 2-30.

LISTING 2-30: Aggregate database function buttons

```
<Button Content="Average" Height="23" HorizontalAlignment="Left"
        Margin="499,166,0,0" Name="buttonAverage" VerticalAlignment="Top"
        Width="92" Click="buttonAverage_Click" />
<Button Content="Minimum" Height="23" HorizontalAlignment="Left"
        Margin="499,195,0,0" Name="buttonMinimum" VerticalAlignment="Top"
        Width="92" Click="buttonMinimum_Click" />
<Button Content="Maximum" Height="23" HorizontalAlignment="Left"
        Margin="499,224,0,0" Name="buttonMaximum" VerticalAlignment="Top"
        Width="92" Click="buttonMaximum_Click" />
<Button Content="Count" Height="23" HorizontalAlignment="Left"
        Margin="499,253,0,0" Name="buttonCount" VerticalAlignment="Top"
        Width="92" Click="buttonCount_Click" />
```

Note that each of the buttons has a `Click` event and an associated method that is called when clicked. The content of the methods are identical other than the `DataGrid` column heading and the value of the named query to execute — for example, `GetCountByTypeHQL`. Listing 2-31 shows the code within the `buttonMaximum_Click()` method found within the `MainWindow.xaml.cs` file of the `GuitarStore` project.

LISTING 2-31: Calling an aggregate database funtion from GuitarStore WPF

```
private void buttonMaximum_Click(object sender, RoutedEventArgs e)
{
  NHibernateInventory nhi = new NHibernateInventory();
  List<string> fields = new List<string>
  {
    "Guitar Type", "Maximum Value"
  };

  IList GuitarInventory = nhi.ExecuteNamedQuery("GuitarMAXValueByTypeHQL");
  dataGridInventory.ItemsSource =
                  BuildDataTable(fields, GuitarInventory).DefaultView;

  SetDatabaseRoundTripImage();
}
```

When the Maximum button is clicked, the `ExecuteNamedQuery()` method receives the `GuitarMAXValueByTypeHQL` named query as a parameter, and then the results are bound to the `DataGrid` of the `GuitarStore` WPF program. The result is a WPF window that resembles Figure 2-10.

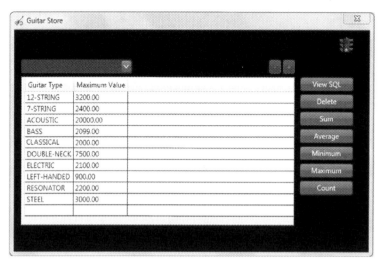

FIGURE 2-10

UNDERSTANDING DETACHEDQUERY

In every example up until now, the query being created has been explicitly attached to a `Session`. Using a detached query enables you to create the query without being initially associated to a `Session`. Once the query has been created and is ready to be executed, it can then be bound to a `Session` and run.

The syntax for accessing and executing a `DetachedQuery` is shown in Listing 2-32.

LISTING 2-32: Example of a DetachedQuery

```
using NHibernate.Impl;

public IList ExecuteDetachedQuery(string searchParameter)
{
  using (ITransaction transaction = Session.BeginTransaction())
  {
    string hqlQuery = "select Builder, Model, Price, Id " +
                      "from Inventory " +
                      "where Model like :search " +
                      "order by Builder";
    IDetachedQuery detachedQuery = new DetachedQuery(hqlQuery)
                                   .SetString("search", searchParameter);

    IQuery executableQuery = detachedQuery.GetExecutableQuery(Session);
    return executableQuery.List();
  }
}

Generated SQL:

select inventory0_.BUILDER as col_0_0_,
```

```
          inventory0_.MODEL as col_1_0_,
          inventory0_.PRICE as col_2_0_,
          inventory0_.ID as col_3_0_
from INVENTORY inventory0_
where inventory0_.MODEL like @p0
order by inventory0_.BUILDER;
@p0 = '%L%' [Type: String (4000)]
```

The `DetachedQuery` class is found within the `NHibernate.Impl` namespace, so the `using NHibernate.Impl;` directive is added to the `NHibernateInventory` class.

To implement the preceding search functionality in the `GuitarStore` WPF program, the following actions are required:

1. Add a `TextBox` control with a `Label` control to the `GuitarStore` WPF window.

2. Add a `Button` control to the GuitarStore WPF window that uses the `ExecuteDetachedQuery()` method and binds the results to the `DataGrid`.

Listing 2-33 shows the XAML code that adds the `TextBox`, `Button`, and `Label` controls to the `MainWindow.xaml` file located in the `GuitarStore` WPF project.

LISTING 2-33 Search controls for the GuitarStore WPF program

```
<TextBox Height="23" HorizontalAlignment="Left" Margin="12,21,0,0"
        Name="textBoxSearch" VerticalAlignment="Top" Width="195" />
<Label Content="Search:" Height="28" HorizontalAlignment="Left"
        Margin="14,4,0,0" Name="labelSearch" VerticalAlignment="Top" />
<Button Content="Search" Height="23" HorizontalAlignment="Left"
        Margin="499,282,0,0" Name="buttonSearch" VerticalAlignment="Top"
        Width="92" Click="buttonSearch_Click"/>
```

Lastly, add the logic to the `buttonSearch_Click()` method found in the `MainWindow.xaml.cs` file of the `GuitarStore` project, as shown in Listing 2-34. This code captures the search criteria from the `TextBox`, passes it to the `ExecuteDetachedQuery()` method, and then binds the results to the `DataGrid`.

LISTING 2-34: Calling the DetachedQuery from the GuitarStore WPF program

```
private void buttonSearch_Click(object sender, RoutedEventArgs e)
{
  NHibernateInventory nhi = new NHibernateInventory();
  List<string> fields = new List<string>
  {
    "Builder", "Model", "Price", "Id"
  };

  IList GuitarInventory =
        nhi.ExecuteDetachedQuery("%" + textBoxSearch.Text + "%");
  dataGridInventory.ItemsSource =
                BuildDataTable(fields, GuitarInventory).DefaultView;

  if (GuitarInventory != null && GuitarInventory.Count > 0)
```

continues

LISTING 2-34 *(continued)*

```
  {
    dataGridInventory.Columns[3].Visibility = System.Windows.Visibility.Hidden;
  }

  SetDatabaseRoundTripImage();
}
```

The detached functionality also enables you to pass the query around to different methods and modify it in whatever way the requirements dictate. For example, Listing 2-35 modifies the method shown in the previous listing to add an AND to the HQL query and call another method, AddPriceLevel(), that modifies the query.

LISTING 2-35: Extended DetachedQuery example

```
public IList ExecuteDetachedQuery(string searchParameter)
{
  using (ITransaction transaction = Session.BeginTransaction())
  {
    string hqlQuery = "select Builder, Model, Price, Id " +
                      "from Inventory " +
                      "where Model like :search " +
                      "AND Cost > :cost ";

    IDetachedQuery detachedQuery = new DetachedQuery(hqlQuery)
                                        .SetString("search", searchParameter);
    AddPriceLevel(detachedQuery);

    IQuery executableQuery = detachedQuery.GetExecutableQuery(Session);
    return executableQuery.List();
  }
}

private void AddPriceLevel(IDetachedQuery query)
{
    query.SetDecimal("cost", 1000);
}

Generated SQL:

select inventory0_.BUILDER as col_0_0_,
       inventory0_.MODEL as col_1_0_,
       inventory0_.PRICE as col_2_0_,
       inventory0_.ID as col_3_0_
from INVENTORY inventory0_
where (inventory0_.MODEL like @p0) and
       inventory0_.COST>@p1
order by inventory0_.BUILDER;
@p0 = '%L%' [Type: String (4000)],
@p1 = 1000 [Type: Decimal (0)]
```

The `AddPriceLevel()` method receives the `DetachedQuery` as a parameter and modifies it. Then the `GetExecutableQuery()` method is called to get the `IQuery` interface associated with the `Session`. Finally, the `List()` method is used to retrieve the results.

When a user enters some search criteria into the search textbox and clicks the Search `Button`, the `DetachedQuery` is executed. The results have been restricted to return only guitars that cost greater than €1,000. Figure 2-11 shows the `GuitarStore` WPF window.

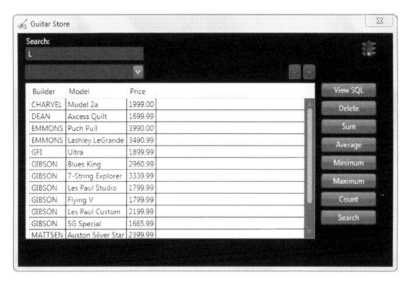

FIGURE 2-11

WORKING WITH DETACHEDNAMEDQUERY

Named queries and detached queries have both been discussed already in this chapter. As you can probably guess, `DetachedNamedQuery` enables you to select a named query and modify it without it being associated to a `Session`.

Similar to how named queries were added previously, another query is added to the `Query.hbm.xml` file, as shown in Listing 2-36.

LISTING 2-36: A named query for DetachedNamedQuery example

```
<query name="InventoryHQLSearch">
  <![CDATA[
    from Inventory where Model like :search
  ]]>
</query>
```

Listing 2-37 shows how to implement the DetachedNamedQuery in the NHibernateInventory class.

LISTING 2-37: Implementing a DetachedNamedQuery

```
public IList<T> ExecuteDetachedNamedQuery<T>
                                (string searchParameter, string QueryName)
{
  using (ITransaction transaction = Session.BeginTransaction())
  {
     IDetachedQuery detachedQuery = new DetachedNamedQuery(QueryName)
                              .SetString("search", searchParameter);

     IQuery executableQuery = detachedQuery.GetExecutableQuery(Session);
     return executableQuery.List<T>();
  }
}

Generated SQL where class is Inventory:

select inventory0_.ID as ID1_,
       inventory0_.TYPEID as TYPEID1_,
       inventory0_.BUILDER as BUILDER1_,
       inventory0_.MODEL as MODEL1_,
       inventory0_.QOH as QOH1_,
       inventory0_.COST as COST1_,
       inventory0_.PRICE as PRICE1_,
       inventory0_.RECEIVED as RECEIVED1_
from INVENTORY inventory0_
where inventory0_.MODEL like @p0;
@p0 = '%L%' [Type: String (4000)]
```

Notice that this example uses a strongly typed generic result set. It's possible to strongly type the DetachedQuery too. Refer to Figure 2-1, which shows the different IQuery interfaces and their execution methods. You can see that GetExecutableQuery() supports both the List() and List<T>() execution methods.

By strongly typing the result set, accessing the properties of the class is simple and clear. Listing 2-32 demonstrates the implementation of the DetachedQuery, which receives a projected List(), and the DetachedNamedQuery, which receives a strongly typed List<T>().

To implement the DetachedNamedQuery() in the GuitarStore WPF program, modify the existing buttonSearch_Click() method of the MainWindow.xaml.cs file. Change the buttonSearch_Click() method to resemble the code shown in Listing 2-38.

LISTING 2-38: Using a DetachedNamedQuery() from the GuitarStore WPF

```
private void buttonSearch_Click(object sender, RoutedEventArgs e)
{
   NHibernateInventory nhi = new NHibernateInventory();
   IList<Inventory> GuitarInventory =
```

```
                nhi.ExecuteDetachedNamedQuery<Inventory>("%" + textBoxSearch.Text + "%",
                                            "InventoryHQLSearch");

        dataGridInventory.ItemsSource = GuitarInventory;

        if (GuitarInventory != null && GuitarInventory.Count > 0)
        {
          dataGridInventory.Columns[0].Visibility = System.Windows.Visibility.Hidden;
          dataGridInventory.Columns[1].Visibility = System.Windows.Visibility.Hidden;
          dataGridInventory.Columns[8].Visibility = System.Windows.Visibility.Hidden;
        }

        labelPaging.Content = "";
        buttonNext.IsEnabled = false;

        SetDatabaseRoundTripImage();
    }
```

UNDERSTANDING FUTURES

As previously noted, you can implement the batching of queries for execution using a single round-trip to the database — if your DBMS supports this. However, if your program needs to support batching because it must function with different DBMSs, some of which can batch queries and some of which can't, then using NHibernate's Futures functionality is the solution. The reason it's possible is because of implementation of the Future<T>() and FutureValue<T>() execution methods, found in both the IQuery and ICriteria APIs.

The implementation methods for Future<T>() and FutureValue<T>() can be found in the AbstractQueryImpl class for IQuery and the CriteriaImpl class for ICriteria. In both execution methods there is a check for MultipleQuery support. If the current database driver does not support multiple queries, a normal List<T> is returned, as shown in Listing 2-39. If the database driver being used does support multiple queries, then it batches the queries as expected. Recall that this differs from using the MultiQuery interface, whereby an error is returned.

LISTING 2-39: Example of the IQuery Future<T>() implementation

```
public IEnumerable<T> Future<T>()
{
    if (!session.Factory.ConnectionProvider.Driver.SupportMultiQueries)
    {
        return List<T>();
    }
    session.FutureQueryBatch.Add<T>(this);
    return session.FutureQueryBatch.GetEnumerator<T>();
}
```

A common implementation of query batching is used with paging. It makes a lot of sense to combine the retrieval of a data result with a query that counts the total number of possible rows. This count gives the user some idea of how many possible results there are. However, there is no restriction on the different types of queries that can be grouped together.

Implementing paging with Futures in the `GuitarStore` solution only requires changing the `GetInventoryPaging()` method of the `NHibenrateInventory` class to use `Future()` methods instead of `CreateMultiQuery()` methods. Listing 2-40 shows the updated `GetInventoryPaging()` using `Future()` methods.

LISTING 2-40: Paging using Futures

```
public int GetInventoryPaging(int MaxResult, int FirstResult, out IList resultSet)
{
  using (ITransaction transaction = Session.BeginTransaction())
  {
    string hqlQuery = "select Builder, Model, Price, Id " +
                        "from Inventory order by Builder";
    IQuery query = Session.CreateQuery(hqlQuery)
                        .SetMaxResults(MaxResult)
                        .SetFirstResult(FirstResult);
    var count = Session.CreateQuery("select count(*) from Inventory")
                        .FutureValue<long>();

    resultSet = query.Future<object>().ToList();
    int totalCount = (int)count.Value;
    return totalCount;
  }
}

Generated SQL:

select count(*) as col_0_0_
from INVENTORY inventory0_;
select TOP (@p0)
       inventory0_.BUILDER as col_0_0_,
       inventory0_.MODEL as col_1_0_,
       inventory0_.PRICE as col_2_0_,
       inventory0_.ID as col_3_0_
from INVENTORY inven;
@p0 = 25 [Type: Int32 (0)].BUILDER;
```

To get the count, the `FutureValue<T>()` execution method is used. It is strongly typed to a `long` data type and then cast to an `int` when returned. The `Future<T>()` execution method requires a strongly typed class to be returned. However, as shown in the `GuitarStore` WPF program, the HQL query passed to this method is projected and requests only a subset of the `Inventory` class. Therefore, it is strongly typed to an object instead of the `object` class. That's kind of a trick, if you ask me, but a good trick.

Although paging is perhaps the most common use of Futures, there is another less common but very useful purpose for this functionality. Because Futures wait to execute until the data retrieved from the query is actually used, you can batch queries together at points in the program and execute the queries only when the data within one of queries is actually needed. For example, as a computer program matures, it is often possible to become more aware of what data is being retrieved and when the retrieval of this data is necessary. For example, a usage pattern may be discovered whereby a user typically wants a specific piece of information when the computer program is started, perhaps the combined value of all inventory.

Instead of simply executing the "always required" queries, such as the population of the DataGrid, which is one round-trip to the database, and then executing a "probable" query later, which is another round-trip to the database, queries with a high probability of being executed can be batched together with "always required" queries, just in case the data is used in the future. The expectation is that the additional "probable" query being batched and executed with the "always required" query results in better overall performance than running each one separately. To implement this concept in the GuitarStore solution, the following actions must be performed:

1. Add a named query that calculates the total value of all guitars in inventory.

2. Add the execution of this named query to the GetInventoryPaging() method using the Future() method and an additional return parameter.

3. Add two class variables to the GuitarStore WPF project (datetime and decimal).

4. Modify PopulateDataGrid() to use the new modified GetInventoryPaging() method and store the inventory value.

5. Add a Button control named Total Value to the GuitarStore WPF project to display the stored value.

First, open the Query.hbm.xml file located in the NHibernate.GuitarStore project. Add a new named query to the file as shown in Listing 2-41.

LISTING 2-41: Named query to select total inventory value

```
<query name="GuitarTotalInventoryValueHQL">
  <![CDATA[
    select SUM(Price) from Inventory
    ]]>
</query>
```

Next, modify the GetInventoryPaging() method found in the NHibernateInventory class so that it uses the NHibernate GetNamedQuery() method to execute the GuitarTotalInventoryValueHQL named query, as shown in Listing 2-42. Also, use the FutureValue<T>() method so that it is batched along with the other queries.

LISTING 2-42: Additonal batched query to use if necessary

```
public int GetInventoryPaging(int MaxResult, int FirstResult,
                        out IList resultSet, out decimal totalInventory)
{
  using (ITransaction transaction = Session.BeginTransaction())
  {
    string hqlQuery = "select Builder, Model, Price, Id " +
                    "from Inventory order by Builder";
    IQuery query = Session.CreateQuery(hqlQuery)
                      .SetMaxResults(MaxResult)
                      .SetFirstResult(FirstResult);
```

continues

LISTING 2-42 *(continued)*

```
        var count = Session.CreateQuery("select count(*) from Inventory")
                        .FutureValue<long>();

        var invTotal = Session.GetNamedQuery("GuitarTotalInventoryValueHQL")
                            .FutureValue<decimal>();

        resultSet = query.Future<object>().ToList();
        int totalCount = (int)count.Value;
        totalInventory = invTotal.Value;

        return totalCount;
    }
  }

Generated SQL (all 3 run using 1 database round-trip):

select count(*) as col_0_0_ from INVENTORY inventory0_;
select SUM(inventory0_.PRICE) as col_0_0_ from INVENTORY inventory0_;
select TOP (@p0)
        inventory0_.BUILDER as col_0_0_,
        inventory0_.MODEL as col_1_0_,
        inventory0_.PRICE as col_2_0_,
        inventory0_.ID as col_3_0_
from INVENTORY inven;
@p0 = 25 [Type: Int32 (0)].BUILDER;
```

Next, in the `MainWindow.xaml.cs` file found in the `GuitarStore` WPF project, modify the `PopulateDataGrid()` method to include the code displayed in Listing 2-43. Notice that two class variables are created.

LISTING 2-43: PopulateDataGrid() using three batched HQL queries

```
decimal totalInventoryValue;
private void PopulateDataGrid()
{
    NHibernateInventory nhi = new NHibernateInventory();
    List<string> fields = new List<string>
    {
        "Builder", "Model", "Price", "Id"
    };
    IList GuitarInventory = null;
    int inventoryCount = nhi.GetInventoryPaging(MaxResult, FirstResult,
                        out GuitarInventory, out totalInventoryValue);
    dataGridInventory.ItemsSource =
                        BuildDataTable(fields, GuitarInventory).DefaultView;

    if (GuitarInventory != null)
    {
        dataGridInventory.Columns[3].Visibility = System.Windows.Visibility.Hidden;
    }

    labelPaging.Content = "Retrieved " + FirstResult.ToString() +
```

```
                              " to " + (FirstResult + GuitarInventory.Count).ToString() +
                              " of " + inventoryCount.ToString();

        totalCount = inventoryCount;
        SetDatabaseRoundTripImage();

    }
```

Next, add a `Button` control to the `MainWindow.xaml` file as shown in Listing 2-44.

LISTING 2-44: Total Value button on the GuitarStore MainWindow

```xaml
<Button Content="Total Value" Height="23" HorizontalAlignment="Left"
        Margin="499,311,0,0" Name="buttonTotalValue" VerticalAlignment="Top"
        Width="92" Click="buttonTotalValue_Click" />
```

Finally, add the code to the `buttonTotalValue_Click()` method that displays the total value of the guitar inventory via the `labelMessage` control. Listing 2-45 shows the contents of the `buttonTotalValue_Click()` method.

LISTING 2-45: The buttonTotalValue_Click() method

```csharp
private void buttonTotalValue_Click(object sender, RoutedEventArgs e)
{
    labelMessage.Content = "Total value of inventory is: " +
                           totalInventoryValue.ToString();
}
```

Running the `GuitarStore` WPF program and pressing the Total Value `Button` displays the total value of guitar inventory, as shown in Figure 2-12.

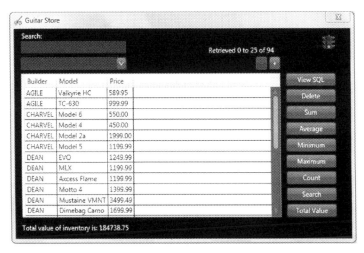

FIGURE 2-12

SUMMARY

HQL and the `IQuery` interface provide some very strong capabilities — arguably the strongest capabilities of any in the NHibernate library. Reduction of database round-trips, storage of static name queries, and runtime modification of queries are but a few examples of this powerful API. You can build any query and use the dot (.) notation to take the complex SQL joins out of the equation, and just let `IQuery` and HQL do all the work for you. It is absolutely impressive.

3

Using ICriteria

In the previous chapter you learned how the Hibernate Query Language (HQL) works and how to implement most of the APIs that make up the library. Most important, you learned how to combine queries so that fewer round-trips can be made to the database, thereby improving the program's performance. This chapter covers using `ICriteria`, which is a more method-based query API versus the SQL-like queries of `IQuery`. In this chapter, you learn about the following:

> ➤ `CreateCriteria`, `CreateMultiCriteria`, `DetachedCriteria`, `QueryOver`, and Futures

> ➤ Implementing paging

> ➤ Lambda expressions

> ➤ `FetchMode`, `Restrictions`, and data transfer objects (DTOs)

INTRODUCTION

The `ICriteria` interface is a feature-rich, method-based query API. When I first started using NHibernate, I chose to use `ICriteria`. As a programmer, the implementation of `ICritera` seemed more programmatic than HQL — meaning that instead of using dot (.) notation in a string, `ICriteria` provides methods, classes, and properties for creating the query. A large number of `ICriteria` methods are accessible via the `Session` to execute a query against the database, and pulling the methods and properties together seems almost intuitive.

Figure 3-1 provides a graphical representation of the methods and their corresponding execution methods for using the `ICriteria` interface, which implements the same functionality described in the previous chapter for `IQuery`. This chapter describes these methods and provides examples demonstrating how to use them.

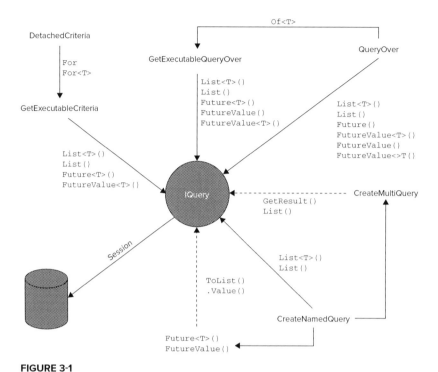

FIGURE 3-1

Figure 3-2 shows the ICriteria, CriteriaImpl, and DetachedCriteria class diagram. ICriteria is the interface that is used to manage and create your query objects. When the Session.CreateCriteria() method is called, it returns an implementation of the ICriteria interface. The methods used to execute an attached query can be found in the NHibernate .Impl namespace within the CriteriaImpl.cs file. The DetachedCriteria class is found in the NHibernate.Criterion namespace.

FIGURE 3-2

The GuitarStore solution used in this book does not require the creation of complex SQL queries. The query shown in Listing 3-1 indicates that it is a little more complicated to create a joined query using ICritera versus IQuery. That's because it is required to programmatically create aliases prior to execution. Whenever you have to dynamically build and then execute a query that joins many tables together, it requires some relatively sophisticated code.

LISTING 3-1: Creating an ICriteria and HQL JOIN query

```
ICriteria:

ICriteria criteria = Session.CreateCriteria<Inventory>("i")
                        .CreateAlias("Guitar", "g")
                        .SetProjection(Projections.ProjectionList()
                           .Add(Projections.Property("i.Builder"))
                           .Add(Projections.Property("i.Model"))
                           .Add(Projections.Property("i.Price"))
                           .Add(Projections.Property("i.Id"))
                           .Add(Projections.Property("g.Type")));
IQuery/HQL:

select i.Builder, i.Model, i.Price, i.Id, g.Type
from Inventory i, Guitar g
where i.TypeId = g.Id
```

Creating the JOIN using ICritera requires a number of different methods and classes to build the query. On the other hand, an HQL query is very similar to the way an SQL query is written. Notice that, as shown in Listing 3-2, ICriteria uses an inner JOIN, whereas IQuery uses a standard equijoin.

LISTING 3-2: ICriteria vs. HQL JOIN SQL

```
ICriteria:
SELECT this_.BUILDER as y0_,
       this_.MODEL as y1_,
       this_.PRICE as y2_,
       this_.ID as y3_,
       g1_.TYPE as y4_
FROM INVENTORY this_ inner JOIN GUITAR g1_ on this_.TYPEID=g1_.ID

IQuery/HQL:
select inventory0_.BUILDER as col_0_0_,
       inventory0_.MODEL as col_1_0_,
       inventory0_.PRICE as col_2_0_,
       inventory0_.ID as col_3_0_,
       guitar1_.TYPE as col_4_0_
from INVENTORY inventory0_, GUITAR guitar1_
where inventory0_.TYPEID=guitar1_.ID
```

In both of the preceding SQL queries, the data returned is identical and there is no noticeable difference in performance. Nonetheless, there are some things about the `ICriteria` interface that are worth mentioning:

> It is less vulnerable to SQL injection.

> Parameter data types are validated using the type value within the mapping file.

> Data can be retrieved dynamically or strongly typed.

> You can use it when the exact structure of the query is not known at design time (i.e., you are not sure what is needed until runtime).

> Methods are used to create data queries, meaning you can't actually see the query.

> It implements fetch strategies by default.

> You can define parameters explicitly using methods such as `Restrictions` `.Eq("propertyName", value)`.

Defining parameters explicitly in a query using `ICriteria` is very straightforward. Simply add a `Restrictions` class, in combination with a property name and the value, and the NHibernate-generated SQL query will include a `WHERE` clause containing the restriction. The `Restrictions` class is found in the `NHibernate.Criterion` namespace. An example is shown in Listing 3-3.

LISTING 3-3: Restrictions class example

```
public IList CriteriaInventoryList(string builder)
{
  using (ITransaction transaction = Session.BeginTransaction())
  {
    try
    {
      ICriteria criteria = Session.CreateCriteria<Inventory>()
        .SetProjection(Projections.ProjectionList()
          .Add(Projections.Property("Builder"))
          .Add(Projections.Property("Model"))
          .Add(Projections.Property("Price"))
          .Add(Projections.Property("Id")))
        .Add(Restrictions.Eq("Builder", builder));

      transaction.Commit();
      return criteria.List();
    }
    catch (Exception ex)
    {
      transaction.Rollback();
      throw;
    }
  }
}

Generated SQL:

SELECT this_.BUILDER as y0_,
```

```
        this_.MODEL as y1_,
        this_.PRICE as y2_,
        this_.ID as y3_
FROM INVENTORY this_
WHERE this_.BUILDER = @p0;
@p0 = 'FENDER' [Type: String (4000)]
```

The `CriteriaInventoryList()` method found within the `NHibernateInventory` class received `"FENDER"` as a parameter. The parameter was added to the `CreateCriteria()` method via the `Add()` method and `Restrictions` class. The NHibernate-generated SQL query contains a WHERE clause that restricts the results of `Inventory` where the `Builder` equals `"FENDER"`.

Another interesting aspect of `ICriteria` is that it implements fetch strategies by default, whereas using HQL via the `IQuery` interface employs lazy loading of data by default. Fetching strategies are put into action on collections initialized within a solution's mapping and class files — for example, the `IList<Inventory>` `Inventory` collection within the `Guitar` class. Placing a `fetch="JOIN"` attribute into the `bag` element of the `Guitar.hbm.xml` file will result in the eager fetching of the `Inventory` collection. Listing 3-4 shows the `Guitar.hbm.xml` file containing the `fetch` attribute.

LISTING 3-4: Eager loading Inventory mapping example using fetch=**JOIN**

```xml
<bag name="Inventory" table="INVENTORY" fetch="JOIN">
  <key     column="TYPEID" />
  <one-to-many class="NHibernate.GuitarStore.Common.Inventory"  />
</bag>
```

Then, if the method in Listing 3-5 retrieves the `Guitar` class, the resulting NHibernate-generated SQL query joins the GUITAR and INVENTORY tables together in a single statement that loads the data from both tables into the `Guitar` class.

LISTING 3-5: Eager loading the Guitar object using ICriteria

```csharp
public IList<T> ExecuteCriteria<T>() where T : class
{
  using (ITransaction transaction = Session.BeginTransaction())
  {
    try
    {
      ICriteria criteria = Session.CreateCriteria<T>();
      transaction.Commit();
      return criteria.List<T>();
    }
    catch (Exception ex)
    {
      transaction.Rollback();
      throw;
    }
```

continues

LISTING 3-5 *(continued)*

```
    }
}

Generated SQL:

SELECT this_.ID as ID0_1_,
       this_.TYPE as TYPE0_1_,
       inventory2_.TYPEID as TYPEID3_,
       inventory2_.ID as ID3_,
       inventory2_.ID as ID1_0_,
       inventory2_.TYPEID as TYPEID1_0_,
       inventory2_.BUILDER as BUILDER1_0_,
       inventory2_.MODEL as MODEL1_0_,
       inventory2_.QOH as QOH1_0_,
       inventory2_.COST as COST1_0_,
       inventory2_.PRICE as PRICE1_0_,
       inventory2_.RECEIVED as RECEIVED1_0_
FROM GUITAR this_
left outer JOIN INVENTORY inventory2_ on
       this_.ID=inventory2_.TYPEID
```

Figure 3-3 shows the List<Guitar> collection, which contains the eagerly loaded Inventory data. No additional database query is needed to access all Inventory for the guitar type.

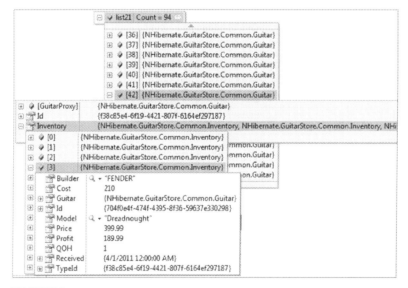

FIGURE 3-3

However, HQL ignores the fetch attribute's value and loads everything lazy by default. Therefore, when executing the HQL query with the Guitar class, shown next in Listing 3-6, only the Guitar is retrieved, not the ILis t<Inventory> Inventory collection, regardless of the fetch value. HQL will wait until the data is accessed before retrieving the collection.

LISTING 3-6: HQL ignoring fetch="**JOIN**" and using lazy loading instead

```
public IList<T> ExecuteHQL<T>(string hqlQuery)
{
    using (ITransaction transaction = Session.BeginTransaction())
    {
        IQuery query = Session.CreateQuery(hqlQuery);
        return query.List<T>();
    }
}

Generated SQL with fetch=JOIN:

select guitar0_.ID as ID0_,
       guitar0_.TYPE as TYPE0_
from GUITAR guitar0_
```

If at a later point the Inventory collection within the Guitar class is requested, an additional SELECT statement is generated to retrieve the Inventory for the specific guitar type.

Note that in two of the preceding listings, Listing 3-1 and Listing 3-3, no "HQL-like" or "SQL-like" query is created when using ICriteria. This may be a positive for programmers who are not strong in SQL-like languages. If this is the case, then using methods, instead of joining tables and forming string-based queries, may be the best option. However, be aware that when using this method-based query API, the overview and visibility of the data being retrieved can easily be lost when the queries become complex, for example, if you need to JOIN several tables, using restrictions, aliases, and projections that use the relationships built within the mapping files.

 NOTE *All NHibernate query constructions are stated in terms of the persistent object model, rather than the database. This means that restrictions are always based on the property values in the mapped object, never in terms of the database column name.*

Understanding the Stateless Session

In Chapter 2, "Using HQL," the ISession interface was used to manage the state of the entities loaded from the database. In this chapter, the IStatelessSession interface is used when data is loaded for display purposes only. If a result set is only used to retrieve data for display in a DataGrid, i.e. read-only, then the IStatelessSession can be used to control memory consumption. It is more difficult to recover from an exception that occurs using a stateful `Session`, which uses the built-in change-tracking capabilities of NHibernate, than when using the `IStatelessSession` (stateless) interface. Recovering from an exception when using the `IStatelessSession` requires that you close the stateless `Session` and reopen a new one using the `OpenStatelessSession()` method found in the `SessionFactory` class. Before implementing this interface, however, you should consider the following two limitations:

➤ Caching is not utilized.

➤ Lazy loading is not supported.

A majority, but not all, of the methods in this chapter use the `StatelessSession` interface to show that it exposes many of the same methods as the statefull `Session`. In most cases you would use the statefull `Session`, as that is where most of NHibernate's power exists. Use the `StatelessSession` interface for simple display-only or for bulk data manipulation.

WORKING WITH CREATECRITERIA

Six different `CreateCriteria` methods are available within the `ISession` interface, as shown in Listing 3-7, each one having a different definition. Two of them support generics; the others expect an alias, a `System.Type`, or the name of the entity as a string.

LISTING 3-7: CreateCriteria methods

```
ICriteria CreateCriteria<T>() where T : class;
ICriteria CreateCriteria<T>(string alias) where T : class;
ICriteria CreateCriteria(System.Type persistentClass);
ICriteria CreateCriteria<T>( System.Type persistentClass, string alias);
ICriteria CreateCriteria(string entityName) ;
ICriteria CreateCriteria(string entityName, string alias);
```

In this section, the `CreateCriteria<T>()` method is used in most of the examples. To implement the `CreateCriteria()` method in the `NHibernate.GuitarStore` class library and the `GuitarStore` WPF project, you will perform the following:

1. Program a `CreateCriteria()` method that returns a dynamic list of all Inventory.

2. Reuse the `BuildDataTable()` method created in Chapter 2 to convert the dynamic result set into a `DataTable`.

3. Bind the result from the `BuildDataTable()` to a `DataGrid`.

4. Create a `CreateCriteria()` method that accepts and uses a guitar type as a parameter to constrain the result set.

5. Implement paging.

Open the `GuitarStore` solution and within the `NHibernate.GuitarStore` project, double-click the `NHibernateInventory.cs` file. Add the method shown in Listing 3-8, which returns a dynamic list of all `Inventory` using the `CreateCriteria()` method.

LISTING 3-8: CreateCriteria method returning project inventory

```
public IList GetDynamicInventoryList()
{
  using (ITransaction transaction = StatelessSession.BeginTransaction())
  {
    try
    {
      ICriteria criteria = StatelessSession.CreateCriteria<Inventory>()
              .SetProjection(Projections.ProjectionList()
                .Add(Projections.Property("Builder"))
                .Add(Projections.Property("Model"))
                .Add(Projections.Property("Price"))
                .Add(Projections.Property("Id")))
              .AddOrder(Order.Asc("Builder"));

      transaction.Commit();
      return criteria.List();
    }
    catch (Exception ex)
    {
      transaction.Rollback();
      throw;
    }
  }
}

Generated SQL:

SELECT this_.BUILDER as y0_,
       this_.MODEL as y1_,
       this_.PRICE as y2_,
       this_.ID as y3_
FROM INVENTORY this_
ORDER BY this_.BUILDER asc
```

Next, in the `GuitarStore` WPF project, open the `MainWindow.xml.cs` file and review the `BuildDataTable()` method created in Chapter 2, found in Listing 2-4.

To retrieve the `Inventory` data from the database, use the `GetDynamicInventoryList()` method created in Listing 3-8. Then bind the result of the `BuildDataTable()` method to the `DataGrid`, as shown in Listing 3-9. Place the code found in Listing 3-9 into the `PopulateDataGrid()` method created in Chapter 2.

LISTING 3-9: Retrieving a dynamic result set and binding it to the DataGrid

```
private void PopulateDataGrid()
{
  NHibernateInventory nhi = new NHibernateInventory();
  List<string> fields = new List<string>
  {
    "Builder", "Model", "Price", "Id"
  };
  IList GuitarInventory = nhi.GetDynamicInventoryList();
  dataGridInventory.ItemsSource =
              BuildDataTable(fields, GuitarInventory).DefaultView;

  if (GuitarInventory != null)
  {
    dataGridInventory.Columns[3].Visibility = System.Windows.Visibility.Hidden;
  }
}
```

The preceding method simply selects the entire inventory from the INVENTORY table and populates the DataGrid with the data. Next, add a new method to the NHibernateInventory class within the NHibernate.GuitarStore project that accepts a guitar type as a parameter and returns only the guitars of that type. Listing 3-10 shows the method that accepts a parameter and returns the matching data.

LISTING 3-10: CreateCriteria returning inventory by guitar type

```
public IList GetDynamicInventoryListByType(Guid Id)
{
   using (ITransaction transaction = StatelessSession.BeginTransaction())
   {
     try
     {
        ICriteria criteria = StatelessSession.CreateCriteria<Inventory>()
              .SetProjection(Projections.ProjectionList()
                  .Add(Projections.Property("Builder"))
                  .Add(Projections.Property("Model"))
                  .Add(Projections.Property("Price"))
                  .Add(Projections.Property("Id")))
                  .Add(Restrictions.Eq("TypeId", Id))
              .AddOrder(Order.Asc("Builder"));

        transaction.Commit();
        return criteria.List();
     }
     catch (Exception ex)
     {
       transaction.Rollback();
       throw;
     }
   }
}
```

```
}

Generate SQL:
SELECT this_.BUILDER as y0_,
       this_.MODEL as y1_,
       this_.PRICE as y2_,
       this_.ID as y3_
FROM INVENTORY this_
WHERE this_.TYPEID = @p0
ORDER BY this_.BUILDER asc;
@p0 = 471c5b3f-19da-4fcb-8e9f-48dd17a00a3d [Type: Guid (0)]
```

Finally, modify the `comboBoxGuitarTypes_SelectionChanged()` method to use the preceding method when a guitar type is selected from the `ComboBox` found on the `GuitarStore` WPF window. The code shown in Listing 3-11 captures the selected guitar type from the `ComboBox` and passes the `Id` to the `GetDynamicInventoryListByType()` method, builds the `DataTable` with the results, and populates the `DataGrid`.

LISTING 3-11: CreateCriteria method from the SelectionChanged method

```csharp
private void comboBoxGuitarTypes_SelectionChanged(object sender,
                                      SelectionChangedEventArgs e)
{
  try
  {
    dataGridInventory.ItemsSource = null;
    Guitar guitar = (Guitar)comboBoxGuitarTypes.SelectedItem;
    Guid guitarType = new Guid(guitar.Id.ToString());

    NHibernateInventory nhi = new NHibernateInventory();
    IList GuitarInventory = nhi.GetDynamicInventoryListByType(guitarType);
    List<string> fields = new List<string>
    {
      "Builder", "Model", "Price", "Id"
    };
    dataGridInventory.ItemsSource =
            BuildDataTable(fields, GuitarInventory).DefaultView;

    if (GuitarInventory != null)
    {
      dataGridInventory.Columns[3].Visibility = System.Windows.Visibility.Hidden;
    }
  }
  catch (Exception ex)
  {
    labelMessage.Content = ex.Message;
  }
}
```

Set the `GuitarStore` project as the startup project and run it. When the guitar type is selected from the `ComboBox`, the resulting list in the `DataGrid` will be restricted to the selection.

Implementing Paging

It is good practice to reduce the number of rows returned from the database, especially if the table being selected from has hundreds of thousands of rows. The current implementation selects all the rows from the INVENTORY table, which is okay in this situation because there are relatively few rows to retrieve at this early stage in this program's life cycle.

The ICriteria interface provides two methods for implementing paging. The names are identical to those in the IQuery interface: SetMaxResults() and SetFirstResult(). The SetMaxResults() method accepts an integer as a parameter that determines the maximum number of rows to be returned with the associated query.

The SetFirstResult() method also accepts an integer as a parameter and is used to determine the first row to be returned from the query. For example, if the value for SetFirstResult() is 500 and the value for SetMaxResults() is 50, then rows 500 to 550 will be returned when the query is executed.

 NOTE *When used with* ICriteria, *the* SetFirstResult() *method expects a 1 as the first row. However, when used with* IQuery, *the value is expected to be 0.*

A method that retrieves the data from the INVENTORY table has already been implemented, as shown previously in Listing 3-8. To implement paging, create a new method in the NHibernateInventory.cs file of the NHibernate.Guitar project that accepts two integer parameters, one for max result and one for first result. Then associate the SetFirstResult() and SetMaxResults() methods to the CreateCriteria method. Listing 3-12 shows how this method would look once completed.

LISTING 3-12: ICriteria paging method

```
public IList GetDynamicInventoryList(int maxResult, int firstResult)
{
  using (ITransaction transaction = StatelessSession.BeginTransaction())
  {
    try
    {
      ICriteria criteria = StatelessSession.CreateCriteria<Inventory>()
          .SetProjection(Projections.ProjectionList()
            .Add(Projections.Property("Builder"))
            .Add(Projections.Property("Model"))
            .Add(Projections.Property("Price"))
            .Add(Projections.Property("Id")))
            .AddOrder(Order.Asc("Builder"))
            .SetMaxResults(maxResult)
            .SetFirstResult(firstResult);

      transaction.Commit();
      return criteria.List();
    }
    catch (Exception ex)
    {
```

```
          transaction.Rollback();
          throw;
       }
     }
   }
}

Generate SQL: (where max=25 and first=1)

SELECT TOP (@p0)
       y0_,
       y1_,
       y2_,
       y3_
FROM (SELECT this_.BUILDER as y0_,
             this_.MODEL as y1_,
             this_.PRICE as y2_,
             this_.ID as y3_,
             ROW_NUMBER()
             OVER(ORDER BY this_.BUILDER) as __hibernate_sort_row
      FROM INVENTORY this_) as query
WHERE query.__hibernate_sort_row > @p1
ORDER BY query.__hibernate_sort_row;
@p0 = 25 [Type: Int32 (0)],
@p1 = 1 [Type: Int32 (0)]
```

Next, create a method that selects a count of all retrievable records from the INVENTORY table. The row count provides a context that indicates where the data contained in the current DataGrid is in relation to all data stored on the table. Add the contents of Listing 3-13, to the NHibernateInventory.cs file of the NHibernate.GuitarStore project.

LISTING 3-13: CriteriaRowCount() method

```
public int CriteriaRowCount<T>() where T : class
{
   using (ITransaction transaction = StatelessSession.BeginTransaction())
   {
     try
     {
        ICriteria rowCount = StatelessSession.CreateCriteria<T>();
        return Convert.ToInt32(
                    rowCount.SetProjection(
                          Projections.RowCount()).UniqueResult());
     }
     catch (Exception ex)
     {
        transaction.Rollback();
        throw;
     }
   }
}

Generated SQL:

SELECT count(*) as y0_
FROM INVENTORY this_
```

Before implementing the code in Listing 3-12 and Listing 3-13 in the `GuitarStore` WPF project, add the code segment shown in Listing 3-14 to the `Main()` method of the `NHibernate.GuitarStore` console application and test to ensure that the expected results are returned.

LISTING 3-14: Testing CreateCriteria paging and row count from the console

```
IList list25 = nhi.GetDynamicInventoryList(25, 1);
System.Console.WriteLine("GetDynamicInventoryList(25, 1): " +
                      list25.Count.ToString() + " results");

int count26 = nhi.CriteriaRowCount<Inventory>();
System.Console.WriteLine("CriteriaRowCount<Inventory>(): " +
                      count26.ToString() + " results");
```

Now open the `MainWindow.xaml.cs` file in the `GuitarStore` WPF project and modify the existing `PopulateDataGrid()` method with the following code in Listing 3-15.

LISTING 3-15: PopulateDataGrid() using ICriteria paging functionality

```
public int FirstResult = 1;
public int MaxResult = 25;
public int totalCount = 0;

private void PopulateDataGrid()
{
  NHibernateInventory nhi = new NHibernateInventory();
  List<string> fields = new List<string>
  {
     "Builder", "Model", "Price", "Id"
  };
  IList GuitarInventory = nhi.GetDynamicInventoryList(MaxResult, FirstResult);
  int inventoryCount = nhi.CriteriaRowCount<Inventory>();
  dataGridInventory.ItemsSource =
                BuildDataTable(fields, GuitarInventory).DefaultView;

  if (GuitarInventory != null)
  {
     dataGridInventory.Columns[3].Visibility = System.Windows.Visibility.Hidden;
  }

  labelPaging.Content = "Retrieved " + FirstResult.ToString() +
               " to " + (FirstResult + GuitarInventory.Count).ToString() +
               " of " + inventoryCount.ToString();
  totalCount = inventoryCount;
}
```

Notice that the stoplight in the following figure, Figure 3-4, is red. This is because three queries are executed using three round-trips to the database during the loading of the `GuitarStore` WPF window. The first loads the guitar types into the `ComboBox`, the second is the `CreateCriteria()`

query that retrieves the `Inventory` for the `DataGrid`, and the third retrieves the total row count on the `INVENTORY` table, for paging.

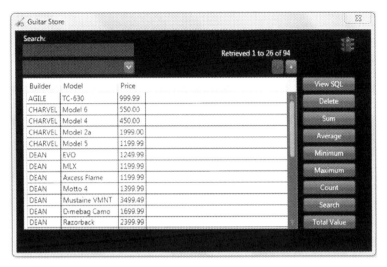

FIGURE 3-4

For many programs, three queries to load a window are acceptable. The implementation of the `QueryCounter`, which exists in the `Utils` class of the `NHibernate.GuitarStore` project (where 1 = green, 2 = yellow, and 3 = red), is used only as an example. The acceptable number of queries per process or transaction will vary according to the program, of course. In this case, three query executions are equated with red.

In the next section, where the `CreateMultiCriteria()` method is implemented, the `Inventory` retrieval and the row count are combined into a single database round-trip; therefore, the stoplight will be yellow instead of red after the `GuitarStore` WPF window is loaded.

IMPLEMENTING CREATEMULTICRITERIA

One of the many nice features found in NHibernate is the capability to batch multiple queries together and execute them using a single trip to the database. Consider that one of the more expensive actions in regard to a database transaction is the time it takes to get from the computer or server where the program is hosted to the database server and back. If you limit the number of round-trips required, you can realize a noticeable performance improvement.

In this section, the focus is on batching two queries together using the `CreateMultiCriteria()` method. To implement the `CreateMultiCriteria()` method in the `NHibernate.GuitarStore` class library and the `GuitarStore` WPF project, you need to perform the following:

1. Program a `CreateMultiCriteria()` method that returns the row count as an integer and a dynamic list of all Inventory as an `out` parameter.

2. Reuse the `BuildDataTable()` method created in Chapter 2 to convert the dynamic result set into a `DataTable`.

3. Bind the result from the `BuildDataTable()` method to a `DataGrid`.

4. Create a `CreateMultiCriteria()` method that accepts and uses a guitar type as a parameter to constrain the result set.

5. Implement paging.

Open the `GuitarStore` solution and within the `NHibernate.GuitarStore` project, double-click the `NHibernateInventory.cs` file. The `CreateMultiCriteria()` method provides the capability to batch queries together. Add the method shown in Listing 3-16, which batches together two queries using the `CreateMultiCriteria()` method. Note that the `ISession` is used here. The `IStatelessSession` interface does not expose an instance of the `CreateMultiCriteria()` method.

LISTING 3-16: Example of the CreateMultiCriteria() method

```
public IList GetDynamicInventoryList(int maxResult, int firstResult,
                                     out int totalCount)
{
  using (ITransaction transaction = Session.BeginTransaction())
  {
    try
    {
      ICriteria criteria = Session.CreateCriteria<Inventory>()
        .SetProjection(Projections.ProjectionList()
          .Add(Projections.Property("Builder"))
          .Add(Projections.Property("Model"))
          .Add(Projections.Property("Price"))
          .Add(Projections.Property("Id")))
        .AddOrder(Order.Asc("Builder"))
        .SetMaxResults(maxResult)
        .SetFirstResult(firstResult);

      ICriteria rowCount = Session.CreateCriteria(typeof(Inventory))
        .SetProjection(Projections.Count(Projections.Id()));

      IMultiCriteria mCriteria = Session.CreateMultiCriteria()
                                 .Add("criteria", criteria)
                                 .Add("count", rowCount);

      IList countResult = (IList)mCriteria.GetResult("count");
      totalCount = Convert.ToInt32(countResult[0]);

      return (IList)mCriteria.GetResult("criteria");

    }
    catch (Exception ex)
    {
      transaction.Rollback();
      throw;
    }
```

```
    }
  }

Generated SQL:

select count(*) as col_0_0_
from INVENTORY inventory0_;
SELECT TOP (@p0)
        col_0_0_,
        col_1_0_,
        col_2_0_,
        col_3_0_
FROM (select inventory0_.BUILDER as col_0_0_,
             inventory0_.MODEL as col_1_0_,
             inventory0_.PRICE as col_2_0_,
             inventory0_.ID as col_3_0_,
             ROW_NUMBER()
             OVER(ORDER BY inventory0_.BUILDER)as __hibernate_sort_row
      from INVENTORY inventory0_) as query
WHERE query.__hiber;
@p0 = 25 [Type: Int32 (0)],
@p1 = 1 [Type: Int32 (0)];
```

The preceding method implements two `CreateCriteria()` methods. The first method creates the query to return the projected dataset from the `INVENTORY` table. The second selects the total number of rows that exist on the table. This count value is displayed in the paging label to identify where the user is in relation to the total number of available records.

The two `CreateCriteria()` methods are bound together using the `Add()` method of the `CreateMultiCriteria()` method, which returns an `IMultiCriteria` interface. A call to the `GetResult()` execution method results in the two generated `CreateCriteria()` SQL queries being batched and executed via a single round-trip to the database.

Next, open the `MainWindow.xaml.cs` file in the `GuitarStore` WPF project and implement the `GetDynamicInventoryList()` method, which uses the `CreateMultiCriteria()` NHibernate method. Listing 3-17 is an example of how it can be implemented using the `PopulateDataGrid()` method.

LISTING 3-17: Using CreateMultiCriteria() from PopulateGridData()

```
private void PopulateDataGrid()
{
    NHibernateInventory nhi = new NHibernateInventory();
    List<string> fields = new List<string>
    {
        "Builder", "Model", "Price", "Id"
    };
    IList GuitarInventory = null;
    int inventoryCount =
            nhi.GetDynamicInventoryList(MaxResult, FirstResult, out GuitarInventory);
    dataGridInventory.ItemsSource =
```

continues

LISTING 3-17 *(continued)*

```
        BuildDataTable(fields, GuitarInventory).DefaultView;

    if (GuitarInventory != null)
    {
      dataGridInventory.Columns[3].Visibility = System.Windows.Visibility.Hidden;
    }

    labelPaging.Content = "Retrieved " + FirstResult.ToString() +
                " to " + (FirstResult + GuitarInventory.Count).ToString() +
                " of " + inventoryCount.ToString();
    totalCount = inventoryCount;
}
```

Run the `GuitarStore` WPF program. As shown in Figure 3-5, the stoplight is yellow, reflecting the query to populate the `ComboBox` with guitar types and the batched query containing the inventory data and the row count.

FIGURE 3-5

This is one of the ways to confirm that the queries have been batched together and executed using a single round-trip to the database. The other way is to select the View SQL button, which enables you to look at the most recently executed NHibernate-generated SQL query.

As already mentioned, not all DBMSs support the batching and execution of queries together. Check the `NHibernate.Driver` namespace for your driver and look for the `SupportMultipleQueries()` method. If you find it, chances are good that the DBMS you currently use supports this capability. If it is not in the driver class, then most likely you will not be able to implement this technology in your programs.

UNDERSTANDING DETACHEDCRITERIA

Sometimes a requirement dictates that a query be built dynamically. There are many ways this could be accomplished. One possibility is to implement the `DetachedCriteria` class, which is found in the `NHibernate.Criterion` namespace. This class allows the passing of a `DetachedCriteria` object between different methods, each of which could perform some actions and modify the object based on the business requirements.

For example, the method in Listing 3-18 is used to search for a specific model of guitar that may exist in the inventory.

LISTING 3-18: A DetachedCriteria example

```
using NHibernate.Criterion;

public IList DetachedSearch(string searchParameter)
{
    using (ITransaction transaction = StatelessSession.BeginTransaction())
    {
      DetachedCriteria detachedCriteria= DetachedCriteria.For<Inventory>()
            .Add(Restrictions.Like("Model", searchParameter));

      return detachedCriteria.GetExecutableCriteriaS(StatelessSession).List();
    }
}

Generated SQL:

SELECT this_.ID as ID1_0_,
       this_.TYPEID as TYPEID1_0_,
       this_.BUILDER as BUILDER1_0_,
       this_.MODEL as MODEL1_0_,
       this_.QOH as QOH1_0_,
       this_.COST as COST1_0_,
       this_.PRICE as PRICE1_0_,
       this_.RECEIVED as RECEIVED1_0_
FROM INVENTORY this_
WHERE this_.MODEL like @p0;
@p0 = '%L%' [Type: String (4000)]
```

To implement the preceding method in the `GuitarStore` WPF program, you need to perform the following:

1. Reuse the search `TextBox` and `Button` controls added in Chapter 2.

2. Modify the `buttonSearch_Click()` method to use the `DetachedSearch()` method.

Open the `MainWindow.xaml.cs` file and modify the `buttonSearch_Click()` method so that it resembles the code in Listing 3-19.

LISTING 3-19: Implementing DetachedCriteria in the GuitarStore WPF program

```
private void buttonSearch_Click(object sender, RoutedEventArgs e)
{
    NHibernateInventory nhi = new NHibernateInventory();
    IList GuitarInventory = nhi.DetachedSearch("%" + textBoxSearch.Text + "%");

    dataGridInventory.ItemsSource = GuitarInventory;

    if (GuitarInventory != null && GuitarInventory.Count > 0)
    {
      dataGridInventory.Columns[0].Visibility =
          System.Windows.Visibility.Hidden;
      dataGridInventory.Columns[1].Visibility =
          System.Windows.Visibility.Hidden;
      dataGridInventory.Columns[8].Visibility =
          System.Windows.Visibility.Hidden;
      dataGridInventory.Columns[9].Visibility =
          System.Windows.Visibility.Hidden;
    }
    labelPaging.Content = "";
    buttonNext.IsEnabled = false;
}
```

The preceding method will return a list of guitar inventory based on the value entered in the `TextBox` control.

Next, to dynamically modify the `DetachedCriteria`, you want to add a method named `SellFirst()` that returns the list of inventory ordered by `Received` and where the `Cost` is greater than €1000. To do this, open the `NHibernateInventory.cs` file found in the `NHibernate.GuitarStore` project and add the method shown in Listing 3-20.

LISTING 3-20: SellFirst() to modify a DetachedCriteria

```
public static void SellFirst(DetachedCriteria criteria)
{
    decimal Amount = 1000;
    criteria.Add(Restrictions.Ge("Cost", Amount));
    criteria.AddOrder(Order.Asc("Received"));
}
```

Then modify the `DetachedSearch()` method to call the `SellFirst()` method, which passes the detached criteria instance for modification. The code is shown in Listing 3-21.

LISTING 3-21: Modifying the DetachedCriteria

```
public IList DetachedSearch(string searchParameter)
{
  using (ITransaction transaction = StatelessSession.BeginTransaction())
  {
    DetachedCriteria detachedCriteria = DetachedCriteria.For<Inventory>()
```

```
            .Add(Restrictions.Like("Model", searchParameter));

    SellFirst(detachedCriteria);

    return detachedCriteria.GetExecutableCriteria(StatelessSession).List();
    }
}

Generated SQL:

SELECT this_.ID as ID1_0_,
       this_.TYPEID as TYPEID1_0_,
       this_.BUILDER as BUILDER1_0_,
       this_.MODEL as MODEL1_0_,
       this_.QOH as QOH1_0_,
       this_.COST as COST1_0_,
       this_.PRICE as PRICE1_0_,
       this_.RECEIVED as RECEIVED1_0_
FROM INVENTORY this_
WHERE this_.MODEL like @p0 and
      this_.COST >= @p1
ORDER BY this_.RECEIVEDasc;
@p0 = '%L%' [Type: String (4000)],
@p1 = 1000 [Type: Decimal (0)]
```

Associating the restrictions with the `DetachedCriteria()` method resulted in the usage of the SQL keyword LIKE and the ≥ symbol.

Now, when the inventory is searched the result set will be restricted to guitars with a `Cost` of more than €1000 and ordered by `Received`. The `GuitarStore` WPF program now resembles Figure 3-6.

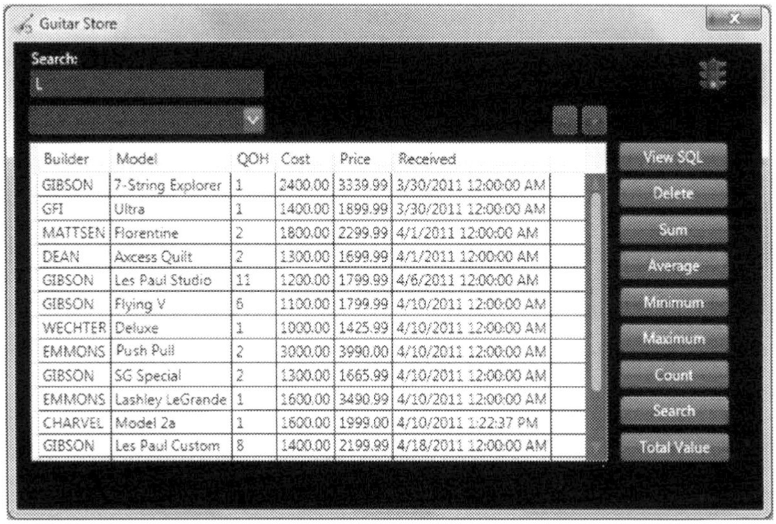

FIGURE 3-6

WORKING WITH QUERYOVER

The driving motivation for the QueryOver API was to provide a type-safe (compile-time) wrapper for the Criteria API. The Criteria API is dependent on fragile string literals that could fail at runtime, so adding this wrapper eliminates that dependency. Figure 3-7 shows the IQueryOver, IQueryOver<TRoot>, and the QueryOver<TRoot, TSubType> class diagram. The NHibernate .Criterion.QueryOver class is an abstract class. It is implemented by the QueryOver<TRoot, TSubType> class found within the same file. QueryOver is built on top of both the ICriteria interface and the CriteriaImpl class. Therefore, the QueryOver capabilities can be considered a lambda expression–based interface into ICriteria. I find the implementation a little more simple and straightforward than using the Criteria API.

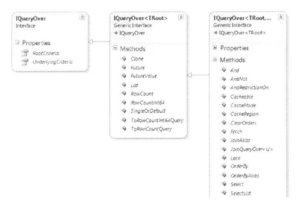

FIGURE 3-7

Listing 3-22 shows an example that compares an ICriteria implementation versus an exact replicated implementation using QueryOver.

LISTING 3-22: Comparison of an ICriteria and QueryOver API with generated SQL

```
ICriteria:
IList<Guitar> result = session.CreateCriteria<Guitar>()
                            .List<Guitar>();
QueryOver:
IList<Guitar> result = session.QueryOver<Guitar>().List();

Generated SQL for the 2 are identical

SELECT this_.ID as ID0_0_,
 this_.TYPE as TYPE0_0_
FROM GUITAR this_
```

Using QueryOver in the GuitarStore WPF project requires the following actions:

1. Create a method named GetInventory() that returns a list of a strongly typed Inventory class.

2. Bind the method to the DataGrid on the GuitarStore WPF window.

3. Create another GetInventory() method that accepts a guitar type and limit the results on that parameter.

4. Implement paging.

First, create a method that uses QueryOver in the NHibernateInventory class found in the NHibernate.GuitarStore project. This method needs to return a result set that is used to populate the GuitarStore WPF DataGrid. Listing 3-23 contains the GetInventory() method.

LISTING 3-23: GetInventory() using QueryOver

```
public IList<Inventory> GetInventory()
{
  using (ITransaction transaction = StatelessSession.BeginTransaction())
  {
    try
    {
      IQueryOver<Inventory> result = StatelessSession.QueryOver<Inventory>()
                          .OrderBy(i => i.Builder).Asc;
      transaction.Commit();
      return result.List<Inventory>();
    }
    catch (Exception ex)
    {
      transaction.Rollback();
      throw;
    }
  }
}

Generated SQL:

SELECT this_.ID as ID1_0_,
       this_.TYPEID as TYPEID1_0_,
       this_.BUILDER as BUILDER1_0_,
       this_.MODEL as MODEL1_0_,
       this_.QOH as QOH1_0_,
       this_.COST as COST1_0_,
       this_.PRICE as PRICE1_0_,
       this_.RECEIVED as RECEIVED1_0_
FROM INVENTORY this_
ORDER BY this_.BUILDER asc
```

Next, open the MainWindow.xaml.cs file and modify the PopulateDataGrid() method so that is uses the GetInventory() method, which utilizes the QueryOver API. Listing 3-24 contains the description of the PopulateDataGrid() method.

LISTING 3-24: PopulateDataGrid() using QueryOver

```
private void PopulateDataGrid()
{
  NHibernateInventory nhi = new NHibernateInventory();
  dataGridInventory.ItemsSource = nhi.GetInventory();

  dataGridInventory.Columns[0].Visibility = System.Windows.Visibility.Hidden;
  dataGridInventory.Columns[1].Visibility = System.Windows.Visibility.Hidden;
  dataGridInventory.Columns[9].Visibility = System.Windows.Visibility.Hidden;
}
```

Next, create another the GetInventory() method that is called when a guitar type is selected from the ComboBox on the GuitarStore WPF window. The method is added to the NHibernateInventory class found within the NHibernate.GuitarStore project. Listing 3-25 contains this new method and shows how to use the Where and OrderBy methods in a lambda expression.

LISTING 3-25: GetInventory() to filter based on guitar type

```
public IList<Inventory> GetInventory(Guid Id)
{
  using (ITransaction transaction = StatelessSession.BeginTransaction())
  {
    try
    {
      IQueryOver<Inventory> result = StatelessSession.QueryOver<Inventory>()
                                         .Where(i => i.TypeId == Id)
                                         .OrderBy(i => i.Builder).Asc;
      transaction.Commit();
      return result.List<Inventory>();
    }
    catch (Exception ex)
    {
      transaction.Rollback();
      throw;
    }
  }
}

Generated SQL:

SELECT this_.ID as ID1_0_,
       this_.TYPEID as TYPEID1_0_,
       this_.BUILDER as BUILDER1_0_,
       this_.MODEL as MODEL1_0_,
       this_.QOH as QOH1_0_,
       this_.COST as COST1_0_,
       this_.PRICE as PRICE1_0_,
       this_.RECEIVED as RECEIVED1_0_
FROM INVENTORY this_
WHERE this_.TYPEID = @p0
ORDER BY this_.BUILDER asc;
@p0 = 471c5b3f-19da-4fcb-8e9f-48dd17a00a3d [Type: Guid (0)]
```

Within the `MainWindow.xaml.cs` file, modify the `comboBoxGuitarTypes_SelectionChanged()` method to use the newly created `GetInventory()` method, as shown in Listing 3-26.

LISTING 3-26: Using QueryOver in the GuitarStore WPF program

```
private void comboBoxGuitarTypes_SelectionChanged(object sender,
                                 SelectionChangedEventArgs e)
{
  try
  {
    dataGridInventory.ItemsSource = null;
    Guitar guitar = (Guitar)comboBoxGuitarTypes.SelectedItem;
    Guid guitarType = new Guid(guitar.Id.ToString());

    NHibernateInventory nhi = new NHibernateInventory();
    dataGridInventory.ItemsSource = nhi.GetInventory(guitarType);
    dataGridInventory.Columns[0].Visibility =
        System.Windows.Visibility.Hidden;
    dataGridInventory.Columns[1].Visibility =
        System.Windows.Visibility.Hidden;
    dataGridInventory.Columns[9].Visibility =
        System.Windows.Visibility.Hidden;
  }
  catch (Exception ex)
  {
    labelMessage.Content = ex.Message;
  }
}
```

Running the `GuitarStore` WPF program and selecting a guitar type from the `ComboBox` results in a window similar to the one shown in Figure 3-8.

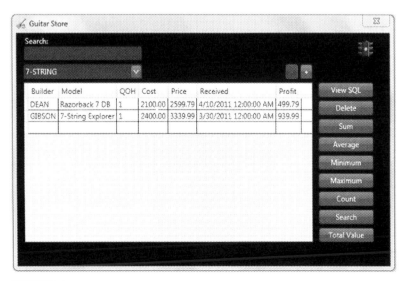

FIGURE 3-8

Lastly, to implement paging using `QueryOver`, add the following method in Listing 3-27 to the `NHibernateInventory` class found within the `NHibernate.GuitarStore` project. Note the use of Futures and the `ISession` interface. Use a statefull `Session` with Futures, as Futures queries are not supported for a stateless `Session`.

LISTING 3-27: QueryOver method implementing paging and using Futures

```
public IEnumerable<Inventory> GetInventory(int maxResult, int firstResult,
                                            out int totalCount)
{
  using (ITransaction transaction = Session.BeginTransaction())
  {
    try
    {
      IQueryOver<Inventory> rowCount =
          Session.QueryOver<Inventory>().ToRowCountQuery();
      IQueryOver<Inventory> result = Session.QueryOver<Inventory>()
                                        .OrderBy(i => i.Builder).Asc
                                        .Take(maxResult)
                                        .Skip(firstResult);

      totalCount = rowCount.FutureValue<int>().Value;

      transaction.Commit();
      return result.Future<Inventory>();
    }
    catch (Exception ex)
    {
      transaction.Rollback();
      throw;
    }
  }
}

Generated SQL:

SELECT TOP (@p0)
        this_.ID as ID1_0_,
        this_.TYPEID as TYPEID1_0_,
        this_.BUILDER as BUILDER1_0_,
        this_.MODEL as MODEL1_0_,
        this_.QOH as QOH1_0_,
        this_.COST as COST1_0_,
        this_.PRICE as PRICE1_0_,
        this_.RECEIVED as RECEIVED1_0_
FROM INVENTORY this_
ORDER BY this_.BUILDER asc;
;@p0 = 25 [Type: Int32 (0)]
INVENTORY this_;
```

Before implementing the preceding code in the `GuitarStore` WPF program, now would be a good time to use the `NHibernate.GuitarStore.Console` application to test the `GetInventory()`

method. The code to perform this test is contained in Listing 3-28 and should be located within the `Main()` method in the `Program.cs` file.

LISTING 3-28: Testing the paging GetInventory() method from the console

```
IEnumerable<Inventory> invListQO31 = null;
int countQO31 = nhi.GetInventory(25, 0, out invListQO31);
Console.WriteLine("GetInventory(25, 0, out invListQO31): " +
                  invListQO31.Count().ToString() + " results");
```

The result will confirm that the `Take()` method applied to the `QueryOver` API returns the number of rows passed via the `maxResult` parameter. Also, if the `show_sql` parameter is enabled within the NHibernate configuration settings, then the SQL can be viewed on the console.

To implement paging using the `QueryOver` API, modify the `PopulateDataGrid()` method within the `MainWindow.xaml.cs` file found in the `GuitarStore` WPF project. The code is shown in Listing 3-29. Don't forget to set the `FirstResult` back to 0; it was changed to 1 when paging was implemented using the `CreateCriteria()` method earlier in this chapter.

LISTING 3-29: Paging within PopulateDataGrid() using the QueryOver API

```
public int FirstResult = 0;

private void PopulateDataGrid()
{
  NHibernateInventory nhi = new NHibernateInventory();
  IEnumerable<Inventory> GuitarInventory = null;
  int inventoryCount = nhi.GetInventory(MaxResult, FirstResult,
                                        out GuitarInventory);
  DataTable dt = new DataTable();
  dt.Columns.Add("Builder", typeof(string));
  dt.Columns.Add("Model", typeof(string));
  dt.Columns.Add("Price", typeof(string));
  dt.Columns.Add("Id", typeof(string));

  foreach (var item in GuitarInventory)
  {
    dt.Rows.Add(item.Builder, item.Model, item.Price.ToString(), item.Id);
  }

  dataGridInventory.ItemsSource = dt.DefaultView;
  labelPaging.Content = "Retrieved " + FirstResult.ToString() +
                " to " + (FirstResult + GuitarInventory.Count()).ToString() +
                " of " + inventoryCount.ToString();
  totalCount = inventoryCount;
}
```

Futures have been implemented with paging from the start using the `QueryOver` API. Therefore, when the `GuitarStore` WPF program is run, the inventory is populated into the `DataGrid` and the row count displayed using a single round-trip to the database. Notice that the stoplight is green in Figure 3-9.

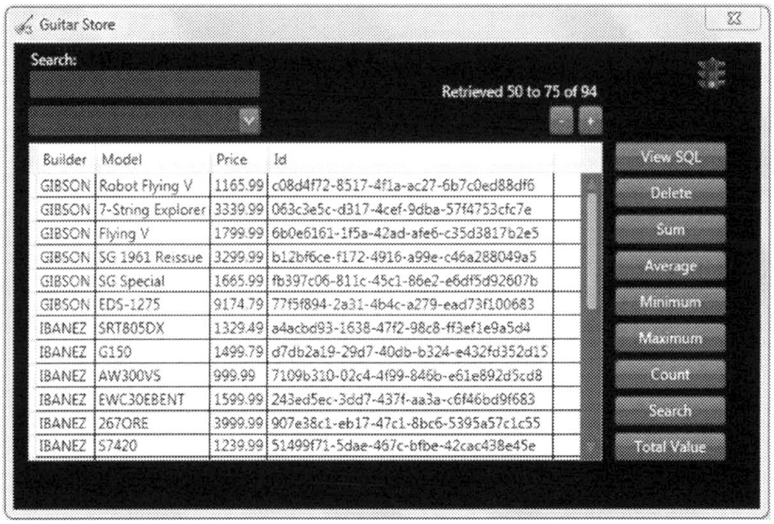

FIGURE 3-9

USING LAMBDA EXPRESSIONS

As with LINQ to NHibernate, discussed in the next chapter, the `QueryOver` class found in the `NHibernate.Criterion` namespace supports the use of lambda expressions. Lambda expressions are synonymous in many ways with anonymous functions in that they don't support assignment to an implicitly typed variable. Lambda expressions simplify the syntax used in anonymous methods by removing the requirement to use the `delegate` keyword.

Listing 3-30 shows the difference between using an anonymous method versus a lambda expression. When the `CalculateProfit` delegate is accessed, it will return the decimal value `Profit`. `Profit` is the result of subtracting the cost of the guitar from the price for which it was sold.

LISTING 3-30: Anonymous method versus lambda expression

```
Anonymous method:

CalculateProfit cProfit = delegate(decimal Profit)
            { return (decimal)inventory.Price - (decimal)inventory.Cost; };


Lambda expression:

CalculateProfit cProfit = (Profit) =>
        { return (decimal)inventory.Price - (decimal)inventory.Cost; };
```

Within NHibernate, the lambda expression capability is used primarily to limit the amount of data returned from a query. Lambda expressions also make the code more readable and user friendly. This enables a better understanding of what the code is doing and makes it easier to modify and maintain. One of the primary motivations for the introduction of lambda expressions was to use the `System.Linq.Expression` constructs for type-safe static reflection. Therefore, you will find many of the common LINQ commands within the `QueryOver` API, such as `And`, `Where`, `WhereNot`, `Select`, `Skip`, `Take`, and so on, all of which are used to retrieve a more precise result set. Nonetheless, however similar LINQ is to lambda expressions, do not make the mistake of thinking they are the same.

UNDERSTANDING FUTURES

The source of the `Future()` methods can be found in the `NHibernate.Impl` namespace within the `CriteriaImpl` class. A more canonical use of `Future()` methods is the retrieval of data as late in a process or transaction as possible, whereby the data is only retrieved if it is actually needed. `Future()` methods also enable the batching of queries so that round-trips to the database for data retrieval can be minimized. For example, if it is known at the beginning of a transaction that the average cost of a guitar type is needed, and then later the minimum price, `Future()` methods could be an option for retrieving both in a single database round-trip, rather than multiple trips. As discussed earlier, it is efficient to batch the queries for paging, whereby the retrieval of the current page of data is combined with the count of all rows on the table.

The `Future<T>()` source code, found in the `CreateImpl` class, is interesting. You can see it in Listing 3-31.

LISTING 3-31: The ICriteria Future<T>() method

```
public IEnumeralbe<T> Future<t>()
{
    if(!session.Factory.ConnectionProvider.Driver.SupportsMultipleQueries)
    {
        return List<T>();
    }
    session.FutureCriteriaBatch.Add<T>(this);
    return session.FutureCriteriaBatch.GetEnumerator<T>();
}
```

Notice that the `if` statement checks to confirm that the DMBS being used supports the batching of SQL queries before trying to execute it. If batching is not supported, the method is intelligent enough to return result sets as a `List<t>` instead of an error. This is not the case when accessing the `CreateMultiCriteria()` method directly, whereby an error is returned instead of a result set.

 TIP *Use Futures when you want to batch SQL queries together to reduce database round-trips or when you want to delay the retrieval of the data for as long as possible.*

Future() methods have already been used in this chapter to implement paging with the QueryOver and Criteria APIs. Using Future() methods also allows the program to wait as long as possible to execute the query so that it can be batched with other queries that potentially need execution. The Future() method is an alternative for the List() method, which will execute the query immediately. The Future() method can also be used in a context other than with paging. For example, the loading of the ComboBox and the DataGrid are executed from two separate methods using a combination of the List() method of the CreateCriteria() and the Future() method of the QueryOver API. They should instead be combined into a single method using the Future() method. Listing 3-32 provides an example of a method called Load() located in the NHibernateInventory class of the NHibernate.GuitarStore project. This method combines all database queries required to load the GuitarStore WPF program into a single round-trip to the database.

LISTING 3-32: Method using Future() methods to load all GuitarStore queries

```
public int Load(int maxResult, int firstResult,
                out IEnumerable<Inventory> resultSetInv,
                out IEnumerable<Guitar> resultSetGuitar)
{
  using (ITransaction transaction = Session.BeginTransaction())
  {
    try
    {
      IQueryOver<Inventory> rowCount =
          Session.QueryOver<Inventory>().ToRowCountQuery();
      IQueryOver<Inventory> result = Session.QueryOver<Inventory>()
                                        .OrderBy(i => i.Builder).Asc
                                        .Take(maxResult)
                                        .Skip(firstResult);
      ICriteria criteriaGuitar = Session.CreateCriteria<Guitar>();

      resultSetInv = result.Future<Inventory>();
      resultSetGuitar = criteriaGuitar.Future<Guitar>();
      transaction.Commit();
      return rowCount.FutureValue<int>().Value;
    }
    catch (Exception ex)
    {
      transaction.Rollback();
      throw;
    }
  }
}

Generated SQL:

SELECT TOP (@p0)
       this_.ID as ID1_0_,
       this_.TYPEID as TYPEID1_0_,
       this_.BUILDER as BUILDER1_0_,
       this_.MODEL as MODEL1_0_,
```

```
        this_.QOH as QOH1_0_,
        this_.COST as COST1_0_,
        this_.PRICE as PRICE1_0_,
        this_.RECEIVED as RECEIVED1_0_
FROM INVENTORY this_
ORDER BY this_.BUILDER asc;
SELECT this_.ID as ID0_0_,
        this_.TYPE as TYPE0_0_
FROM GUITAR this_;
;@p0 = 25 [Type: Int32 (0)]
INVENTORY this_;
```

Implementing this into the `GuitarStore` WPF program requires that the code within the `MainWindow`
`.xaml.cs` file that populates the `ComboBox` is removed and then the `PopulateDataGrid()` method
is modified to use the previously created `Load()` method. Listing 3-33 contains the code for the
`PopulateDataGrid()` method.

LISTING 3-33: Loading all GuitarStore controls with a single database round-trip

```
private void PopulateDataGrid()
{
  NHibernateInventory nhi = new NHibernateInventory();
  IEnumerable<Inventory> GuitarInventory = null;
  IEnumerable<Guitar> GuitarTypes = null;
  int inventoryCount = nhi.Load(MaxResult, FirstResult,
                        out GuitarInventory, out GuitarTypes);

  foreach (var item in GuitarTypes)
  {
    Guitar guitar = new Guitar(item.Id, item.Type);
    comboBoxGuitarTypes.DisplayMemberPath = "Type";
    comboBoxGuitarTypes.SelectedValuePath = "Id";
    comboBoxGuitarTypes.Items.Add(guitar);
  }
  DataTable dt = new DataTable();
  dt.Columns.Add("Builder", typeof(string));
  dt.Columns.Add("Model", typeof(string));
  dt.Columns.Add("Price", typeof(string));
  dt.Columns.Add("Id", typeof(string));

  foreach (var item in GuitarInventory)
  {
    dt.Rows.Add(item.Builder, item.Model, item.Price.ToString(),
              item.Id);
  }

  dataGridInventory.ItemsSource = dt.DefaultView;
  labelPaging.Content = "Retrieved " + FirstResult.ToString() +
            " to " + (FirstResult + GuitarInventory.Count()).ToString() +
            " of " + inventoryCount.ToString();

  totalCount = inventoryCount;
}
```

Finally, notice that in Figure 3-10 the stoplight is now green at the initial startup. This means that all queries are being executed using a single round-trip to the database.

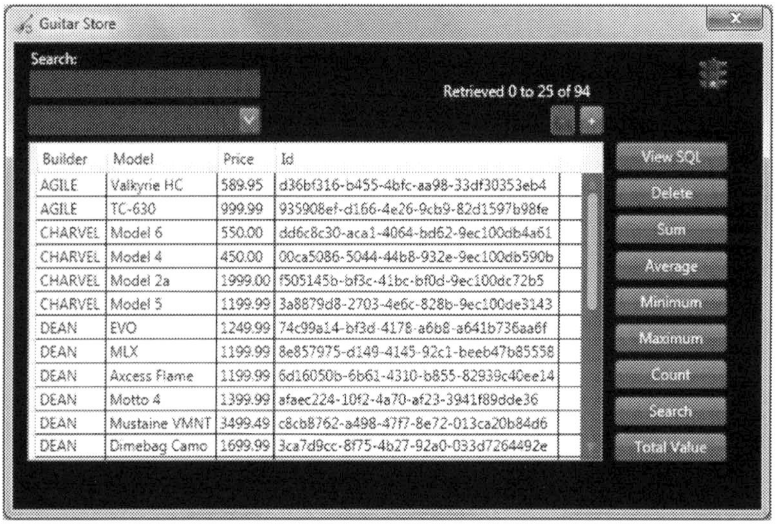

FIGURE 3-10

Selecting the View SQL button on the `GuitarStore` WPF window will display the most recently NHibernate-generated SQL queries, as shown in Figure 3-11.

FIGURE 3-11

USING FETCHMODE

How the data will be retrieved within a program is an important decision that needs to be made during the design phase. The data can be lazy loaded, meaning that it's retrieved only when accessed; or eagerly loaded, meaning the data and corresponding mapped entities are all loaded when the query is executed. The data retrieval strategy may need to be made on a per-query basis or perhaps at a higher level, such as for specific groups of functionality. The ICriteria interface provides designers and programmers with a mechanism to define such strategies within the program. This mechanism is referred to as FetchMode. The FetchMode enumerator can be found in the NHibernate namespace and it is implemented using the SetFetchMode() method within the NHibernate.Impl.CriteriaImpl class.

 NOTE *HQL ignores the* fetch *attribute's value and loads everything lazy by default. If no* FetchMode *is set,* ICriteria *will default to lazy loading.*

FetchMode can be configured either in the mapping files or during the ICriteria query configuration.

Configuring FetchMode in the Mapping Files

The default setting for a data collection, i.e., set, bag, list, and so on, is lazy="true"; however, if the fetch value is set to JOIN within the collection, then it is similar to setting lazy="false". Listing 3-34 shows the fetch attribute added to the Guitar.hbm.xml mapping file.

LISTING 3-34: Fetch attribute example

```
<bag   name="Inventory"   table="INVENTORY" fetch="JOIN" >
  <key column="TYPEID" />
  <one-to-many class="NHibernate.GuitarStore.Common.Inventory" />
</bag>
```

When the code in Listing 3-35 is executed, it may not be obvious that all data from both the GUITAR and the INVENTORY tables has been retrieved from the database and loaded into memory. However, when looking at the generated SQL query, it is clear that a JOIN was performed between the tables and that all the data from both tables was selected.

LISTING 3-35: Loading the Guitar class with fetch=JOIN

```
ICriteria criteria = Session.CreateCriteria<Guitar>();
return criteria.List<Guitar>();

Generated SQL:

SELECT this_.ID as ID0_1_,
```

continues

LISTING 3-35 *(continued)*

```
        this_.TYPE as TYPE0_1_,
        inventory2_.TYPEID as TYPEID3_,
        inventory2_.ID as ID3_,
        inventory2_.ID as ID1_0_,
        inventory2_.TYPEID as TYPEID1_0_,
        inventory2_.BUILDER as BUILDER1_0_,
        inventory2_.MODEL as MODEL1_0_,
        inventory2_.QOH as QOH1_0_,
        inventory2_.COST as COST1_0_,
        inventory2_.PRICE as PRICE1_0_,
        inventory2_.RECEIVED as RECEIVED1_0_
FROM GUITAR this_ left outer JOIN INVENTORY inventory2_
        on this_.ID=inventory2_.TYPEID
```

Configuring FetchMode Programmatically

Setting the FetchMode programmatically, as shown in Listing 3-36, is required for each mapped relationship, just like in the mapping files. There is no global way to set the FetchMode for all relationships within the class. Not being able to set the FetchMode globally may seem like a hindrance initially, but developers soon realize that they can set the FetchMode for each relationship within each class as appropriate. Some requirements may necessitate the eager loading of related classes, while other classes only need to be loaded when referred to within the code. This gives you the flexibility and functionality to support a system's needs in the most optimal way.

LISTING 3-36: Setting FetchMode programmatically

```
public IList<Guitar> GetGuitar()
{
  using (ITransaction transaction = Session.BeginTransaction())
  {
    try
    {
      ICriteria criteria = Session.CreateCriteria<Guitar>()
                           .SetFetchMode("Inventory", FetchMode.Join);

      transaction.Commit();
      return criteria.List<Guitar>();
    }
    catch (Exception ex)
    {
      transaction.Rollback();
      throw;
    }
  }
}

Generated SQL:

SELECT this_.ID as ID0_1_,
```

```
             this_.TYPE as TYPE0_1_,
             inventory2_.TYPEID as TYPEID3_,
             inventory2_.ID as ID3_,
             inventory2_.ID as ID1_0_,
             inventory2_.TYPEID as TYPEID1_0_,
             inventory2_.BUILDER as BUILDER1_0_,
             inventory2_.MODEL as MODEL1_0_,
             inventory2_.QOH as QOH1_0_,
             inventory2_.COST as COST1_0_,
             inventory2_.PRICE as PRICE1_0_,
             inventory2_.RECEIVED as RECEIVED1_0_
    FROM GUITAR this_ left outer JOIN INVENTORY inventory2_
         on this_.ID=inventory2_.TYPEID
```

The preceding code generates the same SQL query you would get when the fetch mode is set from within the mapping file. Table 3-1 describes the different fetch mode settings.

TABLE 3-1: Fetch Mode Options

VALUE	DESCRIPTION
FetchMode.Default	Uses the settings in the .hbm.xml mapping file
FetchMode.Eager	Loads mapped relationships as if lazy=false, using a left outer JOIN
FetchMode.Join	Loads mapped relationships as if lazy=false, using a left outer JOIN
FetchMode.Lazy	Loads mapped relationships as if lazy=true
FetchMode.Select	Loads mapped relationships as if lazy=true

A review of the NHibernate.FetchMode source code shows that Eager = Join and Lazy = Select. Therefore, one can rightly assume that because they are set as equal, as shown in Listing 3-37, they will act the same. This is probably the reason why IntelliSense, when configuring the Fetch in the mapping file, only displays select and JOIN as options.

LISTING 3-37: NHibernate FetchMode enum source code

```
namespace NHibernate
{
  [Serializable]
  public enum FetchMode
  {
    /// <summary>
    /// Default to the setting configured in the mapping file.
    /// </summary>
    Default = 0,
    /// <summary>
```

continues

LISTING 3-37 *(continued)*

```
    /// Fetch eagerly, using a separate select. Equivalent to
    /// <c>fetch="select"</c> (and <c>outer-JOIN="false"</c>)
    /// </summary>
    Select = 1,
    /// <summary>
    /// Fetch using an outer JOIN.  Equivalent to
    /// <c>fetch="JOIN"</c> (and <c>outer-JOIN="true"</c>)
    /// </summary>
    Join = 2,

    Lazy = Select,
    Eager = Join
  }
}
```

 NOTE *Avoid using eager and lazy FetchMode values, as they exist only for backward compatibility with older NHibernate-dependent projects.*

Lastly, recall from Listing 2-6 in Chapter 2 where `IQuery` is covered how parameters were set: `IQuery` exposes a large set of methods that specifically define the value type of the parameter being passed to the query. `ICriteria` does not have this capability. Instead, `ICriteria` uses the types defined in the mapping files to confirm that the value being supplied matches the database type. Listing 3-38 shows a comparison between setting a parameter in `IQuery` vs. `ICriteria`.

LISTING 3-38: Setting query parameters — HQL vs. ICriteria

```
HQL- uses reflection to validate data type of Id:

IQuery query = session.CreateQuery(HQLQuery)
                      .SetGuid("TypeId", Id);

ICriteria- uses mapping file type to validate data type of Id:

ICriteria criteria = session.CreateCriteria(typeof(Inventory))
                            .Add(Restrictions.Eq("TypeId", Id));
```

IMPLEMENTING AGGREGATE DATABASE FUNCTIONS

Aggregate database methods provide the programmer with a quick and simple way to average, count, or find the minimum or maximum values in a database table. Not all database aggregates are supported by NHibernate. A review of the `Projection` class, found in the `NHibernate.Criterion` namespace, shows that the functions described in Table 3-2 are supported.

TABLE 3-2: Supported Aggregate Functions

AGGREGATE	DESCRIPTION
Distinct	Creates a distinct projection from a projection
RowCount	The query row count, i.e., Count(*)
Count	A property value count
CountDistinct	A distinct property value count
MAX	A property maximum value
MIN	A property minimum value
AVG	A property average value
SUM	A property value sum
Group	A grouping property value accessible via lambda expression

To implement aggregate database functions using ICriteria in the GuitarStore WPF program, you need to perform the following:

1. Add Avg, Min, Max, and Count methods to the NHibernateInventory class.

2. Modify the Click event of the AVG, MIN, MAX, and COUNT buttons created in Chapter 2.

Open the NHibernateInventory.cs file located in the NHibernate.GuitarStore project and add the following methods shown in Listings 3-39 through 3-42.

LISTING 3-39: Avg ICriteria aggregate function

```
public IList GetInventoryAveragePrice()
{
  using (ITransaction transaction = Session.BeginTransaction())
  {
    try
    {
      ICriteria criteria = Session.CreateCriteria<Guitar>("g")
            .CreateAlias("Inventory", "i")
            .SetProjection(Projections.ProjectionList()
                .Add(Projections.GroupProperty("g.Type"))
                .Add(Projections.Avg("i.Price")));

      transaction.Commit();
      return criteria.List();
    }
    catch (Exception ex)
    {
      transaction.Rollback();
```

continues

LISTING 3-39 *(continued)*

```
        throw;
      }
    }
}

Generated SQL:

SELECT this_.TYPE as y0_,
       avg(cast(i1_.PRICE as DOUBLE PRECISION)) as y1_
FROM GUITAR this_ inner JOIN INVENTORY i1_
     on this_.ID=i1_.TYPEID
GROUP BY this_.TYPE
```

The preceding code calculates the average Price by guitar type and returns a list grouped by guitar types.

LISTING 3-40: Min ICriteria aggregate function

```
public IList GetInventoryMinimumPrice()
{
  using (ITransaction transaction = Session.BeginTransaction())
  {
    try
    {
      ICriteria criteria = Session.CreateCriteria<Guitar>("g")
          .CreateAlias("Inventory", "i")
          .SetProjection(Projections.ProjectionList()
              .Add(Projections.GroupProperty("g.Type"))
              .Add(Projections.Min("i.Price")));
      transaction.Commit();
      return criteria.List();
    }
    catch (Exception ex)
    {
      transaction.Rollback();
      throw;
    }
  }
}

Generated SQL:

SELECT this_.TYPE as y0_,
      min(i1_.PRICE) as y1_
FROM GUITAR this_ inner JOIN INVENTORY i1_
     on this_.ID=i1_.TYPEID
GROUP BY this_.TYPE
```

The preceding code returns the guitar with the lowest Price by guitar type and a list grouped by guitar type.

LISTING 3-41: Max ICriteria aggregate function

```
public IList GetInventoryMaximumPrice()
{
  using (ITransaction transaction = Session.BeginTransaction())
  {
    try
    {
      ICriteria criteria = Session.CreateCriteria<Guitar>("g")
          .CreateAlias("Inventory", "i")
          .SetProjection(Projections.ProjectionList()
             .Add(Projections.GroupProperty("g.Type"))
             .Add(Projections.Max("i.Price")));
      transaction.Commit();
      return criteria.List();
    }
    catch (Exception ex)
    {
      transaction.Rollback();
      throw;
    }
  }
}

Generated SQL:

SELECT this_.TYPE as y0_,
       max(i1_.PRICE) as y1_
FROM GUITAR this_ inner JOIN INVENTORY i1_
on this_.ID=i1_.TYPEID
GROUP BY this_.TYPE
```

The preceding list returns the guitar with the highest Price by guitar type and a list grouped by guitar type.

LISTING 3-42: Count ICriteria aggregate function

```
public IList GetInventoryCountADF()
{
  using (ITransaction transaction = Session.BeginTransaction())
  {
    try
    {
      ICriteria criteria = Session.CreateCriteria<Guitar>("g")
          .CreateAlias("Inventory", "i")
          .SetProjection(Projections.ProjectionList()
             .Add(Projections.GroupProperty("g.Type"))
             .Add(Projections.RowCount()));
```

continues

LISTING 3-42 *(continued)*

```
      transaction.Commit();
      return criteria.List();
    }
    catch (Exception ex)
    {
      transaction.Rollback();
      throw;
    }
  }
}

Generated SQL:

SELECT this_.TYPE as y0_,
       count(*) as y1_
FROM GUITAR this_ inner JOIN INVENTORY i1_
     on this_.ID=i1_.TYPEID
GROUP BY this_.TYPE
```

The preceding list returns the total number of guitars by guitar type and a list grouped by guitar type.

 NOTE *Both* IQuery *and* ICriteria *support the use of aggregates.*

The next step is to change the existing code for the buttonCount_Click() method, which is called when the Count button is clicked from the GuitarStore WPF window. An example of the COUNT implementation is shown in Listing 3-43.

LISTING 3-43: Using the ICriteria Count button from the GuitarStore WPF

```
private void buttonCount_Click(object sender, RoutedEventArgs e)
{
  NHibernateInventory nhi = new NHibernateInventory();
  List<string> fields = new List<string>
  {
    "Guitar Type", "Total Count"
  };
  IList GuitarInventory = nhi.GetInventoryCountADF();
  dataGridInventory.ItemsSource =
        BuildDataTable(fields, GuitarInventory).DefaultView;
}
```

Starting the `GuitarStore` WPF program and clicking the Count button will display a WPF window like the one shown in Figure 3-12.

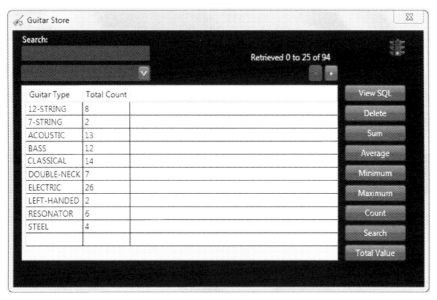

FIGURE 3-12

To implement the remaining aggregate database functions using the `ICriteria` API, simply modify the code in the `MainWindow.xaml.cs` file to use the newly created aggregate database methods.

UNDERSTANDING RESTRICTIONS AND EXPRESSIONS

The `Restrictions` and `Expression` classes can be found in the `NHibernate.Criterion` namespace. These classes hold an abundant number of methods that support the implementation of projection and value comparison logic. *Projection* reduces the amount of data returned from a query and is implemented with SQL by using the `WHERE` clause, or with the `ICriteria` API by using the `Restrictions` class. Conversely, *value comparison logic* uses operators, such as $\leq$, $\neq$, or $\geq$, for example, to limit the data result. Most of the value comparison operators and terms are supported via the `Restrictions` class. Table 3-3 describes the restriction methods and comparison operators/terms found within the `Restrictions` class.

TABLE 3-3: Restrictions Methods and Operators

RESTRICTION	OPERATOR	DESCRIPTION
Eq	=	Applies an "equal" constraint to the named property
Like	LIKE	Applies a "like" constraint to the named property
Gt	>	Applies a "greater than" constraint to the named property
Lt	<	Applies a "less than" constraint to the named property
Le	<=	Applies a "less than or equal" constraint to the named property
Ge	>=	Applies a "greater than or equal" constraint to the named property
BETWEEN	BETWEEN	Applies a "between" constraint to the named property
In	IN	Applies an "in" constraint to the named property
IsNull		Applies an "is null" constraint to the named property
IsNotNull		Applies an "is not null" constraint to the named property
And	AND	Returns the conjunction of two expressions
Or	OR	Returns the disjunction of two expressions
Not	NOT	Returns the negation of an expression
Where	WHERE	Lambda expression support for ICriteria (e.g., Expression<func<T, bool>>)

It is very common for a data-driven program to need to constrain the queries that return information used for decision making. You will find that the Restrictions class plays a significant role in the data retrieval process and provides the programmer with the capabilities necessary for creating such data-driven programs.

NOTE *The* Expression *class inherits from the* Restrictions *class. Avoid using* Expressions, *as the class is marked as semi-deprecated and exists only for backward compatibility.*

By adding query restrictions to a CreateCriteria or DetachedCriteria method, the query will be constrained and return only the data that complies with the restriction. The following actions are performed in this section to implement the Between, In, Not, and Or Restrictions into the GuitarStore WPF program.

1. Create four new methods within the NHibernateInventory class found in the NHibernate .GuitarStore project: one method for each restriction implemented.

2. Enhance the search capabilities of the GuitarStore WPF program to utilize the new search capabilities.

3. Populate the search results in the DataGrid.

First, open the NHibernateInventory class found within the NHibernate.GuitarStore project and add the four methods shown in Listing 3-44, 3-45, 3-47, and 3-48. Listing 3-44 will return a list of guitars whose price is between the low and high values passed to the method.

LISTING 3-44: Between restriction using the ICriteria Restrictions class

```
public IList GetGuitarBetween(decimal low, decimal high)
{
  using (ITransaction transaction = StatelessSession.BeginTransaction())
  {
    try
    {
      ICriteria criteria = StatelessSession.CreateCriteria<Inventory>()
                .SetProjection(Projections.ProjectionList()
                    .Add(Projections.Property("Builder"))
                    .Add(Projections.Property("Model"))
                    .Add(Projections.Property("Price"))
                    .Add(Projections.Property("Id")))
                .AddOrder(Order.Asc("Builder"))
                .Add(Restrictions.Between("Cost", low, high));

      transaction.Commit();
      return criteria.List();
    }
    catch (Exception ex)
    {
      transaction.Rollback();
      throw;
    }
  }
}

Generated SQL:

SELECT this_.BUILDER as y0_,
       this_.MODEL as y1_,
       this_.PRICE as y2_,
       this_.ID as y3_
FROM INVENTORY this_
WHERE this_.COST between @p0 and @p1
ORDER BY this_.BUILDER asc;
@p0 = 1000 [Type: Decimal (0)],
@p1 = 2000 [Type: Decimal (0)]
```

Listing 3-45 provides an example of how to implement the In restriction using the ICriteria API. The query returns all guitars in the inventory that are built by Fender, Ibanez, and Takamine.

LISTING 3-45: In restriction using the ICriteria Restrictions class

```
public IList GetGuitarIn(object[] Builders)
{
  using (ITransaction transaction = StatelessSession.BeginTransaction())
  {
    try
    {
      ICriteria criteria = StatelessSession.CreateCriteria<Inventory>()
                .SetProjection(Projections.ProjectionList()
                  .Add(Projections.Property("Builder"))
                  .Add(Projections.Property("Model"))
                  .Add(Projections.Property("Price"))
                  .Add(Projections.Property("Id")))
                .AddOrder(Order.Asc("Builder"))
                .Add(Restrictions.In("Builder", Builders));

      transaction.Commit();
      return criteria.List();
    }
    catch (Exception ex)
    {
      transaction.Rollback();
      throw;
    }
  }
}

Generated SQL:

SELECT this_.BUILDER as y0_,
       this_.MODEL as y1_,
       this_.PRICE as y2_,
       this_.ID as y3_
FROM INVENTORY this_
WHERE this_.BUILDER in (@p0, @p1, @p2)
ORDER BY this_.BUILDER asc;
@p0 = 'FENDER' [Type: String (4000)],
@p1 = 'IBANEZ' [Type: String (4000)],
@p2 = 'TAKAMINE' [Type: String (4000)]
```

Now would be a good time to test the preceding method using the NHibernate.GuitarStore .Console application. By doing this you can be certain that the method works prior to attempting its implementation in the GuitarStore WPF program. It will also help you to understand the format of the parameter data required to utilize the method. Add the following code in Listing 3-46 to the Main() method of the Program class found in the NHibernate.GuitarStore .Console application. Then set the project as the startup project, run it, and confirm it runs as expected.

```
object[] Builders40 = new object[] { "FENDER", "IBANEZ", "TAKAMINE" };
IList list40 = nhi.GetGuitarIn(Builders40);
Console.WriteLine("GetGuitarIn(Builders40): "
                    + list40.Count.ToString() + " results");
```

Next, add the method that uses the Not restriction. This method, shown in Listing 3-47, returns a list of guitars that are not built by Fender, Ibanez, or Takamine.

LISTING 3-47: Not restriction using the ICriteria Restrictions class

```
public IList GetGuitarNot(object[] Builders)
{
  using (ITransaction transaction = StatelessSession.BeginTransaction())
  {
    try
    {
      ICriteria criteria = StatelessSession.CreateCriteria<Inventory>()
                  .SetProjection(Projections.ProjectionList()
                    .Add(Projections.Property("Builder"))
                    .Add(Projections.Property("Model"))
                    .Add(Projections.Property("Price"))
                    .Add(Projections.Property("Id")))
                  .AddOrder(Order.Asc("Builder"))
                  .Add(Restrictions.Not(Restrictions.In("Builder", Builders)));

      transaction.Commit();
      return criteria.List();
    }
    catch (Exception ex)
    {
      transaction.Rollback();
      throw;
    }
  }
}

Generated SQL:

SELECT this_.BUILDER as y0_,
       this_.MODEL as y1_,
       this_.PRICE as y2_,
       this_.ID as y3_
FROM INVENTORY this_
WHERE not (this_.BUILDER in (@p0, @p1, @p2))
ORDER BY this_.BUILDER asc;
@p0 = 'FENDER' [Type: String (4000)],
@p1 = 'IBANEZ' [Type: String (4000)],
@p2 = 'TAKAMINE' [Type: String (4000)]
```

The last method that implements the Or restriction is shown in Listing 3-48. This query will result in a list of guitars that are built by Fender, Ibanez, or Takamine or whose price is between the low and high value passed as the parameter.

LISTING 3-48: Or restriction using the ICriteria Restrictions class

```
public IList GetGuitarOr(object[] Builders, decimal low, decimal high)
{
  using (ITransaction transaction = StatelessSession.BeginTransaction())
  {
    try
    {
      ICriteria criteria = StatelessSession.CreateCriteria<Inventory>()
                .SetProjection(Projections.ProjectionList()
                  .Add(Projections.Property("Builder"))
                  .Add(Projections.Property("Model"))
                  .Add(Projections.Property("Price"))
                  .Add(Projections.Property("Id")))
                .AddOrder(Order.Asc("Builder"))
                .Add(Restrictions.Or(Restrictions.In("Builder", Builders),
                    Restrictions.Between("Cost", low, high)));

      transaction.Commit();
      return criteria.List();
    }
    catch (Exception ex)
    {
      transaction.Rollback();
      throw;
    }
  }
}

Generated SQL:

SELECT this_.BUILDER as y0_,
       this_.MODEL as y1_,
       this_.PRICE as y2_,
       this_.ID as y3_
FROM INVENTORY this_
WHERE (this_.BUILDER in (@p0, @p1, @p2)
       or this_.COST between @p3 and @p4)
ORDER BY this_.BUILDER asc;
@p0 = 'FENDER' [Type: String (4000)],
@p1 = 'IBANEZ' [Type: String (4000)],
@p2 = 'TAKAMINE' [Type:String (4000)],
@p3 = 1000 [Type: Decimal (0)],
@p4 = 2000 [Type: Decimal (0)]
```

To implement the Between restriction shown earlier in Listing 3-44 in the GuitarStore WPF program, open the MainWindow.xaml file within the GuitarStore project and add two Label controls and two TextBox controls. Figure 3-13 shows the result. The XAML code is shown in Listing 3-49.

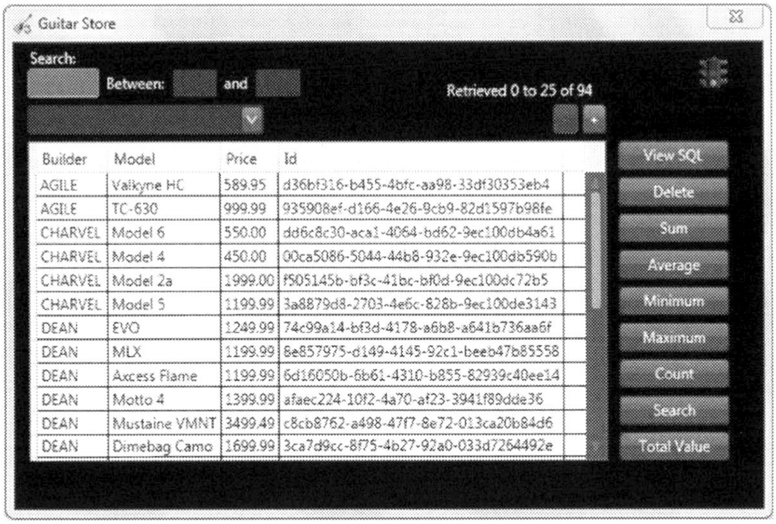

FIGURE 3-13

LISTING 3-49: XAML code for Between restriction WPF implementation

```
<Label Content="Between:" Height="28" HorizontalAlignment="Left"
       Margin="77,24,0,0" Name="labelBetween" VerticalAlignment="Top" />
<TextBox Height="23" HorizontalAlignment="Left" Margin="131,21,0,0"
        Name="textBoxLow" VerticalAlignment="Top" Width="38" />
<Label Content="and" Height="28" HorizontalAlignment="Left"
       Margin="174,24,0,0" Name="labelAnd" VerticalAlignment="Top" />
<TextBox Height="23" HorizontalAlignment="Left" Margin="200,21,0,0"
        Name="textBoxHigh" VerticalAlignment="Top" Width="38" />
```

Now open the MainWindow.xaml.cs file and modify the buttonSearch_Click() method so that is resembles what is shown in Listing 3-50.

LISTING 3-50: Between restriction in the GuitarStore WPF program

```
private void buttonSearch_Click(object sender, RoutedEventArgs e)
{
  NHibernateInventory nhi = new NHibernateInventory();
  IList GuitarInventory = nhi.GetGuitarBetween(Convert.ToDecimal(textBoxLow.Text),

Convert.ToDecimal(textBoxHigh.Text));
```

continues

LISTING 3-50 *(continued)*

```
  List<string> fields = new List<string>
  {
    "Builder", "Model", "Price", "Id"
  };
  dataGridInventory.ItemsSource =
                  BuildDataTable(fields, GuitarInventory).DefaultView;
}
```

Lastly, to implement the Or restriction into the GuitarStore WPF program, add three CheckBox controls to the MainWindow.xaml window. Listing 3-51 provides the XAML code.

LISTING 3-51: XAML code for Or restriction WPF implementation

```
<CheckBox Content="Fender" Height="16" HorizontalAlignment="Left"
          Margin="142,54,0,0" Name="checkBoxFender" VerticalAlignment="Top" />
<CheckBox Content="Ibanez" Height="16" HorizontalAlignment="Left"
          Margin="205,54,0,0" Name="checkBoxIbanez" VerticalAlignment="Top" />
<CheckBox Content="Takamine" Height="16" HorizontalAlignment="Left"
          Margin="267,54,0,0" Name="checkBoxTakamine" VerticalAlignment="Top" />
```

Then modify the buttonSearch_Click() method so that it resembles the code shown in Listing 3-52.

LISTING 3-52: Or restriction in the GuitarStore WPF program

```
private void buttonSearch_Click(object sender, RoutedEventArgs e)
{
  NHibernateInventory nhi = new NHibernateInventory();
  object[] Builders = new object[3];

  if (checkBoxFender.IsChecked == true)
  {
    Builders[0] = "FENDER";
  }
  if (checkBoxIbanez.IsChecked == true)
  {
    Builders[1] = "IBANEZ";
  }
  if (checkBoxTakamine.IsChecked == true)
  {
    Builders[2] = "TAKAMINE";
  }

  IList GuitarInventory = nhi.GetGuitarOr(Builders,
                     Convert.ToDecimal(textBoxLow.Text),
                     Convert.ToDecimal(textBoxHigh.Text));
  List<string> fields = new List<string>
```

```
{
    "Builder", "Model", "Price", "Id"
};
dataGridInventory.ItemsSource =
        BuildDataTable(fields, GuitarInventory).DefaultView;
}
```

When the `GuitarStore` WPF program is run after €4000 is entered as the low `Cost`, €5000 is entered as the high `Cost`, and Fender and Ibanez are checked, the window shown in Figure 3-14 is produced. The `DataGrid` displays all Fender and Ibanez guitars, plus guitars that have a `Cost` between €4000 and €5000.

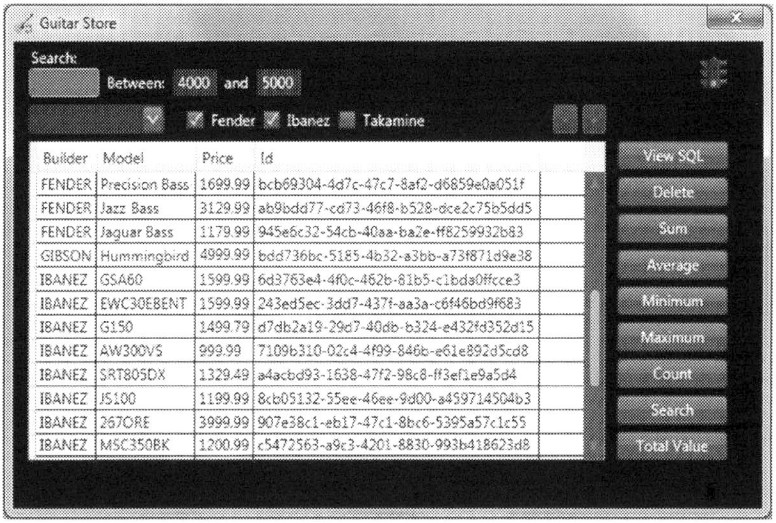

FIGURE 3-14

WORKING WITH DATA TRANSFER OBJECTS

There is a very powerful feature in NHibernate that supports the conversion of any result set to a business object-like class or data transfer object (DTO). This capability is supported through the `Transformers` class, found within the `NHibernate.Transform` namespace. Although this capability is available via the `IQuery` interface, it is easier to leverage when accessed via `ICriteria` because of the continued use of methods to build the query.

In all the examples within the `GuitarStore` solution up to now, when projection has been implemented to reduce the number of columns returned from a query, the fact that the result set was dynamic has not been an issue. This is because in every case, the result set has been immediately added to a `DataTable` and then bound to a `DataGrid`.

In other programs, it may be an absolute requirement that all result sets be strongly typed. As shown in Listings 2-18 and 2-19 in Chapter 2 and Listings 3-23 and 3-25 in this chapter, when the result set is strongly typed as a class, accessing the properties within the class is much easier.

NHibernate provides programmers with the capability to transform a dynamically retrieved dataset into a strongly typed class. This is accomplished by using the `AliasToBean()` method, found within the `Transformers` class, in the `NHibernate.Transform` namespace.

> **NOTE** Both `IQuery` and `ICriteria` *support the transformation of a dynamically retrieved result set to a strongly typed class.*

To implement a DTO to store the projected result set into the `GuitarStore` WPF program, you need to do the following:

1. Create a new class named `InventoryDTO`.

2. Create a new mapping file named `InventoryDTO.hbm.xml`.

3. Add a method named `GetInventoryDTO()` to the `NHibernateInventory` class that retrieves a projected result set and then converts it to the `InventoryDTO` class.

4. Implement the `GetInventoryDTO()` method into the `GuitarStore` WPF program.

To create a new class in the `NHibernate.GuitarStore` project, right-click the `Common` folder, and select Add ⇨ Class. Then add **InventoryDTO.cs** as the name of the class and select OK. Modify the `InventoryDTO` class so that it resembles the code shown in Listing 3-53.

LISTING 3-53: InventoryDTO class description

```
namespace NHibernate.GuitarStore.Common
{
    public class InventoryDTO
    {
        public InventoryDTO() { }

        public virtual Guid Id { get; set; }
        public virtual string Builder { get; set; }
        public virtual string Model { get; set; }
        public virtual decimal? Price { get; set; }
        public virtual string Type { get; set; }
    }
}
```

The `InventoryDTO` class is created just like any other class that is used to store retrieved data via NHibernate. The mapping file is a little different from all the previous mapping files, as shown in Listing 3-54. As there is no associated database table, the properties do not need mappings. To add the file to the `NHibernate.GuitarStore` project, right-click the `Mapping` directory and select Add ⇨ New Item. Select XML File and enter **InventoryDTO.hbm.xml** as the name.

LISTING 3-54: Inventory DTO mapping file example

```xml
<?xml version="1.0" encoding="utf-8" ?>
<hibernate-mapping xmlns="urn:nhibernate-mapping-2.2">
  <import class="NHibernate.GuitarStore.Common.
InventoryDTO, NHibernate.GuitarStore" />
</hibernate-mapping>
```

There is no database table directly related to this class and mapping file. Therefore, no actual SQL query is generated to populate this object. These files are used simply as storage containers for the dynamically generated result set. The `import` element in the mapping file makes NHibernate aware of the type, enabling NHibernate to manipulate it.

 NOTE *It is required to set all* `.hbm.xml` *files in your project to Embedded Resource via the Properties window or place them within the program working directory; otherwise, you are likely to get an exception at compile time or your program simply will not display any data.*

The `GuitarStore` solution should now resemble Figure 3-15.

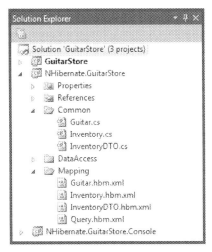

FIGURE 3-15

Next, add a method named `GetInventoryDTO()` to the `NHibernateInventory` class found within the `NHibernate.GuitarStore` project. The code segment should resemble Listing 3-55. Notice that the `NHibernate.Transform` directive has been added to the `NHibernateInventory` class.

LISTING 3-55: GetInventoryDTO() using AliasToBean()

```
using NHibernate.Transform;

public IList<InventoryDTO> GetInventoryDTO()
{
  using (ITransaction transaction = StatelessSession.BeginTransaction())
  {
    try
    {
      ICriteria criteria = StatelessSession.CreateCriteria<Guitar>("g")
                .CreateAlias("Inventory", "i")
                .SetProjection(Projections.ProjectionList()
                  .Add(Projections.Property("i.Id"), "Id")
                  .Add(Projections.Property("i.Builder"), "Builder")
                  .Add(Projections.Property("i.Model"), "Model")
                  .Add(Projections.Property("i.Price"), "Price")
                  .Add(Projections.Property("g.Type"), "Type"))
                .AddOrder(Order.Asc("g.Type"));

      criteria.SetResultTransformer(Transformers.AliasToBean<InventoryDTO>());
      return criteria.List<InventoryDTO>();
    }
    catch (Exception ex)
    {
      transaction.Rollback();
      throw;
    }
  }
}

Generated SQL:

SELECT i1_.ID as y0_,
       i1_.BUILDER as y1_,
       i1_.MODEL as y2_,
       i1_.PRICE as y3_,
       this_.TYPE as y4_
FROM GUITAR this_ inner JOIN INVENTORY i1_
     on this_.ID=i1_.TYPEID
ORDER BY this_.TYPE asc
```

The result is a strongly typed dataset that provides the programmer with direct access to the properties of the class. To implement the DTO into the `GuitarStore` WPF program, the

PopulateDataGrid() method within the MainWindow.xaml.cs file should resemble what is shown in Listing 3-56.

LISTING 3-56: Implementing a DTO into the GuitarStore WPF program

```
private void PopulateDataGrid()
{
  NHibernateInventory nhi = new NHibernateInventory();
  IList<InventoryDTO> GuitarInventory = nhi.GetInventoryDTO();
  dataGridInventory.ItemsSource = GuitarInventory;

  if (GuitarInventory != null)
  {
    dataGridInventory.Columns[0].Visibility =
    System.Windows.Visibility.Hidden;
  }
}
```

When you run the GuitarStore WPF program, the window produced should look like the one shown in Figure 3-16.

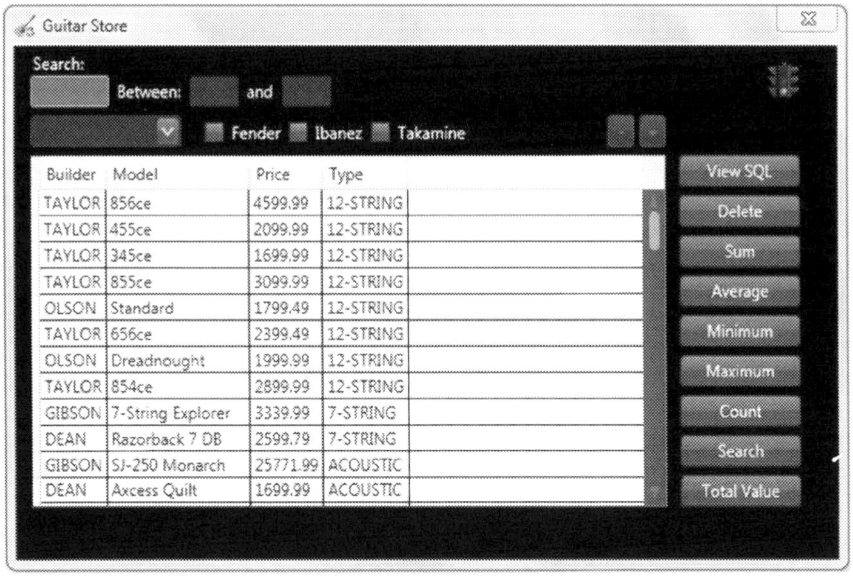

FIGURE 3-16

SUMMARY

Choosing which interface to use with an NHibernate implementation can be difficult. Both Chapter 1 and Chapter 2 have demonstrated that the ICriteria and the IQuery APIs contain powerful features, and each has the capabilities and functionality to support a vast majority of common database activities. My recommendation is simply to choose the interface that matches your programming philosophy and stick with it throughout the lifetime of your project. As you have seen in this chapter, ICriteria is as feature-rich as IQuery, but it also includes the QueryOver API, which utilizes lambda expressions. The ICriteria API has a very strong projection library that can be used to reduce the amount of data retrieved and to more precisely retrieve the data from a data source, by using the methods found within the Restrictions class. The next chapter covers another NHibernate Query API, LINQ to NHibernate, which has been available since the release of NHibernate version 3.0.

4

Using LINQ to NHibernate

In the previous chapter, the `ICritera` API, a programmatic method of data retrieval, was discussed. Recall that the `ICriteria` interface contains the `QueryOver` API, which is a type-safe compile-time wrapper for the `ICriteria` API. It is possible to use lambda expressions in both `QueryOver` and LINQ to NHibernate. In this chapter, you will learn the following:

➤ Working with LINQ to NHibernate

➤ Using LINQ to NHibernate with lambda expressions

➤ Implementing paging using LINQ to NHibernate

➤ Understanding aggregate database functions with LINQ to NHibernate

INTRODUCTION

The release of NHibernate 3.0 included LINQ capabilities for use with NHibernate. LINQ is a very powerful querying tool that exists for objects, SQL, XML, and many other extensions for querying information sources. The LINQ to NHibernate provider implements most of the .NET LINQ operators found in the `System.Linq` namespace. Table 4-1 shows the operator types and execution method(s) provided with the LINQ to NHibernate provider.

TABLE 4-1: LINQ Operators

OPERATOR	EXECUTION METHODS
Aggregates	Count, Sum, Min, Max, and Average
Conversion	ToArray, ToList, ToDictionary, and OfType
Element	First, FirstOrDefault, ElementAt
Generation	Range, and Repeat

continues

TABLE 4-1 *(continued)*

OPERATOR	EXECUTION METHODS
Grouping	GroupBy
Join	Cross, Group, and Left Outer
Ordering	OrderBy, OrderByDescending, ThenBy, ThenByDescending, and Reverse
Partitioning	Take, Skip, TakeWhile, and SkipWhile
Projection	Select and SelectMany
Quantifiers	Any and All
Restriction	Where
Set	Distinct, Union, Intersect, and Except

The LINQ to NHibernate provider is deeply integrated with the .NET LINQ capabilities, and programmers can expect similar performance and functionality.

Figure 4-1 shows the numerous NHibernate classes used in the creation of LINQ to NHibernate capabilities. Recall from Chapter 1, "Getting Started with NHibernate 3," the list of binaries required to utilize the NHibernate functionality. Prior to NHibernate 3.1, there was an additional component named Remotion.Data.Linq.dll. With NHibernate 3.1, ILMerge is used to combine two previously standalone DLLs into the NHibernate.dll. You need to know this because when the NHibernate source code is downloaded, the code for the QueryableBase<T>() class from which the NhQuerable<T> class inherits is not part of the package. The QueryableBase<T>() class is found in the Remotion.Data.Linq namespace and must be downloaded separately from the NHibernate source code. It is a very powerful library and worth downloading and studying.

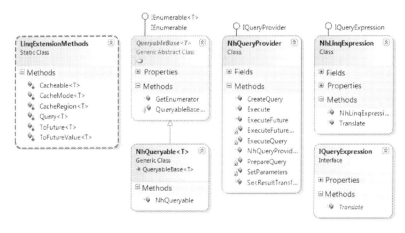

FIGURE 4-1

Like the IQuery, ICriteria, and QueryOver capabilities, LINQ to NHibernate is simply a different API for querying your database with NHibernate. It is most similar to the syntax found in the QueryOver class, as lambda expressions are commonly used. However, there is no dependency between the QueryOver and the NHibernate LINQ provider. Listing 4-1 shows the IQuery, QueryOver, and LINQ to NHibernate methods, all of which render the same result set. Notice also that the NHibernate-generated SQL queries are the same.

LISTING 4-1: IQuery, QueryOver, and LINQ queries for comparison

```
NHibernate LINQ:

IList<Inventory> result = (from inv in session.Query<Inventory>()
                           where inv.TypeId == Id
                           orderby inv.Builder
                           select inv).ToList();

select inventory0_.ID as ID1_,
       inventory0_.TYPEID as TYPEID1_,
       inventory0_.BUILDER as BUILDER1_,
       inventory0_.MODEL as MODEL1_,
       inventory0_.QOH as QOH1_,
       inventory0_.COST as COST1_,
       inventory0_.PRICE as PRICE1_,
       inventory0_.RECEIVED as RECEIVED1_
from INVENTORY inventory0_
where inventory0_.TYPEID=@p0
orderby inventory0_.BUILDER asc;
@p0 = e6f2a2ab-ca6d-4874-8874-6bb9baccffcb [Type: Guid (0)]

QueryOver:

IList<Inventory> result = session.QueryOver<Inventory>()
                                 .Where(i => i.TypeId == Id)
                                 .OrderBy(i => i.Builder).Asc
                                 .List<Inventory>();

SELECT this_.ID as ID1_0_,
       this_.TYPEID as TYPEID1_0_,
       this_.BUILDER as BUILDER1_0_,
       this_.MODEL as MODEL1_0_,
       this_.QOH as QOH1_0_,
       this_.COST as COST1_0_,
       this_.PRICE as PRICE1_0_,
       this_.RECEIVED as RECEIVED1_0_
FROM INVENTORY this_
WHERE this_.TYPEID = @p0
ORDER BY this_.BUILDER asc;
@p0 = e6f2a2ab-ca6d-4874-8874-6bb9baccffcb [Type: Guid (0)]

IQuery:

IQuery query
```

continues

LISTING 4-1 *(continued)*

```
        = session.CreateQuery("from Inventory where TypeId = :TypeId order by Builder")
                .SetGuid("TypeId", Id);

select inventory0_.ID as ID1_,
       inventory0_.TYPEID as TYPEID1_,
       inventory0_.BUILDER as BUILDER1_,
       inventory0_.MODEL as MODEL1_,
       inventory0_.QOH as QOH1_,
       inventory0_.COST as COST1_,
       inventory0_.PRICE as PRICE1_,
       inventory0_.RECEIVED as RECEIVED1_
from INVENTORY inventory0_
where inventory0_.TYPEID=@p0
orderby inventory0_.BUILDER;
@p0 = e6f2a2ab-ca6d-4874-8874-6bb9baccffcb [Type: Guid (0)]
```

WORKING WITH LINQ TO NHIBERNATE

The interface into LINQ to NHibernate is via the `Query<T>()` method, which can be found in the `LinqExtentionMethods` class located in the `NHibernate.Linq` namespace. The `Query<T>()` method returns an `IQueraryable<T>` implementation, which is an implementation of the `System.Linq.IQueryProvider` via the `NhQueryProvider` class. Note that several methods in the `NhQueryProvider` create and pass instances of `IQuery`. There is some commonality between LINQ to NHibernate and the `IQuery` capabilities. For example, both the `NhQueryProvider.Execute()` and the `NhQueryProvider.ExecuteFuture()` methods create and use an instance of an `IQuery` interface. Each of those methods passes that `IQuery` object to other LINQ to NHibernate methods, to be used with the `IQuery` `CreateQuery()` and `SetParamter()` methods. These methods help with the generation of the SQL query executed via LINQ to NHibernate.

Implementing and using LINQ to NHibernate within the `GuitarStore` WPF solution can be done in the same way `IQuery`, `ICriteria`, or `QueryOver` are implemented. In this section, you will accomplish the following:

➤ Create a new method named `GetLINQInventory()` that populates the `DataGrid` with data from the `INVENTORY` table.

➤ Create a new method named `GetLINQFilteredInventory()` that filters the result set based on a selected guitar type.

➤ Create a new method named `SearchInventoryLINQ()` that accepts a search parameter and returns the matching results.

➤ Modify the `GetLINQInventory()` method to support paging.

➤ Modify the `GetLINQInventory()` method to use Futures.

➤ Implement all methods into the `GuitarStore` WPF program.

First, open the NHibernateInventory.cs file, which is found in the NHibernate.GuitarStore project, and add the method called GetLINQInventory(). The method should resemble what is shown in Listing 4-2. Notice that the LINQ capabilities require the addition of the NHibernate.Linq using directive.

LISTING 4-2: LINQ to NHibernate query to retrieve the guitar inventory

```
using NHibernate.Linq;

public IList GetLINQInventory()
{
  using (ITransaction transaction = Session.BeginTransaction())
  {
    IQueryable<Inventory> query = (from l in Session.Query<Inventory>()
                                   select l);
    return query.ToList();
  }
}

Generated SQL:

select inventory0_.ID as ID1_,
       inventory0_.TYPEID as TYPEID1_,
       inventory0_.BUILDER as BUILDER1_,
       inventory0_.MODEL as MODEL1_,
       inventory0_.QOH as QOH1_,
       inventory0_.COST as COST1_,
       inventory0_.PRICE as PRICE1_,
       inventory0_.RECEIVED as RECEIVED1_
from INVENTORY inventory0_
```

Next, open the MainWindow.xaml.cs file and modify the PopulateDataGrid() method so that it uses the method created in Listing 4-2. Listing 4-3 shows how it should look. Note that the GetLINQInventory() method returns a strongly typed result set; therefore, you don't need to create a DataTable before binding the result set to the DataGrid. The result of the method is bound directly to the DataGrid.

LISTING 4-3: Using LINQ to NHibernate in the GuitarStore WPF program

```
private void PopulateDataGrid()
{
  NHibernateInventory nhi = new NHibernateInventory();
  IList GuitarInventory = nhi.GetLINQInventory();
  dataGridInventory.ItemsSource = GuitarInventory;

  if (GuitarInventory != null)
  {
    dataGridInventory.Columns[0].Visibility = System.Windows.Visibility.Hidden;
    dataGridInventory.Columns[1].Visibility = System.Windows.Visibility.Hidden;
    dataGridInventory.Columns[9].Visibility = System.Windows.Visibility.Hidden;
  }
}
```

Now create a new method in the `NHibernateInventory` class, in the `NHibernate.GuitarStore` project, that accepts a guitar type as a parameter and returns a list of matching data. The code segment should resemble the method shown in Listing 4-4.

LISTING 4-4: LINQ to NHibernate method with Where clause

```
public IList GetLINQInventory(Guid Id)
{
  using (ITransaction transaction = Session.BeginTransaction())
  {
    try
    {
      IQueryable<Inventory> query =  (from inv in Session.Query<Inventory>()
                                      where inv.TypeId == Id
                                      orderby inv.Builder
                                      select inv);

      transaction.Commit();
      return query.ToList();
    }
    catch (Exception ex)
    {
      transaction.Rollback();
      throw;
    }
  }
}

Generated SQL:

select inventory0_.ID as ID1_,
       inventory0_.TYPEID as TYPEID1_,
       inventory0_.BUILDER as BUILDER1_,
       inventory0_.MODEL as MODEL1_,
       inventory0_.QOH as QOH1_,
       inventory0_.COST as COST1_,
       inventory0_.PRICE as PRICE1_,
       inventory0_.RECEIVED as RECEIVED1_
from INVENTORY inventory0_
where inventory0_.TYPEID=@p0
orderby inventory0_.BUILDER asc;
@p0 = 471c5b3f-19da-4fcb-8e9f-48dd17a00a3d [Type: Guid (0)]
```

Next, modify the `comboBoxGuitarTypes_SelectionChanged()` method found in the `MainWindow` `.xaml.cs` file of the `GuitarStore` project so that it calls the method created in Listing 4-4. Listing 4-5 provides an example of the modified `SelectionChanged()` method.

LISTING 4-5: Implementing the filtered LINQ to NHibernate method

```
private void comboBoxGuitarTypes_SelectionChanged(object sender,
                               SelectionChangedEventArgs e)
{
  try
```

```
  {
    dataGridInventory.ItemsSource = null;
    Guitar guitar = (Guitar)comboBoxGuitarTypes.SelectedItem;
    Guid guitarType = new Guid(guitar.Id.ToString());

    NHibernateInventory nhi = new NHibernateInventory();

    dataGridInventory.ItemsSource = nhi.GetLINQInventory(guitarType);
    dataGridInventory.Columns[0].Visibility = System.Windows.Visibility.Hidden;
    dataGridInventory.Columns[1].Visibility = System.Windows.Visibility.Hidden;
    dataGridInventory.Columns[9].Visibility = System.Windows.Visibility.Hidden;
  }
  catch (Exception ex)
  {
    labelMessage.Content = ex.Message;
  }
}
```

After implementing and executing the `GuitarStore` WPF program, selecting a guitar type from the `ComboBox` will result in a `DataGrid` being populated with a list of guitar inventory matching that guitar type. Figure 4-2 shows an example of how the `GuitarStore` WPF program looks.

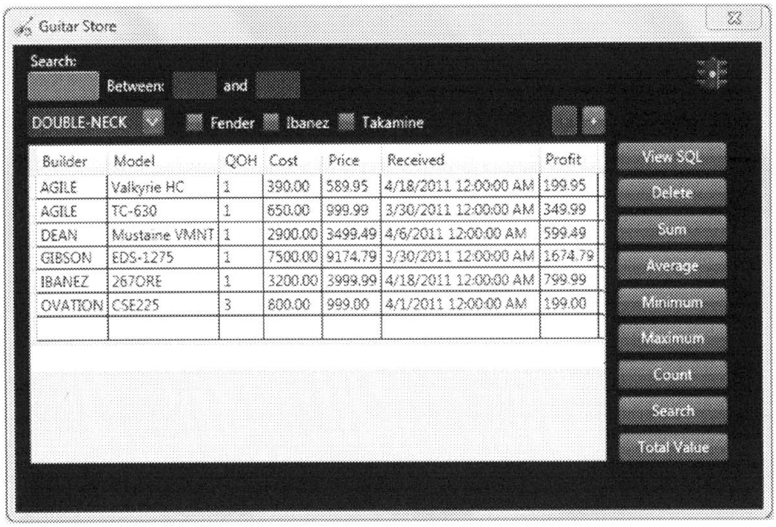

FIGURE 4-2

The next requirement to implement is the search capability when using LINQ to NHibernate. The LINQ to NHibernate provider exposes an execution method called `Contains()` that works nicely with searches. Listing 4-6 shows how to use LINQ to retrieve all models from the INVENTORY table that match the user-entered search parameter.

LISTING 4-6: Using the Contains() method with LINQ to search

```
public IList SearchInventoryLINQ(string guitarType)
{
  using (ITransaction transaction = Session.BeginTransaction())
  {
    try
    {
      IQueryable<Inventory> query = (from inv in Session.Query<Inventory>()
                                     where inv.Model.Contains(guitarType)
                                     orderby inv.Builder
                                     select inv);
      transaction.Commit();
      return query.ToList();
    }
    catch (Exception ex)
    {
      transaction.Rollback();
      throw;
    }
  }
}

Generated SQL:

select inventory0_.ID as ID1_,
       inventory0_.TYPEID as TYPEID1_,
       inventory0_.BUILDER as BUILDER1_,
       inventory0_.MODEL as MODEL1_,
       inventory0_.QOH as QOH1_,
       inventory0_.COST as COST1_,
       inventory0_.PRICE as PRICE1_,
       inventory0_.RECEIVED as RECEIVED1_
from INVENTORY inventory0_
where inventory0_.MODEL like ('%'+@p0+'%')
order by inventory0_.BUILDER asc;

@p0 = '%L%' [Type: String (4000)]
```

The returned list is strongly typed; therefore, the properties within the IList can be accessed directly.

Adding more capabilities to a program is what makes a system feature rich and useful. LINQ provides many logical operators that support almost any program requirement. For example, Listing 4-7 includes a method that returns the inventory received in a specified time period.

LISTING 4-7: LINQ query using the AddDays() method

```
public IList GetRecentInventory(double daysAgo)
{
  using (ITransaction transaction = Session.BeginTransaction())
  {
    IQueryable<Inventory> query= (from inv in Session.Query<Inventory>()
```

```
                                        where inv.Received >
        DateTime.Today.AddDays(daysAgo)
                                        orderby inv.Builder
                                        select inv);
        return query.ToList();
    }
}
```

Generated SQL:

```
select inventory0_.ID as ID1_,
        inventory0_.TYPEID as TYPEID1_,
        inventory0_.BUILDER as BUILDER1_,
        inventory0_.MODEL as MODEL1_,
        inventory0_.QOH as QOH1_,
        inventory0_.COST as COST1_,
        inventory0_.PRICE as PRICE1_,
        inventory0_.RECEIVED as RECEIVED1_
from INVENTORY inventory0_
where inventory0_.RECEIVED>@p0
order by inventory0_.BUILDER asc;
@p0 = 5/16/2011 12:00:00 AM [Type: DateTime (0)]
```

By setting the daysAgo parameter to -5 and passing it to the preceding method, NHibernate generates the presented SQL query.

IMPLEMENTING PAGING

The methods used to implement paging with LINQ are Take() and Skip(). Each method takes an integer as a parameter. Take() is similar to the IQuery and ICriteria SetMaxResult() methods, while the Skip() method is equivalent to the SetFirstResult() method. Listing 4-8 shows the implementation of paging using LINQ from within the NHibernate.GuitarStore class.

LISTING 4-8: Paging with LINQ

```
public IList<Inventory> GetLINQInventory(int take, int skip, out int totalCount)
{
    using (ITransaction transaction = Session.BeginTransaction())
    {
        try
        {
            IQueryable<Inventory> query = (from inv in Session.Query<Inventory>()
                                          orderby inv.Builder
                                          select inv).Take(take).Skip(skip);
            IQueryable<Inventory> countResult = Session.Query<Inventory>();
            totalCount = countResult.Count();

            transaction.Commit();
            return query.ToList<Inventory>();
        }
```

continues

LISTING 4-8 *(continued)*

```
    catch (Exception ex)
    {
      transaction.Rollback();
      throw;
    }
  }
}

Generated SQL using 2 database round-trips:
select cast(count(*) as INT) as col_0_0_ from INVENTORY inventory0_
select TOP (@p0)
       inventory0_.ID as ID1_,
       inventory0_.TYPEID as TYPEID1_,
       inventory0_.BUILDER as BUILDER1_,
       inventory0_.MODEL as MODEL1_,
       inventory0_.QOH as QOH1_,
       inventory0_.COST as COST1_,
       inventory0_.PRICE as PRICE1_,
       inventory0_.RECEIVED as RECEIVED1_
from INVENTORY inventory0_
order by inventory0_.BUILDER asc;
@p0 = 25 [Type: Int32 (0)]
```

Next, implement the `GetLINQInventory()` method into the `GuitarStore` WPF program by modifying the `PopulateDataGrid()` method, as shown in Listing 4-9.

LISTING 4-9: Implementing paging into the GuitarStore progam using LINQ

```
private void PopulateDataGrid()
{
  NHibernateInventory nhi = new NHibernateInventory();
  IList<Inventory> GuitarInventory = null;
  int inventoryCount = nhi.GetLINQInventory(MaxResult, FirstResult,
                                            out GuitarInventory);

  dataGridInventory.ItemsSource = GuitarInventory;

  if (GuitarInventory != null)
  {
    dataGridInventory.Columns[0].Visibility = System.Windows.Visibility.Hidden;
    dataGridInventory.Columns[1].Visibility = System.Windows.Visibility.Hidden;
    dataGridInventory.Columns[9].Visibility = System.Windows.Visibility.Hidden;
  }
  labelPaging.Content = "Retrieved " + FirstResult.ToString() +
                " to " + (FirstResult + GuitarInventory.Count).ToString() +
                " of " + inventoryCount.ToString();

  totalCount = inventoryCount;
}
```

The GuitarStore WPF program now resembles Figure 4-3. Notice that the stoplight is yellow, meaning two database round-trips were required to populate the DataGrid.

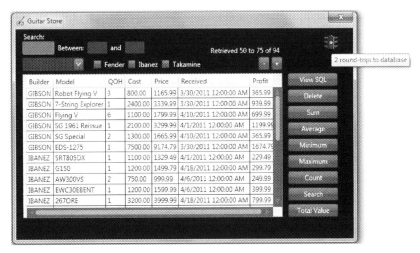

FIGURE 4-3

When implementing paging, it is always a good idea to batch the queries together. Although Futures can be used to load data as late in a process as possible, it is still useful to batch queries together to reduce the number of round-trips to the database. Listing 4-10 shows the GetLINQInventory() method, which now includes the ToFuture() method. The ToFuture() method batches the queries together and executes them all using a single database round-trip. Notice that when using the ToFuture() method, an IEnumerable<out T> is returned.

LISTING 4-10: Using Futures with LINQ to NHibernate

```
public IList<Inventory> GetLINQInventory(int take, int skip, out int totalCount)
{
  using (ITransaction transaction = Session.BeginTransaction())
  {
    try
    {
      IEnumerable<Inventory> query = (from inv in Session.Query<Inventory>()
                                      orderby inv.Builder
                                      select inv).Take(take).Skip(skip)
                                     .ToFuture<Inventory>();
      IEnumerable<Inventory> countResult = Session.Query<Inventory>().ToFuture();
      totalCount = countResult.Count();

      transaction.Commit();
      return query.ToList<Inventory>();
    }
    catch (Exception ex)
```

continues

LISTING 4-10 *(continued)*

```
      {
        transaction.Rollback();
        throw;
      }
    }
  }
}

Generated SQL using single database round-trip and FirstResult = 26:

SELECT TOP (@p0)
       ID1_,
       TYPEID1_,
       BUILDER1_,
       MODEL1_,
       QOH1_,
       COST1_,
       PRICE1_,
       RECEIVED1_
FROM (select inventory0_.ID as ID1_,
             inventory0_.TYPEID as TYPEID1_,
             inventory0_.BUILDER as BUILDER1_,
             inventory0_.MODEL as MODEL1_,
             inventory0_.QOH as QOH1_,
             inventory0_.COST as COST1_,
             inventory0_.PRICE as PRICE1_,
             inventory0_.RECEIVED as RECEIVED1_,
             ROW_NUMBER()
             OVER(ORDER BY inventory0_.BUILDER) as __hibernate_sort_row
      from INVENTORY inventory0_) as query
WHERE query.__hibernate_sort_row > @p1
ORDER BY query.__hibernate_sort_row;
select inventory0_.ID as ID1_,
       inventory0_.TYPEID as TYPEID1_,
       inventory0_.BUILDER as BUILDER1_,
       inventory0_.MODEL as MODEL1_,
       inventory0_.QOH as QOH1_,
       inventory0_.COST as COST1_,
       inventory0_.PRICE as PRICE1_,
       inventory0_.RECEIVED as RECEI;
@p0 = 25 [Type: Int32 (0)],
@p1 = 26 [Type: Int32 (0)]
```

The preceding method implements the `Take()` and `Skip()` methods along with the `ToFuture()` execution method. The `ToFuture()` method batches the LINQ query, which selects the page of data, together with the query for selecting the total count. Both queries are executed via a single round-trip to the database. As shown in Figure 4-4, when running the paging from the LINQ tab in the `GuitarStore` WPF program, the stoplight is green, indicating that the two queries are being batched together. Selecting the View SQL button reinforces this.

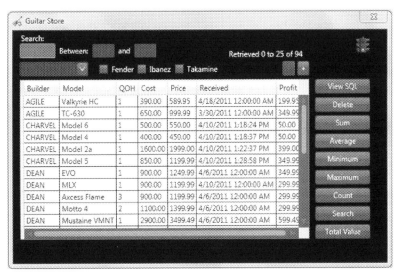

FIGURE 4-4

UNDERSTANDING LINQ TO NHIBERNATE WITH LAMBDA EXPRESSIONS

LINQ to NHibernate supports the use of lambda expressions. In the previous section, the long form of LINQ was used to retrieve the data from the INVENTORY table, to limit the results based on a selected guitar type, and to implement batching using the ToFuture() method. In this section, lambda expressions are used with the Query<T>() method to do the following:

➤ Populate the DataGrid with data from the INVENTORY table using a new method named GetLINQInventoryLE().

➤ Filter the result set based on a selected guitar type.

➤ Limit the result set using a search parameter and return the matching results using a new method called SearchInventoryLINQLE().

➤ Use paging with the ToFuture() method.

The first action to take is to add a new method named GetLINQInventoryLE() to the NHibernateInventory class found in the NHibernate.GuitarStore project. Listing 4-11 shows the code for the GetLINQInventoryLE() method.

NOTE *Sometimes project names can get a little confusing, so here's a reminder: There is a GuitarStore solution, a GuitarStore WPF project, and an NHibernate .GuitarStore project. The last two are projects within the GuitarStore solution.*

LISTING 4-11: Retrieving the guitar inventory using a lambda expression

```
using NHibernate.Linq;

public IList GetLINQInventoryLE()
{
  using (ITransaction transaction = Session.BeginTransaction())
  {
    IQueryable<Inventory> query = Session.Query<Inventory>();
    return query.ToList();
  }
}

Generated SQL:

select inventory0_.ID as ID1_,
       inventory0_.TYPEID as TYPEID1_,
       inventory0_.BUILDER as BUILDER1_,
       inventory0_.MODEL as MODEL1_,
       inventory0_.QOH as QOH1_,
       inventory0_.COST as COST1_,
       inventory0_.PRICE as PRICE1_,
       inventory0_.RECEIVED as RECEIVED1_
from INVENTORY inventory0_
```

Next, add another method to the `NHibernateInventory` class that accepts a search parameter and filters the result set using the provided value. Listing 4-12 provides an example of how this is achieved.

LISTING 4-12: LINQ Where clause using a lambda expression

```
public IList GetLINQInventoryLE(Guid Id)
{
  using (ITransaction transaction = Session.BeginTransaction())
  {
    IQueryable<Inventory> query = Session.Query<Inventory>()
                                  .Where(ti => ti.TypeId == Id);
    return query.ToList();
  }
}

Generated SQL:

select inventory0_.ID as ID1_,
       inventory0_.TYPEID as TYPEID1_,
       inventory0_.BUILDER as BUILDER1_,
       inventory0_.MODEL as MODEL1_,
       inventory0_.QOH as QOH1_,
       inventory0_.COST as COST1_,
       inventory0_.PRICE as PRICE1_,
       inventory0_.RECEIVED as RECEIVED1_
from INVENTORY inventory0_
where inventory0_.TYPEID=@p0
orderby inventory0_.BUILDER asc;
@p0 = 471c5b3f-19da-4fcb-8e9f-48dd17a00a3d [Type: Guid (0)]
```

Implement the preceding method into the `GuitarStore` WPF program by modifying the `comboBoxGuitarTypes_SelectionChanged()` method. Open the `MainWindow.xaml.cs` file and change the `SelectionChanged()` method so that it reflects what is shown Listing 4-13.

LISTING 4-13: Implementing LINQ lambda expression Where clause into WPF

```
private void comboBoxGuitarTypes_SelectionChanged(object sender,
                                    SelectionChangedEventArgs e)
{
  try
  {
    dataGridInventory.ItemsSource = null;
    Guitar guitar = (Guitar)comboBoxGuitarTypes.SelectedItem;
    Guid guitarType = new Guid(guitar.Id.ToString());

    NHibernateInventory nhi = new NHibernateInventory();
    dataGridInventory.ItemsSource = nhi.GetLINQInventoryLE(guitarType);
    dataGridInventory.Columns[0].Visibility = System.Windows.Visibility.Hidden;
    dataGridInventory.Columns[1].Visibility = System.Windows.Visibility.Hidden;
    dataGridInventory.Columns[9].Visibility = System.Windows.Visibility.Hidden;
  }
  catch (Exception ex)
  {
    labelMessage.Content = ex.Message;
  }
}
```

The result of running the `GuitarStore` WPF program and selecting a guitar type from the `ComboBox` is shown in Figure 4-5.

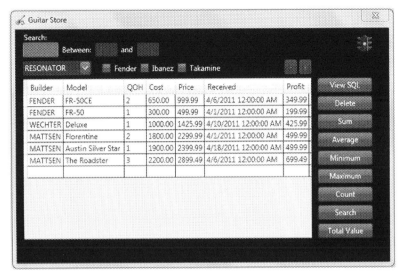

FIGURE 4-5

Next, create the `SearchInventoryLINQLE()` method, which accepts a search parameter and returns a list containing the matching data results. Listing 4-14 provides an example of this method.

LISTING 4-14: Using a lambda expression to search for data

```
public IList SearchInventoryLINQLE(string guitarType)
{
  using (ITransaction transaction = Session.BeginTransaction())
  {
    IQueryable<Inventory> query = Session.Query<Inventory>()
                          .Where(m => m.Model.Contains(guitarType));
    return query.ToList();
  }
}

Generated SQL:

select inventory0_.ID as ID1_,
        inventory0_.TYPEID as TYPEID1_,
        inventory0_.BUILDER as BUILDER1_,
        inventory0_.MODEL as MODEL1_,
        inventory0_.QOH as QOH1_,
        inventory0_.COST as COST1_,
        inventory0_.PRICE as PRICE1_,
        inventory0_.RECEIVED as RECEIVED1_
from INVENTORY inventory0_
where inventory0_.MODEL like ('%'+@p0+'%');
@p0 = '%l%' [Type: String (4000)]
```

Before proceeding to the implementation of the `SearchInventoryLINQLE()` method into the `GuitarStore` WPF program, it would be beneficial to test the method in the `NHibernate .GuitarStore` console application. To do this, open the `Program.cs` file found within the `NHibernate.GuitarStore.Console` project and add the code shown in Listing 4-15 to the `Main()` method.

LISTING 4-15: Testing the lambda expression from a console application

```
IList list52 = nhi.SearchInventoryLINQLE("%l%");
Console.WriteLine("SearchInventoryLINQLE(% l %): " +
                  list52.Count.ToString() + " results");
```

Set the `NHibernate.GuitarStore.Console` application as the startup project and press F5. If the method returns the expected results, then you have some assurance that the implementation will go smoothly.

Next, implement the method shown in Listing 4-14 into the `GuitarStore` WPF program by modifying the `buttonSearch_Click()` method found in the `MainWindow.xaml.cs` file of the `GuitarStore` project so that it is identical to the code shown in Listing 4-16.

LISTING 4-16: Implementing search using lambda expressions into a WPF program

```
private void buttonSearch_Click(object sender, RoutedEventArgs e)
{
  NHibernateInventory nhi = new NHibernateInventory();
  IList GuitarInventory = nhi.SearchInventoryLINQLE("%" +
                                      textBoxSearch.Text + "%");

  dataGridInventory.ItemsSource = GuitarInventory;

  if (GuitarInventory != null && GuitarInventory.Count > 0)
  {
    dataGridInventory.Columns[0].Visibility = System.Windows.Visibility.Hidden;
    dataGridInventory.Columns[1].Visibility = System.Windows.Visibility.Hidden;
    dataGridInventory.Columns[8].Visibility = System.Windows.Visibility.Hidden;
    dataGridInventory.Columns[9].Visibility = System.Windows.Visibility.Hidden;
  }
}
```

Ordering the retrieved data helps make a program more useful. Although most `DataGrid` controls allow users to perform this action, it is good practice to provide the data in the format required from the beginning. Two methods can be used to implement the ordering of data: `OrderBy()` and `ThenByDecending()`. Modify the `GetLINQInventory()` method to use these two methods with lambda expressions. Listing 4-17 provides an example of the modified methods.

LISTING 4-17: Using a lambda expression with OrderBy() and ThenByDecending()

```
public IList GetLINQInventoryLE()
{
  using (ITransaction transaction = Session.BeginTransaction())
  {
    IQueryable<Inventory> query = Session.Query<Inventory>()
                                  .OrderBy(i => i.Builder)
                                  .ThenByDescending(i => i.Price);
    return query.ToList();
  }
}

Generated SQL:

select inventory0_.ID as ID1_,
       inventory0_.TYPEID as TYPEID1_,
       inventory0_.BUILDER as BUILDER1_,
       inventory0_.MODEL as MODEL1_,
       inventory0_.QOH as QOH1_,
       inventory0_.COST as COST1_,
       inventory0_.PRICE as PRICE1_,
       inventory0_.RECEIVED as RECEIVED1_
from INVENTORY inventory0_
order by inventory0_.BUILDER asc,
         inventory0_.PRICE desc
```

Figure 4-6 shows how the data within the `DataGrid` on the `GuitarStore` WPF window is presented using the `OrderBy()` and `ThenByDecending()` methods.

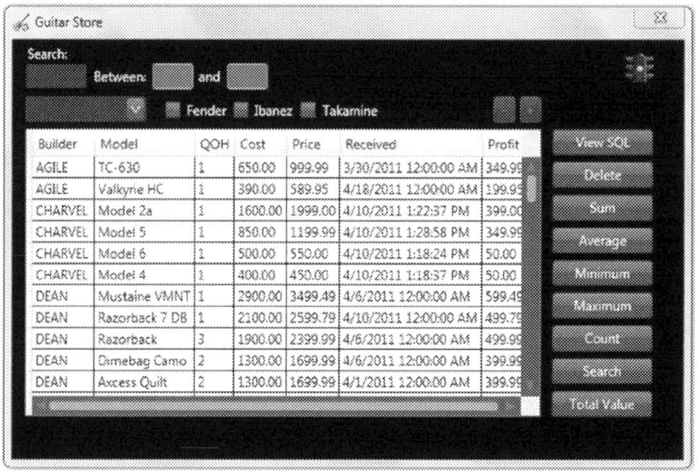

FIGURE 4-6

The last action to take in this section is to create a method for paging using LINQ with lambda expressions and the `ToFuture()` method. Listing 4-18 gives you an idea of how a method like this should look.

LISTING 4-18: LINQ with lambda expressions that implement paging

```
public int GetLINQInventoryLE(int take, int skip, out IList<Inventory> resultSet)
{
  using (ITransaction transaction = Session.BeginTransaction())
  {
    try
    {
      IEnumerable<Inventory> query = Session.Query<Inventory>()
                                     .Take(take).Skip(skip)
                                     .ToFuture<Inventory>();

      IEnumerable<Inventory> countResult = Session.Query<Inventory>().ToFuture();
      int totalCount = countResult.Count();
      resultSet = query.ToList<Inventory>();

      transaction.Commit();
      return totalCount;
    }
    catch (Exception ex)
    {
      transaction.Rollback();
      throw;
    }
```

```
    }
}

Generated SQL using 1 database round-trip:

select TOP (@p0)
        inventory0_.ID as ID1_,
        inventory0_.TYPEID as TYPEID1_,
        inventory0_.BUILDER as BUILDER1_,
        inventory0_.MODEL as MODEL1_,
        inventory0_.QOH as QOH1_,
        inventory0_.COST as COST1_,
        inventory0_.PRICE as PRICE1_,
        inventory0_.RECEIVED as RECEIVED1_
from INVENTORY inventory0_;
select inventory0_.ID as ID1_,
        inventory0_.TYPEID as TYPEID1_,
        inventory0_.BUILDER as BUILDER1_,
        inventory0_.MODEL as MODEL1_,
        inventory0_.QOH as QOH1_,
        inventory0_.COST as COST1_,
        inventory0_.PRICE as PRICE1_,
        inventory0_.RECEIVED as RECEI;
@p0 = 25 [Type: Int32 (0)]ory0_;
```

Implement this method into the `GuitarStore` WPF program by using it from within the `PopulateDataGrid()` method within the `MainWindow.xaml.cs` file located in the `GuitarStore` project. Listing 4-19 presents an example of the code segment.

LISTING 4-19: Implement paging using LINQ with lambda expressions in WPF

```
private void PopulateDataGrid()
{
  NHibernateInventory nhi = new NHibernateInventory();
  IList<Inventory> GuitarInventory = null;
  int inventoryCount = nhi.GetLINQInventoryLE(MaxResult, FirstResult,
                                              out GuitarInventory);
  dataGridInventory.ItemsSource = GuitarInventory;

  if (GuitarInventory != null)
  {
    dataGridInventory.Columns[0].Visibility = System.Windows.Visibility.Hidden;
    dataGridInventory.Columns[1].Visibility = System.Windows.Visibility.Hidden;
    dataGridInventory.Columns[9].Visibility = System.Windows.Visibility.Hidden;
  }

  labelPaging.Content = "Retrieved " + FirstResult.ToString() +
                " to " + (FirstResult + GuitarInventory.Count).ToString() +
                " of " + inventoryCount.ToString();

  totalCount = inventoryCount;
}
```

Figure 4-7 illustrates the `GuitarStore` WPF window after implementation of the preceding `GetLINQInventoryLE()` paging method. Notice that the stoplight is green. The green stoplight and the tool tip note confirm that the multiple methods required to support paging of the guitar inventory are being batched and executed using a single round-trip to the database.

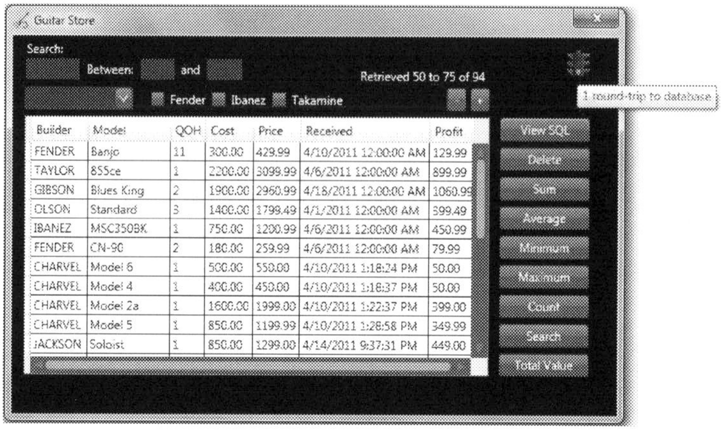

FIGURE 4-7

UNDERSTANDING AGGREGATE DATABASE FUNCTIONS

Aggregates are discussed in more detail in both Chapters 2 and 3, which cover the `IQuery` and `ICriteria` interfaces, respectively. The common aggregate methods (`SUM`, `MIN`, `MAX`, and `AVG`) can be run via the LINQ to NHibernate provider. In this section, the aggregate database functions will be implemented with LINQ using a combination of the long form and lambda expressions. The following actions should be taken to implement aggregate database functions into the `GuitarStore` solution using LINQ to NHibernate:

➤ Create a new class, `AggregateResults`, to store the results of the aggregate database queries.

➤ Add `SUM`, `MIN`, `MAX`, and `AVG` methods to the `NHibernateInventory` class.

➤ Modify the `Click` event of the `SUM`, `MIN`, `MAX`, and `AVG` buttons created in Chapter 2.

First, add a new class named `AggregateResults` to the `DataAccess` folder of the `NHibernate .GuitarStore` project. Listing 4-20 provides the example code for this class.

LISTING 4-20: The AggregateResults class

```
namespace NHibernate.GuitarStore.DataAccess
{
    public class AggregateResults
    {
        public string GuitarType { get; set; }
        public decimal? Value { get; set; }
    }
}
```

Next, open the `NHibernateInventory.cs` file located in the `NHibernate.GuitarStore` project and add the following methods shown in Listings 4-21 through 4-24.

LISTING 4-21: SUM LINQ aggregate function

```
public IList<AggregateResults> GetInventorySum()
{
  using (ITransaction transaction = Session.BeginTransaction())
  {
    try
    {
      IQueryable<AggregateResults> linqSUM =
                (from g in Session.Query<Guitar>()
                 join i in Session.Query<Inventory>() on g.Id equals i.TypeId
                 group i by g.Type into r
                 select new AggregateResults
                 {
                   GuitarType = r.Key, Value = r.Sum(i => i.Price)
                 });

      transaction.Commit();
      return linqSUM.ToList();
    }
    catch (Exception ex)
    {
      transaction.Rollback();
      throw;
    }
  }
}

Generated SQL:

select guitar0_.TYPE as col_0_0_,
       cast(sum(inventory1_.PRICE) as DECIMAL(19,5)) as col_1_0_
from GUITAR guitar0_,
     INVENTORY inventory1_
where inventory1_.TYPEID=guitar0_.ID
group by guitar0_.TYPE
```

LISTING 4-22: MIN LINQ aggregate function

```
public IList<AggregateResults> GetInventoryMin()
{
  using (ITransaction transaction = Session.BeginTransaction())
  {
    try
    {
      IQueryable<AggregateResults> linqMIN =
                (from g in Session.Query<Guitar>()
                 join i in Session.Query<Inventory>() on g.Id equals i.TypeId
```

continues

LISTING 4-22 *(continued)*

```
                group i by g.Type into r
                select new AggregateResults
                {
                  GuitarType = r.Key,
                  Value = r.Min(i => i.Price)
                });
      transaction.Commit();
      return linqMIN.ToList();
    }
    catch (Exception ex)
    {
      transaction.Rollback();
      throw;
    }
  }
}
```

Generated SQL:

```
select guitar0_.TYPE as col_0_0_,
       cast(min(inventory1_.PRICE) as DECIMAL(19,5)) as col_1_0_
from GUITAR guitar0_,
     INVENTORY inventory1_
where inventory1_.TYPEID=guitar0_.ID
group by guitar0_.TYPE
```

LISTING 4-23: MAX LINQ aggregate function

```
public IList<AggregateResults> GetInventoryMax()
{
  using (ITransaction transaction = Session.BeginTransaction())
  {
    try
    {
      IQueryable<AggregateResults> linqMAX =
                  (from g in Session.Query<Guitar>()
                   join i in Session.Query<Inventory>() on g.Id equals i.TypeId
                   group i by g.Type into r
                   select new AggregateResults
                   {
                     GuitarType = r.Key,
                     Value = r.Max(i => i.Price)
                   });
      transaction.Commit();
      return linqMAX.ToList();
    }
    catch (Exception ex)
    {
      transaction.Rollback();
      throw;
    }
  }
```

```
}

Generated SQL:

select guitar0_.TYPE as col_0_0_,
       cast(max(inventory1_.PRICE) as DECIMAL(19,5)) as col_1_0_
from GUITAR guitar0_,
     INVENTORY inventory1_
where inventory1_.TYPEID=guitar0_.ID
group by guitar0_.TYPE
```

LISTING 4-24: AVG LINQ aggregate function

```
public IList<AggregateResults> GetInventoryAvg()
{
  using (ITransaction transaction = Session.BeginTransaction())
  {
    try
    {
      IQueryable<AggregateResults> linqAVG =
                   (from g in Session.Query<Guitar>()
                    join i in Session.Query<Inventory>() on g.Id equals i.TypeId
                    group i by g.Type into r
                    select new AggregateResults
                    {
                      GuitarType = r.Key,
                      Value = r.Average(i => i.Price)
                    });
      transaction.Commit();
      return linqAVG.ToList();
    }
    catch (Exception ex)
    {
      transaction.Rollback();
      throw;
    }
  }
}

Generated SQL:

select guitar0_.TYPE as col_0_0_,
       cast(avg(inventory1_.PRICE) as DECIMAL(19,5)) as col_1_0_
from GUITAR guitar0_,
     INVENTORY inventory1_
where inventory1_.TYPEID=guitar0_.ID
group by guitar0_.TYPE
```

The final step is to implement the aggregate database functions into the GuitarStore WPF program. To do this, open the MainWindow.xaml.cs file found within the GuitarStore WPF project and modify the Click event for each of the four aggregate Button controls (SUM, MIN, MAX, and AVG). Listing 4-25 presents the code required to implement the MIN aggregate database function into the buttonMinimum_Click() method within the GuitarStore WPF window.

LISTING 4-25: Implementing the MIN aggregate function into WPF

```
private void buttonMinimum_Click(object sender, RoutedEventArgs e)
{
  NHibernateInventory nhi = new NHibernateInventory();
  dataGridInventory.ItemsSource = nhi.GetInventoryMin();
}
```

Running the `GuitarStore` WPF program and clicking the Minimum button will render what is shown in Figure 4-8.

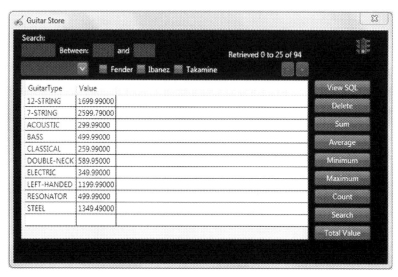

FIGURE 4-8

SUMMARY

In this chapter, you learned that the LINQ to NHibernate API supports two implementation approaches. The first is the SQL/long form method whereby the `from X in Y select` format is used. The second approach uses lambda expressions, as discussed in Chapter 3, "Using ICriteria," in regard to the `QueryOver` API. Both LINQ to NHibernate approaches are rooted in the `Query()` method, which is based on the .NET LINQ libraries. In the next chapter, the primary topic is no longer the retrieval of data, which has been the focus so far, but the insertion of data and how to manage an entity's state.

5

Managing State and Saving Data

In the previous chapter, the LINQ to NHibernate API was discussed. Like the `IQuery`, `ICriteria`, and `QueryOver` APIs, LINQ to NHibernate provides functionality that enables the retrieval of data from a database in an object-oriented manner. Up to now, only the retrieval of data has been covered. This chapter, however, covers data insertion and entity state management. This is where many of NHibernate's strengths lie. It is also a more complicated aspect of NHibernate, however, and therefore more difficult to comprehend and implement. This chapter clarifies the following topics:

- ➤ An overview of concurrency
- ➤ Using NHibernate versioning
- ➤ Implementing a custom data type using `IUserType`
- ➤ Inserting data into a database
- ➤ Using the first- and second-level caches
- ➤ Understanding the `Evict()`, `Merge()`, and `Persist()` methods
- ➤ Implementing batch processing

INTRODUCTION

Of course, a discussion about NHibernate isn't complete without covering the management and manipulation of data. It is relatively difficult to find good examples of inserting data using NHibernate, probably because there are so many options and implementation possibilities. The task, or program requirement, at hand determines which technique is the best in a given situation.

Before using NHibernate's methods, such as `Save()`, `SaveOrUpdate()`, `Update()`, and so on, which add or modify data on the database, it is important to understand the three different instance states an object can have: *transient*, *persistent*, or *detached*. Figure 5-1 displays which NHibernate methods can be used to change the state of an object or entity.

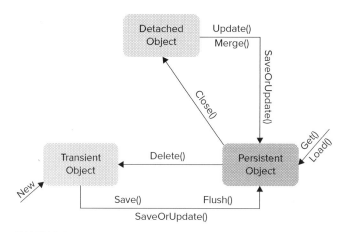

FIGURE 5-1

A *transient object* is an object that has never been associated with an NHibernate `Session` and therefore does not exist in the `ISession`'s Identity Map, meaning it is not change-tracked. Creating an instance of a mapped class, such as `Guitar guitar = new Guitar()`, within a program results in the creation of a transient instance of an object. Associating values to the properties does not cause NHibernate to track the object. Only after the instance of the class has been associated with a `Session` is the object capable of changing to a persistent state, and then possibly later to a detached object.

There are two primary differences between objects in the persistent and detached states. First, a persistent object is currently associated with an NHibernate `Session`, whereas a detached object is not, but has been at some point in the past. The second difference is related to whether or not NHibernate can guarantee that the object stored in memory is equal to the data stored in the database, or which will be stored in the database. A persistent object has this guarantee, whereas a detached object does not.

A detached object could be represented by a `List<T>` bound to a `DataGrid`. At one point, the objects within the list were associated with a `Session`; however, once bound, the association or `Session` is no longer needed and is closed. Converting a detached object to a persistent object is achieved by using the `Update()`, `SaveOrUpdate()`, `Persist()`, or `Merge()` methods. For example, you can convert a transient object to a persistent object by using, for example, the `Save()`, `SaveOrUpdate()`, or `Flush()` methods.

UNDERSTANDING CONCURRENCY

A program that is used by more than one person and allows simultaneous updates or deletes needs to implement a *concurrency strategy*. A concurrency solution requires a lot of thought in regard to the following concurrency strategy components:

➤ Choosing the isolation level

➤ Choosing optimistic or pessimistic concurrency

➤ Deciding how to resolve concurrency conflicts

➤ Deciding how to recover from a concurrency violation

The isolation level that is implemented can have a significant impact on the system due to its effect on performance and data integrity. Table 5-1 provides a brief description of each isolation level, from safest to fastest.

TABLE 5-1: Isolation Levels

ISOLATION LEVEL	DESCRIPTION
Serializable	A range lock is placed on the dataset until the transaction is complete, which prevents other users from updating or inserting rows into the dataset.
Snapshot	Stores a version of the data used by one program to read while another is modifying the same data. One transaction cannot see changes made by another transaction.
RepeatableRead	Locks are placed on all data used in a query, preventing other users from updating the data. Phantom rows are still possible, but non-repeatable reads are prevented.
ReadCommitted	Shared locks are applied while the data is being read, avoiding dirty reads; however, data can be changed before the end of the transaction, which can result in non-repeatable reads or phantom data.
ReadUncommitted	No shared locks are issued and no exclusive locks are honored, meaning dirty reads are possible.

 TIP *These descriptions can be found in the* System.Data.IsolationLevel *metadata.*

The default isolation level for NHibernate is ReadCommitted and is configurable at either the transaction and/or program level. Recall from Chapter 1, Listing 1-15, where the strongly typed configuration and app.config configuration in Listing 1-12 represent how and where the configuration is set up. You can use these two listings to better understand where to place the isolation configuration based on the chosen configuration method. If you need to change the isolation level from the default, a change to either of those configuration methods will be needed. Adding the isolation level at the program level requires setting an additional property, as shown in Listing 5-1.

LISTING 5-1: Setting the isolation level value

```
Strongly Typed Configuration:

dbi.IsolationLevel = IsolationLevel.ReadUncommitted;

app.config Configuration:

<property name="connection.isolation">ReadUncommitted</property>
```

You can set the isolation level for a specific transaction by passing the isolation level as a parameter to the `BeginTransaction()` method. Listing 5-2 provides an example of this.

LISTING 5-2: Setting the isolation level for a transaction

```
using (ISession session = SessionFactory.OpenSession())
{
  using (ITransaction transaction =
                  session.BeginTransaction(IsolationLevel.ReadUncommitted))
  {
     // Todo: ...
  }
}
```

Setting the isolation level is one part of a data concurrency strategy. When the correct settings have been found per program or per transaction, the program will perform optimally. However, there is another significant aspect of data concurrency and data integrity: *concurrency control*. Concurrency control refers to the two main approaches to managing database modifications: optimistic or pessimistic. Pessimistic control is not an option for high-concurrency programs because it blocks a transaction if it violates the current isolation level rules. This blocking will have serious implications on performance because it will wait in a queue until the transaction can complete. The best solution for enterprise or web solutions is optimistic concurrency control with versioning. If it violates the current isolation level, implementing optimistic concurrency results in the transaction failing and returning an exception. This exception can be handled in a way specific to the program, for example retrying the transaction or notifying the user of the program to please try again at a later time.

Concurrency control is important in programs in which a user can update stale data, or a single business transaction spans several database transactions. When data is selected from the database and stored in a local disconnected dataset that allows updates, what happens if user 1 has updated the data after user 2 has retrieved it, and then user 2 attempts to update that same data? This is commonly referred to as the *lost update problem*, whereby a second transaction overwrites a first transaction. In this case, the modification made by user 1 will be lost. Figure 5-2 provides a graphical representation of this problem.

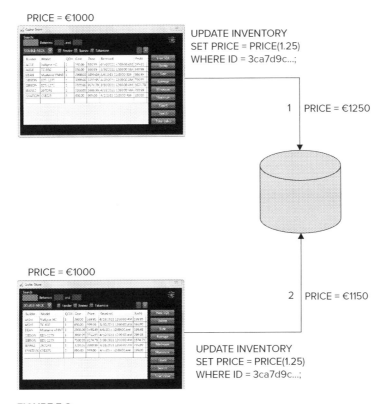

PRICE = €1000

UPDATE INVENTORY
SET PRICE = PRICE(1.25)
WHERE ID = 3ca7d9c...;

1 | PRICE = €1250

PRICE = €1000

2 | PRICE = €1150

UPDATE INVENTORY
SET PRICE = PRICE(1.25)
WHERE ID = 3ca7d9c...;

FIGURE 5-2

In this case, two instances of the `GuitarStore` WPF program are running at the same time. Each one has a local copy of the inventory data. Transaction 1 updates a guitar price by 25 percent, which results in an update statement being generated and executed on the database. The current amount stored on the database for the guitar is now €1250. However, transaction 2 still has the original value of €1000 in the `GuitarStore` WPF program. If user 2 updates that same guitar price by 15 percent, then the amount saved to the database would be €1150. That's a problem.

Managing this type of issue is primarily the responsibility of the application tier and not solely the DBMS. However, NHibernate provides a solution for this: *versioning*. Some of the source that supports this capability can be found in the `NHibernate.Engine.Versioning` class.

The following actions are required to implement versioning in NHibernate for our `GuitarStore` application:

1. Add a column to the `INVENTORY` data table for which versioning will be implemented to store the row version.

2. Add and configure the version element to the `Inventory.hbm.xml` file.

3. Add the version property to the `Inventory.cs` file.

4. Add an additional catch block for the `StaleObjectException` where the exception can occur.

First, add a column named VERSION to the INVENTORY table with type timestamp and which allows nulls. The new INVENTORY table will resemble Figure 5-3.

FIGURE 5-3

Add the element shown in Listing 5-3 directly below the existing id element, to the Inventory .hbm.xml mapping file located in the Mapping directory of the NHibernate.GuitarStore project. The value for the name attribute is the database column name used for the versioning of this entity.

 NOTE *The <version ...> element must immediately follow the <id...> element in the mapping file; otherwise, you will receive a* MappingException *when you attempt to run the program.*

LISTING 5-3: Adding the versioning element to the .hbm.xml mapping file

```
<version name="VERSION" generated="always" type="BinaryBlob" />
```

Next, add the property to the Inventory.cs file located in the Common directory of the NHibernate.GuitarStore project, as shown in Listing 5-4.

LISTING 5-4: Adding the versioning property to the class

```
public virtual Byte[] VERSION { get; set; }
```

After versioning has been implemented, each time a row on the database is updated, the value in the VERSION column will be changed. NHibernate adds the VERSION column as part of the WHERE clause in the generated SQL query, as shown in Listing 5-5.

LISTING 5-5: NHibernate-generated versioned SQL

```
UPDATE INVENTORY SET MODEL = @p0
WHERE ID = @p1 AND VERSION = @p2;
@p0 = '1956 Jazzmaster' [Type: String (4000)],
@p1 = d9055045-f347-424f-995a-1db6a7a61e65 [Type: Guid (0),
@p2 = 0x00000000000007FC [Type: Binary (2147483647)]
```

If the query cannot update due to versioning, a `StaleObjectException` is thrown with the text "Row was updated or deleted by another transaction (or unsaved-value mapping was incorrect)." Therefore, it is a good idea to add the logic shown in Listing 5-6 to specifically catch this exception. Adding this catch block enables the application to recover from this exception in a manner that best suits the needs of the program's requirements.

LISTING 5-6: Catching a StaleObjectException

```
catch (StaleObjectStateException soe)
{
    // Recovery logic : ...
}
```

 TIP If a `StaleObjectException` occurs, one of many possible solutions is to select the most current data from the database and present it to the user along with the attempted update values and highlight the difference. Then enable the user to decide how to proceed.

CREATING AN IUSERTYPE

Although the .NET Framework supports most of the data types required for building quality programs, you may occasionally require a custom data type — for example, a monetary value whose type needs a decimal value combined with a currency type, or a name that is a combination of the first, middle, and last names. NHibernate provides the `IUserType` interface, which is found in the `NHibernate.UserTypes` namespace, to implement a custom data type.

The following tasks can be used to implement an `IUserType` into a program:

1. Create an abstract base class that implements `IUserType`.
2. Create a class that implements the base class to override the method needed.
3. Create a class that represents the custom data type.
4. Modify the NHibernate mapping and class files.
5. Use the custom data type in a program.

To implement the preceding steps in the `GuitarStore` WPF program, the following example assumes that the guitar store using this program is located in Europe, and has recently been purchased by an American company. The program needs to begin tracking the currency type used within the program. An agreement has been made that when the costs and prices are saved, local currency will be used; however, prior to storing these values in the database, the value will be converted to USD ($). This means all values in the database have a currency type of USD ($).

The `IUserType` interface implements 11 methods. Add an abstract class named `BaseUserType` to the `DataAccess` directory of the `NHibernate.GuitarStore` project. Listing 5-7 shows an example of the `BaseUserType` abstract class.

LISTING 5-7: Implementing the IUserType in a base class

```
using NHibernate.SqlTypes;
using NHibernate.UserTypes;
using System.Data;

namespace NHibernate.GuitarStore.DataAccess
{
  public abstract class BaseUserType<T> : IUserType
  {
      public abstract SqlType[] SqlTypes { get; }

      public System.Type ReturnedType { get { return typeof(T); } }

      public new bool Equals(object x, object y)
      {
          if (object.ReferenceEquals(x, y)) return true;
          if (x == null || y == null) return false;
          return x.Equals(y);
      }

      public int GetHashCode(object x) { return x.GetHashCode(); }

      public abstract object NullSafeGet(IDataReader dr, string[] names,
                                          object owner);

      public abstract void NullSafeSet(IDbCommand cmd, object value, int index);

      public object DeepCopy(object value) { return value; }

      public bool IsMutable { get { return false; } }

      public object Replace(object original, object target, object owner)
        { return original; }

      public object Assemble(object cached, object owner)
        { return DeepCopy(cached); }

      public object Disassemble(object value) { return DeepCopy(value); }
  }
}
```

Implementing the IUserType interface into a base abstract class enables you to avoid
applying (copying and pasting) all the methods to more than one custom data type class. Instead,
you can inherit from the base class and override only the methods required for the specific
implementation. Listing 5-8 inherits from the base class; uses the class CurrencyAmount,
which will be created next in Listing 5-9; and overrides two methods: NullSafeGet() and
NullSafeSet(). Add the CurrencyUserType calls to the DataAccess directory of the
NHibernate.GuitarStore project.

LISTING 5-8: CurrencyUserType class inherited from the base class

```
using NHibernate;
using NHibernate.SqlTypes;
using System.Data;

namespace NHibernate.GuitarStore.DataAccess
{
  public class CurrencyUserType : BaseUserType<CurrencyAmount>
  {
    public override object NullSafeGet(IDataReader dr, string[] names,
                                       object owner)
    {
      var currentAmount = ((decimal?)NHibernateUtil.Decimal
                                  .NullSafeGet(dr, names[0]));

      if (currentAmount.HasValue)
      {
        return new CurrencyAmount(currentAmount.Value, "USD");
      }
      else
      {
        return CurrencyAmount.SetToZero;
      }
    }

    public override void NullSafeSet(IDbCommand cmd, object value, int index)
    {
      var currencyAmount = (CurrencyAmount)value;
      object theValue;

      if (currencyAmount != null)
      {
        CurrencyAmount.Convert(currencyAmount, "USD");
        theValue = currencyAmount.Amount;
      }
      else
      {
        theValue = DBNull.Value;
      }
      NHibernateUtil.Decimal.NullSafeSet(cmd, theValue, index);
    }

    public override SqlType[] SqlTypes
    {
      get { return new[] { SqlTypeFactory.Decimal }; }
    }
  }
}
```

The NullSafeGet() method is called during retrieval of the data and sets the retrieved currency type to USD ($). The NullSafeSet() method is called during a save and is overridden to convert the currency amount from local currency into USD ($). The conversion is performed by calling the Convert() method of the CurrencyAmount class, as shown in Listing 5-9. Add the CurrencyAmount class to the DataAccess directory of the NHibernate.GuitarStore project.

LISTING 5-9: CurrencyAmount class example

```
namespace NHibernate.GuitarStore.DataAccess
{
  public class CurrencyAmount
  {
    public CurrencyAmount(decimal amount, string symbol)
    {
        Amount = amount;
        Symbol = symbol;
    }

    public decimal? Amount { get; set; }
    public string Symbol { get; set; }

    public static CurrencyAmount SetToZero
    {
        get { return new CurrencyAmount(0, null); }
    }

    public static CurrencyAmount Convert(CurrencyAmount ca,
                                  string targetCurrency)
    {
      if (targetCurrency == "USD" && ca.Symbol == "EUR")
      {
          ca.Amount = ca.Amount * 1.37;
      }
      else if (targetCurrency == "USD" && ca.Symbol == "JPY")
      {
          ca.Amount = ca.Amount * .24;
      }
      else if (targetCurrency == "USD" && ca.Symbol == "GBP")
      {
          ca.Amount = ca.Amount * 1.64;
      }
      return ca;
    }
  }
}
```

Now that the IUserType interface, the custom data type class, and the CurrencyAmount class have been implemented, the next step is to modify the .hbm.xml mapping file and class file. Listing 5-10 shows the modified Cost and Price properties contained within the Inventory.hbm.xml and Inventory.cs files, both of which are located in the NHibernate.GuitarStore project.

LISTING 5-10: Changing the Cost and Price properties to custom data types

```
<property name="Cost"
          column="COST"
          type="NHibernate.GuitarStore.DataAccess.CurrencyUserType,
                  NHibernate.GuitarStore" />
<property name="Price"
```

```
            column="PRICE"
            type="NHibernate.GuitarStore.DataAccess.CurrencyUserType,
                NHibernate.GuitarStore" />

public virtual CurrencyAmount Cost { get; set; }
public virtual CurrencyAmount Price { get; set; }
```

Note that the mapped type is now of type `CurrencyUserType`, which is a derived class from `BaseUserType` that implements the `IUserType` interface. In addition, `Cost` and `Price` are no longer type `decimal?` — they are type `CurrencyAmount`, which contains both an amount and a currency type.

When the preceding is compiled, errors will be generated because `Cost` and `Price` are no longer decimal. Therefore, two additional modifications are required within the `NHibernateInventory` class found within the `DataAccess` directory of the `NHibernate.GuitarStore` project. You need to change `Cost` and `Price` to `Cost.Amount` and `Price.Amount`, respectively.

> **NOTE** Converting `Cost` and `Price` to the `CurrencyAmount` data type is easy if you use the `NHibernate.GuitarStore` console application. This is because throughout this book all the `GuitarStore` methods have been added to the `NHibernate.GuitarStore.Console` application, and, by running the application, errors are generated where modifications need to take place to support this transition from the `decimal?` data type to the `CurrencyAmount` data type.

The final step is to implement the `CurrencyAmount` class into the `GuitarStore` WPF Program. There are two places where modifications are needed. The first is within the method that saves a new `Inventory` class. Instead of setting the `Cost` and `Price` to a `decimal` value, they are set to new instances of the `CurrencyAmount` class, as shown in Listing 5-11.

LISTING 5-11: Instantiating an Inventory class with a custom user type

```
Inventory inventory = new Inventory
{
    Builder = textBoxBuilder.Text,
    Model = textBoxModel.Text,
    QOH = 1,
    Cost = new CurrencyAmount(Convert.ToDecimal(textBoxCost.Text), "EUR"),
    Price = new CurrencyAmount(Convert.ToDecimal(textBoxPrice.Text), "EUR"),
    Received = DateTime.Now,
    TypeId = guitar.Id,
    Guitar = guitar
};
```

As mentioned earlier, the `Cost` and `Price` are inserted as local currency, in this case EUR (€) and then converted to USD ($) from the `CurrencyAmount.Convert()` method via the overridden `CurrencyUserType.NullSafeSet()` method.

The second change is a bit more complex and requires a number of code changes. That's because in order to access the `Cost.Amount` and `Price.Amount` values so that they are shown in the `DataGrid` correctly, a strongly typed result set is used. Modify the `PopulateDataGrid()` method found within the `MainWindow.xaml.cs` file of the `GuitarStore` WPF project so that it resembles Listing 5-12.

LISTING 5-12: Implementing the custom user type into the GuitarStore WPF

```
private void PopulateDataGrid()
{
  NHibernateInventory nhi = new NHibernateInventory();
  int inventoryCount;
  IList<Inventory> GuitarInventory = nhi.GetLINQInventory(MaxResult,
                            FirstResult, out inventoryCount);
  DataTable dt = new DataTable();
  dt.Columns.Add("Builder", typeof(string));
  dt.Columns.Add("Model", typeof(string));
  dt.Columns.Add("Price", typeof(string));
  dt.Columns.Add("Id", typeof(string));

  foreach (Inventory item in GuitarInventory)
  {
    dt.Rows.Add(item.Builder, item.Model, item.Price.Amount.ToString() +
              " " + item.Price.Symbol, item.Id);
  }

  dataGridInventory.ItemsSource = dt.DefaultView;
  totalCount = inventoryCount;
  labelPaging.Content = "Retrieved " + FirstResult.ToString() +
                  " to " + (FirstResult + GuitarInventory.Count).ToString() +
                  " of " + inventoryCount.ToString();
  SetDatabaseRoundTripImage();
}
```

Notice two things specific to the preceding implementation. First the list returned from the `GetLINQInventory()` method is, as expected, strongly typed. The reason this is significant and required is because later in the code segment where the result set is added to the `DataTable` within the `foreach` loop, instead of accessing the `Price` property directly, as in previous examples, the `Price.Amount` and `Price.Symbol` values are captured and added to the `DataGridRow`. It is not possible to directly access the `Price.Amount` and `Price.Symbol` values using a dynamic result set without further modifications.

INSERTING DATA

This section provides two examples of inserting data that demonstrate the following:

➤ Creating insert capabilities in the `GuitarStore` WPF program

➤ Inserting a single row into a database

➤ Creating a custom id generator

➤ Inserting a parent/child into a database

Before an insertion can take place, the insertion capability needs to be built into the `GuitarStore` WPF window. Modify the `MainWindow.xaml` file so that it results in a window resembling Figure 5-4.

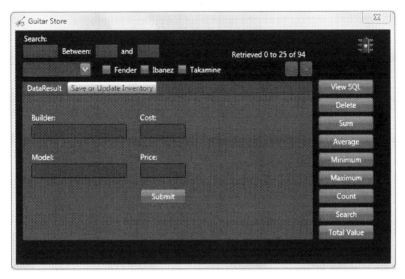

FIGURE 5-4

This is achieved by dragging and dropping a `TabControl`, some `TextBox` controls, a `Button` control, and some `Label` controls onto the WPF `MainWindow`. The XAML code is provided in Listing 5-13.

LISTING 5-13: GuitarStore Save or Update TabControl XAML code

```
<TabControl Height="253" HorizontalAlignment="Left"
            Margin="11,81,0,0" Name="tabControlGuitarStore"
            VerticalAlignment="Top" Width="478">
  <TabItem Header="DataResult" Name="tabItemDataResult">
    <Grid>
      <DataGrid AutoGenerateColumns="True" HorizontalAlignment="Stretch"
            Margin="6,0,6,6" Name="dataGridInventory"
            VerticalAlignment="Stretch" />
    </Grid>
  </TabItem>
  <TabItem Header="Save or Update Inventory" Name="tabItemInsertInventory">
    <Grid>
      <TextBox Height="23" HorizontalAlignment="Left"
            Margin="15,46,0,0" Name="textBoxBuilder"
            VerticalAlignment="Top" Width="157" />
      <TextBox Height="23" HorizontalAlignment="Left"
            Margin="15,109,0,0" Name="textBoxModel"
            VerticalAlignment="Top" Width="157" />
      <TextBox Height="23" HorizontalAlignment="Left"
            Margin="194,46,0,0" Name="textBoxCost"
            VerticalAlignment="Top" Width="75" />
```

continues

LISTING 5-13 *(continued)*

```
    <TextBox Height="23" HorizontalAlignment="Left"
            Margin="194,109,0,0" Name="textBoxPrice"
            VerticalAlignment="Top" Width="75" />
    <Label Content="Builder:" Height="28"
            HorizontalAlignment="Left" Margin="15,27,0,0"
            Name="labelBuilder" VerticalAlignment="Top" />
    <Label Content="Model:" Height="28"
            HorizontalAlignment="Left" Margin="15,90,0,0"
            Name="labelModel" VerticalAlignment="Top" />
    <Label Content="Cost:" Height="28"
            HorizontalAlignment="Left" Margin="194,27,0,0"
            Name="labelCost" VerticalAlignment="Top" />
    <Label Content="Price:" Height="28"
            HorizontalAlignment="Left" Margin="194,90,0,0"
            Name="labelPrice" VerticalAlignment="Top" />
    <Button Content="Submit" Height="23" HorizontalAlignment="Left"
            Margin="194,150,0,0" Name="buttonSubmit"
            VerticalAlignment="Top" Width="75"
            Click="buttonSubmit_Click"/>
   </Grid>
  </TabItem>
 </TabControl>
```

Inserting a single row is relatively straightforward. Using the methods found within the `IQuery`, `ICriteria`, `QueryOver`, or LINQ classes is not required to insert. All you need to do is call the `Save()` method from the `Session` and pass the entity as a parameter.

Create the `SaveInventory()` method within the `NHibernateInventory` class, as shown in Listing 5-14.

LISTING 5-14: Saving a guitar to the **INVENTORY** table

```
public bool SaveInventory(Inventory inventory)
{
  try
  {
    using (ITransaction transaction = Session.BeginTransaction())
    {
      Session.Save(inventory);
      transaction.Commit();
    }
    return true;
  }
  catch (Exception ex)
  {
    return false;
  }
}
```

Next, open the `MainWindow.xaml.cs` file of the `GuitarStore` WPF project and add the following code shown in Listing 5-15 to the `buttonSubmit_Click()` method.

LISTING 5-15: Saving a Guitar to Inventory from GuitarStore WPF

```
private void buttonSubmit_Click(object sender, RoutedEventArgs e)
{

  Guitar guitar = (Guitar)comboBoxGuitarTypes.SelectedItem;

  Inventory inventory = new Inventory();
  inventory.Id = Guid.NewGuid();
  inventory.Builder = textBoxBuilder.Text;
  inventory.Model = textBoxModel.Text;
  inventory.QOH = 1;
  inventory.Cost = Convert.ToDecimal(textBoxCost.Text);
  inventory.Price = Convert.ToDecimal(textBoxPrice.Text);
  inventory.Received = DateTime.Now;
  inventory.Guitar = guitar;

  NHibernateInventory nhi = new NHibernateInventory();

  if (nhi.SaveInventory(inventory))
  {
    labelMessage.Content = "Save was successful.";
  }
  else
  {
    labelMessage.Content = "Save failed.";
  }
}
```

The preceding Save() method results in the NHibernate-generated SQL query shown in Figure 5-5. It is a result of clicking the View SQL button directly after the saving a guitar to inventory.

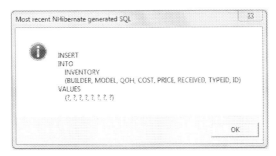

FIGURE 5-5

One of the more complex decisions to make when inserting data is which type of id generator to use. The type of id generator is configured in the hbm.xml file for each class. Until now, this element has been left out of the mapping files because it wasn't needed. Listing 5-16 shows a standard configuration of an id generator using a guid.comb.

LISTING 5-16: Id generator mapping configuration

```
<id name="Id" column="ID" type="System.Guid">
  <generator class="guid.comb" />
</id>
```

If no value is provided, `Assigned` (the default) is used. This means NHibernate expects to be provided with the Id from the implementation and before the `Save()` method is used. Some of the more popular generators are described in Table 5-2.

TABLE 5-2: Commonly Used NHibernate id Generators

GENERATOR	DESCRIPTION
Assigned	The program itself provides the id before the `Save()` method is used. This is the default setting if no element is provided.
Foreign	Uses the id of another related object.
Guid	Uses a `GUID` as the key.
guid.comb	Uses a `GUID` sequence, which reduces table fragmentation
Hilo	Generates a `HI` and a `LOW` value as the id; see `.NHibernate.ID .TableHiLoGenerator.Generate()` for the source code.
Identity	Provides support for `IDENTITY` database columns.
Native	Uses either `IDENTITY`, `SEQUENCE`, or `HILO`, depending on the utilized database.
Seqhillo	Uses a named database `SEQUENCE` to generate `HI/LOW` ids.
Sequence	Provides support for the `SEQUENCE` database method.

If none of the preceding id generators meets the current requirements, it is possible to create a custom id generator. This is done, for example, by inheriting from the class `TableGenerator` or `TableHiLoGenerator` found in the `NHibernate.Id` namespace and overriding the `Generate()` method. The code within the `Generate()` method can be modified to return a value specific to the requirements. An overridden `Generate()` method is show in Listing 5-17. It returns a `Guid` in this example, but the method can be programmed to return any unique identifier. Notice that the return type is an `object`. Add the `CustomIdGenerator` class to the `DataAccess` folder of the `NHibernate .GuitarStore` project.

LISTING 5-17: Custom id generator example

```
using NHibernate.Id;
using NHibernate.Engine;

public class CustomIdGenerator : TableGenerator
```

```
{
  public override object Generate(ISessionImplementor session, object obj)
  {
    Guid guid = Guid.NewGuid();
    return guid;

    //return base.Generate(session, obj);
  }
}
```

The preceding code listing is only an example. NHibernate already has its own GUID generator; therefore, you would not implement the code in Listing 5-17. You can add your own algorithm to create an id in a way that meets the needs of the current project.

Then, within the mapping file of the class that uses the CustomIdGenerator, associate the namespace.class to be used to generate the id, as shown in Listing 5-18.

LISTING 5-18: Mapping a customer id generator

```
<id name="Id" column="ID" type="System.Guid">
  <generator class="NHibernate.GuitarStore.DataAccess.CustomIdGenerator,
                    NHibernate.GuitarStore" />
</id>
```

Inserting a Parent/Child into a Database

Inserting a parent and then its children into the database is a common action in many programs. This section demonstrates one way to insert data using the many-to-one and one-to-many relationships. Listing 5-19 shows how the mappings should be configured to support inserting. Add a bag element to the Guitar.hbm.xml file and a many-to-one element to the Inventory .hbm.xml file, both of which are located in the Mapping directory of the NHibernate .GuitarStore project.

LISTING 5-19: Parent/child insert mapping configuration

```
PARENT - Guitar

<bag      name="Inventory"  table="INVENTORY" cascade="all">
  <key     column="TYPEID" />
  <one-to-many class="NHibernate.GuitarStore.Common.Inventory"  />
</bag>

CHILD - Inventory

<property name="TypeId"   column="TYPEID"   type="System.Guid" insert="false"/>
<many-to-one  name="Guitar" column="TYPEID" />
```

TIP *By adding the* `insert="false"` *attribute to the child mapping file, the "Invalid Index for this SqlParameterCollection with count=" error is avoided. This error is caused by the declaration of the* `TYPEID` *as a property and a foreign key in the* `many-to-one` *element. It should only be declared once for inserts and updates.*

Next, add the initialization of the `List<Inventory>()` to the constructor of the `Guitar` class located in the `Common` directory of the `NHibernate.GuitarStore` project, as shown in Listing 5-20.

LISTING 5-20: Instantiating the Inventory list in the Guitar constructor

```
public Guitar()
{
    Inventory = new List<Inventory>();
}
```

The basic approach for inserting a parent and child is to create an instance of the parent, create the children, add the children to the parent, and then perform a `Save()`. Listing 5-21 shows an example. This approach works fine, but performing a save in this manner results in two `INSERT` statements and an additional but unnecessary `UPDATE` statement.

LISTING 5-21: Standard NHibernate Save() example

```
public bool InsertParentChild(Guitar guitar, Inventory inventory)
{
  try
  {
    using (ITransaction transaction = Session.BeginTransaction())
    {
      guitar.Inventory.Add(inventory);
      Session.Save(guitar);
      transaction.Commit();
    }
    return true;
  }
  catch (Exception ex)
  {
    return false;
  }
}

Generated SQL:

INSERT INTO GUITAR (TYPE, ID) VALUES (@p0, @p1);
@p0 = 'ELECTRIC - ACOUSTIC' [Type: String (4000)],
@p1 = 945e108f-536a-4a93-8953-e7856e33f77f [Type: Guid (0)]

INSERT INTO INVENTORY (BUILDER, MODEL, QOH, COST, PRICE, RECEIVED, TYPEID,
```

```
        ID) VALUES (@p0, @p1, @p2, @p3, @p4, @p5, @p6, @p7);
@p0 = 'CHARVEL' [Type: String (4000)],
@p1 = 'Model 5' [Type: String (4000)],
@p2 = 1 [Type: Int32 (0)],
@p3 = 600 [Type: Decimal (0)],
@p4 = 899 [Type: Decimal (0)],
@p5 = 4/10/2011 10:40:05 AM [Type: DateTime (0)],
@p6 = NULL [Type: Guid (0)],
@p7 = 32f45e7e-861c-4c7b-afa8-9ec100afce25 [Type: Guid (0)]

UPDATE INVENTORY SET TYPEID = @p0 WHERE ID = @p1;
@p0 = 945e108f-536a-4a93-8953-e7856e33f77f [Type: Guid (0)],
@p1 = 32f45e7e-861c-4c7b-afa8-9ec100afce25 [Type: Guid (0)]
```

The initial insertion of the child sets the foreign key to NULL and then the child is updated with the foreign key after the INSERT. You can avoid the additional UPDATE by adding the INVERSE attribute to the parent's mapping file, as shown in Listing 5-22.

LISTING 5-22: Adding an **INVERSE** attribute to mapping for insert optimization

```xml
<bag       name="Inventory"  table="INVENTORY" inverse="true" cascade="all">
  <key     column="TYPEID" />
  <one-to-many class="NHibernate.GuitarStore.Common.Inventory"  />
</bag>

INSERT INTO GUITAR (TYPE, ID) VALUES (@p0, @p1);
@p0 = 'ELECTRIC - ACOUSTIC' [Type: String (4000)],
@p1 = eb6d6ef2-ce25-4817-957e-062ee75f7e2c [Type: Guid (0)]

INSERT INTO INVENTORY (BUILDER, MODEL, QOH, COST, PRICE, RECEIVED, TYPEID,
    ID) VALUES (@p0, @p1, @p2, @p3, @p4, @p5, @p6, @p7);
@p0 = 'CHARVEL' [Type: String (4000)],
@p1 = 'Model 5' [Type: String (4000)],
@p2 = 1 [Type: Int32 (0)],
@p3 = 600 [Type: Decimal (0)],
@p4 = 899 [Type: Decimal (0)],
@p5 = 4/10/2011 10:49:39 AM [Type: DateTime (0)],
@p6 = eb6d6ef2-ce25-4817-957e-062ee75f7e2c [Type: Guid (0)],
@p7 = 91392dcb-bab3-4c04-b5dc-9ec100b26f09 [Type: Guid (0)]
```

After updating the mapping files with an Id generator type, properly configuring the attributes, and calling the Save() method from methods within the NHibernateInventory class, the capability to insert new Inventory and new Guitar items is complete and usable from within the GuitarStore WPF program.

UNDERSTANDING NHIBERNATE CACHING

Caching is a mechanism that stores data transparently, enabling requests to execute faster when the stored data is again requested. NHibernate provides two methods of caching, first-level and second-level. These caching methods help improve a program's performance by reducing or eliminating the generation and execution of database queries. Figure 5-6 visually describes the life spans of first- and second-level caches in combination with the data retrieval process of the `Get()`, `Load()`, and `List()` methods.

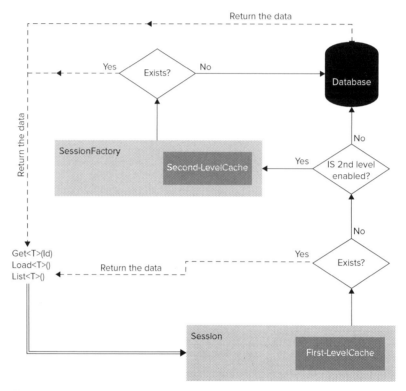

FIGURE 5-6

Using the First-Level Cache

The first-level cache, which is enabled by default in NHibernate, has a life span equal to that of the current NHibernate `Session`. When an entity is loaded into the identity map, whose primary responsibility is to confirm that only a single instance of a database record exists in a `Session`, all future requests for that entity will be loaded from the first-level cache. You can consider the identity map and the first-level cache as the same thing.

 NOTE *You must employ the stateful* `Session`, *as the stateless* `Session` *does not update the cache.*

NHibernate provides two methods for loading an entity into the identity map: `Get()` and `Load()`. They are exposed via the NHibernate `Session`.

Using Get() and Load()

After an initial save, it may be necessary to add more children to the parent. This requires retrieval of the parent so that the newly created children can be associated and saved. As shown in Figure 5-7, using the Get() method creates an instance of the class, while the Load() method creates a proxy.

FIGURE 5-7

When the Get() method is used as shown in Listing 5-23, NHibernate performs a SELECT statement to retrieve the persisted data of the parent only if the entity does not already exist in the identity map. If the entity is not present in the identity map, then it is loaded into it and all future requests for that entity within the context of the Session are retrieved from memory.

LISTING 5-23: Using the Get() method

```
Guitar guitar = session.Get<Guitar>(Id);

SELECT guitar0_.ID as ID0_0_,
       guitar0_.TYPE as TYPE0_0_
FROM GUITAR guitar0_
WHERE guitar0_.ID=@p0;
@p0 = e6f2a2ab-ca6d-4874-8874-6bb9baccffcb [Type: Guid (0)]
```

If a fully populated entity is not required, and you are certain that the entity exists on the database, then you can use the Load() method. For example, if the Id is known, you can simply use the code in Listing 5-24 to create a proxy class for the child to use, then set the foreign key and perform the Save(). A SELECT is executed only if the code specifically accesses a property of the parent class.

LISTING 5-24: Using the Load() method and creating a child

```
Guitar guitar = session.Load<Guitar>(Id);

Inventory inventory = new Inventory
{
    Builder = textBoxBuilder.Text,
    Model = textBoxModel.Text,
    QOH = 1,
    Cost = Convert.ToDecimal(textBoxCost.Text),
    Price = Convert.ToDecimal(textBoxPrice.Text),
    Received = DateTime.Now,
    TypeId = guitar.Id,
    Guitar = guitar
};
```

Implementing the Second-Level Cache

The second-level cache has a life span equal to that of the `SessionFactory` and is not enabled by default. Using the second-level cache requires the following configurations:

➤ Identify which type of caching to use.

➤ Configure NHibernate to use the second-level cache.

In this example, the `NHibernate.Cache.HashtableCacheProvider` cache provider is used. This is not a recommended provider for a production environment. For real production usage, use one of the many cache providers that are part of the NHibernate contribution project. Before selecting a provider, be sure to do sufficient research to determine which one is best suited for your program requirements.

 NOTE *You must commit transactions; otherwise, caching does not work.*

Table 5-3 describes the most common cache providers.

TABLE 5-3: Cache Providers

NAME	DESCRIPTION
Velocity	Uses Microsoft Velocity, now called AppFabric, a highly scalable in-memory cache
SharedCache	Supports the distribution and replication of in-memory object caching
SysCache	Relies on the ASP.NET `System.Web.Caching.Cache` class as the cache provider
SysCache2	Can configure certain cache regions to expire automatically when certain data in the database changes
Prevalence	Based on `Bamboo.Prevalence` and provides persistent caching in client applications
MemCache	In simple terms, a distributed hash table that is primarily used for speeding up web applications

The first action to take when configuring the second-level cache is to set the `cache.provider_class` and the `(cache.use_second_level_cache)` properties. This can be done within the `app.config` file or by using the strongly typed configuration method. Listing 5-25 shows what the `app.config` file should look like after adding the two properties.

LISTING 5-25: Second-level cache app.config configuration

```
<?xml version="1.0"?>
<configuration>
 <configSections>
  <section name="hibernate-configuration"
        type="NHibernate.Cfg.ConfigurationSectionHandler, NHibernate"/>
```

```
    </configSections>
    <hibernate-configuration xmlns="urn:nhibernate-configuration-2.2">
      <session-factory>
        <property name="connection.isolation">ReadCommitted</property>
        <property name="dialect">NHibernate.Dialect.MsSql2008Dialect</property>
        <property name="connection.driver_class">
                            NHibernate.Driver.SqlClientDriver</property>
        <property name="connection.connection_string_name">GuitarStore</property>
        <property name="connection.provider">
                     NHibernate.Connection.DriverConnectionProvider</property>
        <property name="cache.provider_class">
                     NHibernate.Cache.HashtableCacheProvider</property>
        <property name="cache.use_second_level_cache">true</property>
        <property name="show_sql">true</property>
      </session-factory>
    </hibernate-configuration>
    <connectionStrings>
      <add name="GuitarStore"
           connectionString="Data Source=W7;Initial Catalog=myGuitarStore;/>
      <add name="GuitarStoreOracle"
           connectionString="user id=*****;password=*****;
                            datasource=(DESCRIPTION=(ADDRESS=(PROTOCOL=tcp)
                            (HOST=192.168.1.1)(PORT=1521))
                            (CONNECT_DATA=(SERVICE_NAME=ora11g)))"/>
    </connectionStrings>
    <appSettings>
      <add key="SerializedFilename" value="nhibernate.guitarstore.serialized.cfg"/>
    </appSettings>
  </configuration>
```

You can also configure second-level caching using the strongly typed configuration. To do so, open the NHibernateBase.cs file in the DataAccess directory of the NHibernate.GuitarStore project. Change the ConfigureNHibernate() method so that it resembles Listing 5-26.

LISTING 5-26: Second-level cache strongly typed configuration

```
using NHibernate.Cfg.Loquacious;

public static Configuration ConfigureNHibernate(string assembly)
{
  Configuration = new NHibernate.Cfg.Configuration();

  Configuration.DataBaseIntegration(dbi =>
  {
    dbi.Dialect<MsSql2008Dialect>();
    dbi.Driver<SqlClientDriver>();
    dbi.ConnectionProvider<DriverConnectionProvider>();
    dbi.IsolationLevel = IsolationLevel.ReadCommitted;
    dbi.Timeout = 15;
  });

  Configuration.Cache(ca =>
```

continues

LISTING 5-26 *(continued)*

```
{
    ca.Provider<NHibernate.Cache.HashtableCacheProvider>();
});

Configuration.AddAssembly(assembly);

return Configuration;
}
```

 NOTE *When configuring the second-level cache via the* `app.config` *file, the* `cache.use_second_level_cache` *attribute is* `false`. *If you use the strongly typed configuration, the default is* `true`. *However, in both configuration methods, if* `cache.use_second_level_cache` *is added to the* `app.config` *file and set to* `false`, *it will turn off the second-level cache.*

Next, add the `cache` element to the mapping file of the `Inventory` entity. Open the `Inventory.hbm.xml` file located in the `Mapping` directory of the `NHibernate.GuitarStore` project. Listing 5-27 shows an updated `Inventory` mapping file containing the `cache` element.

LISTING 5-27: Enabling the second-level cache for the Inventory entity

```xml
<?xml version="1.0" encoding="utf-8" ?>
<hibernate-mapping xmlns="urn:nhibernate-mapping-2.2"
                   assembly="NHibernate.GuitarStore">
  <class name="NHibernate.GuitarStore.Common.Inventory, NHibernate.GuitarStore"
         table="INVENTORY">
   <cache usage="read-write"/>
   <id       name="Id"        column="ID"        type="System.Guid">
     <generator class="guid.comb" />
   </id>
   <version name="VERSION" generated="always" type="BinaryBlob" />
   <property name="TypeId"   column="TYPEID"   type="System.Guid" insert="false"/>
   <property name="Builder"  column="BUILDER"  type="System.String" />
   <property name="Model"    column="MODEL"    type="System.String" />
   <property name="QOH"      column="QOH"      type="System.Int32" />
   <property name="Cost"     column="COST"     type="System.Decimal" />
   <property name="Price"    column="PRICE"    type="System.Decimal" />
   <property name="Received" column="RECEIVED" type="System.DateTime" />
   <many-to-one  name="Guitar" column="TYPEID" />
  </class>
</hibernate-mapping>
```

In this example, the read-write caching strategy has been implemented. Table 5-4 describes the caching strategy types. As mentioned earlier, the caching strategy should be implemented based on your current program requirements.

TABLE 5-4: Caching Strategies

STRATEGY TYPE	DESCRIPTION
read-only	The program needs to read but not modify a persistent class.
read-write	Use this when the program will update the data. Locking is not supported.
nonstrict-read-write	The program rarely updates data, and is unlikely to update same entity simultaneously.
transactional	This provides support for cache providers that implement transactional cache functionality.

To confirm that the second-level cache is working, set the cache.use_second_level_cache attribute to false and add the code shown in Listing 5-28 to the Main() method within the Program.cs file of the NHibernate.GuitarStore.Console application.

LISTING 5-28: Testing second-level caching from the console application

```
Guid guitar59 = new Guid("c8cb8762-a498-47f7-8e72-013ca20b84d6");

using (ISession session = sessionFactory.OpenSession())
{
  Inventory inventory59 = session.Get<Inventory>(guitar59);
}

using (ISession session = sessionFactory.OpenSession())
{
  Inventory inventory60 = session.Get<Inventory>(guitar59);
}
```

Notice in Figure 5-8 that two SELECT statements are generated and executed on the database.

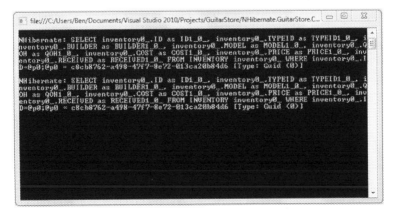

FIGURE 5-8

Now set the `cache.use_second_level_cache` attribute to `true` and rerun `NHibernate` `.GuitarStore.Console` application. As shown in Figure 5-9, only a single `SELECT` statement is generated and executed on the database. The first `Get<T>(Id)` method retrieves the data and loads it into the second-level cache. The second call to the `Get<T>(Id)` retrieves the data from the second-level cache. The data for this entity is retrieved from the cache for the life span of the associated `SessionFactory`.

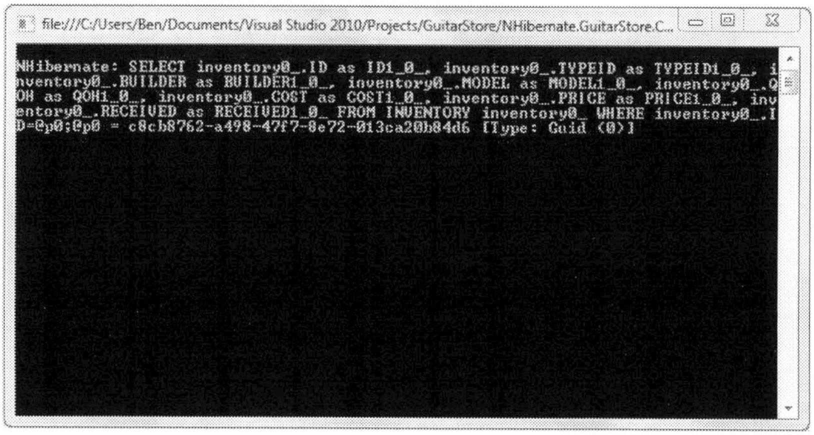

file:///C:/Users/Ben/Documents/Visual Studio 2010/Projects/GuitarStore/NHibernate.GuitarStore.C...

```
NHibernate: SELECT inventory0_.ID as ID1_0_, inventory0_.TYPEID as TYPEID1_0_, i
nventory0_.BUILDER as BUILDER1_0_, inventory0_.MODEL as MODEL1_0_, inventory0_.Q
OH as QOH1_0_, inventory0_.COST as COST1_0_, inventory0_.PRICE as PRICE1_0_, inv
entory0_.RECEIVED as RECEIVED1_0_ FROM INVENTORY inventory0_ WHERE inventory0_.I
D=@p0;@p0 = c8cb8762-a498-47f7-8e72-013ca20b84d6 [Type: Guid (0)]
```

FIGURE 5-9

UNDERSTANDING EVICT(), MERGE(), AND PERSIST()

Before you begin reading the section, I recommend that you download the NHibernate source code and view the `ISession.cs` file, which contains very good descriptions for the `Evict()`, `Merge()`, and `Persist()` methods, along with summaries of many other NHibernate features. These three methods, in particular, can be used to help manage the state (transient, detached, and persistent) of the object being used in a specific business transaction within the scope of the `Session`.

Using Evict()

The `Evict()` method stops the synchronization of an entity to the database and removes it from the first-level cache. This means that if modifications are made to an `Inventory` object and the `Evict()` method is called before a `Flush()`, `Save()`, or `SaveOrUpdate()`, then the modification will not be persisted to the database. At the same time, the object will be removed from the first-level cache. If later a `Get()`, `Load()`, or `List()` method is used to retrieve inventory data, the modifications made prior to the `Evict()` method call will not be realized. A possible usage for the `Evict()` method is when loading or processing a large number of objects whereby some objects need to be skipped, removed, or specifically marked for saving based on a program requirement data value. Listing 5-29 provides an example implementation.

LISTING 5-29: Using the Evict() method

```
using (ITransaction transaction = Session.BeginTransaction())
{
  IQueryable<Inventory> inventory62 = (from inv in Session.Query<Inventory>()
                                       orderby inv.Id
                                       select inv);
  IList<Inventory> inventoryList62 = inventory62.ToList();

  foreach (Inventory item in inventoryList62)
  {
    item.Price = item.Price * 1.15M;
    if (item.Price > 5000)
    {
      Session.Evict(item);  //Don't save it
    }
    Session.Flush();
  }
}
```

If the `Price` is more than €5,000, then evict the object from the update and remove it from the first-level cache.

> **NOTE** The code shown in Listing 5-29 exists only to demonstrate the behavior of the `Evict()` method. This method, while powerful, exists to address some unique cases that many typical programs don't experience. The implementation pattern is sub-optimal and should not be replicated.

Using Merge()

The `Merge()` method provides the capability to move a transient or detached object into a persistent state. If an entity with the same identifier has already been persisted, then the transient entity will be merged with the current entity stored in the first-level cache. Conversely, if the transient entity does not exist in the first-level cache, then it will be loaded from the database and stored into memory. Take, for example, the loading of `Inventory` into the `DataGrid` in the `GuitarStore` WPF program using a stateful `Session`. This results in persisted `Inventory` entities.

Before getting deeper into the `Merge()` method, add a `MouseDoubleClick` that captures the values in the columns and populates the `TextBox` controls on the Save Or Update `TabControl`. The first action to take is to open the `MainWindow.xaml` file found in the `GuitarStore` WPF project. The `DataGrid` XAML should resemble the code in Listing 5-30.

LISTING 5-30: DataGrid MouseDoubleClick XAML code

```
<DataGrid AutoGenerateColumns="True" HorizontalAlignment="Stretch"
          Margin="6,0,6,6" Name="dataGridInventory"
          VerticalAlignment="Stretch"
          MouseDoubleClick="dataGridInventory_MouseDoubleClick" />
```

Next, open the `MainWindow.xaml.cs` file found in the `GuitarStore` WPF project and add the following code to the `dataGridInventory_MouseDoubleClick()` method, as shown in Listing 5-31.

LISTING 5-31: DataGrid double-click event

```
private void dataGridInventory_MouseDoubleClick(object sender,
                                                MouseButtonEventArgs e)
{
  Inventory inventory = dataGridInventory.SelectedItem as Inventory;
  tabItemInsertInventory.Focus();

  textBoxBuilder.Text = inventory.Builder;
  textBoxModel.Text = inventory.Model;
  textBoxCost.Text = inventory.Cost.ToString();
  textBoxPrice.Text = inventory.Price.ToString();
}
```

This code segment captures the double-clicked row, sets the focus to the Save or Update Inventory `TabControl`, and sets the modifiable property values to the corresponding `TextBox` value.

Next, open the `NHibernateInventory.cs` file located in the `DataAccess` folder of the `NHibernate.GuitarStore` project and modify the `SaveInventory()` method, as shown in Listing 5-32.

LISTING 5-32: SaveInventory() method

```
public bool SaveInventory(Inventory inventory)
{
  try
  {
    using (ITransaction transaction = Session.BeginTransaction())
    {
      Inventory inventoryDetached = new Inventory();
      inventoryDetached.Id = inventory.Id;
      inventoryDetached.Builder = inventory.Builder;
      inventoryDetached.Model = inventory.Model;
      inventoryDetached.Cost = inventory.Cost;
      inventoryDetached.Price = inventory.Price;

      Session.SaveOrUpdate(inventory);
      transaction.Commit();
    }
    return true;
  }
  catch (Exception ex)
  {
    return false;
  }
}
```

Finally, modify the `buttonSubmit_Click()` method found within the `MainWindow.xaml.cs` file of the `GuitarStore` WPF project so that it calls the previously created `SaveInventory()` method, passing it an `Inventory` class as a parameter. Listing 5-33 provides an example.

LISTING 5-33: Using the SaveInventory() method from the GuitarStore WPF program

```
private void buttonSubmit_Click(object sender, RoutedEventArgs e)
{
  Inventory inventory = new Inventory();
  inventory.Id = dgId;
  inventory.Builder = textBoxBuilder.Text;
  inventory.Model = textBoxModel.Text;
  inventory.Cost = Convert.ToDecimal(textBoxCost.Text);
  inventory.Price = Convert.ToDecimal(textBoxPrice.Text);
  inventory.QOH = 1;

  NHibernateInventory nhi = new NHibernateInventory();
  if (nhi.SaveInventory(inventory))
  {
    labelMessage.Content = "Save was successful.";
  }
  else
  {
    labelMessage.Content = "Save failed.";
  }
}
```

When the `GuitarStore` WPF program is executed and a save is attempted, the save will fail. This is because Listing 5-33 created a *transient* `Inventory` class, populated it with data from an identical already *persisted* `Inventory` class, and attempted to save the transient entity. The result is an `NHibernate.NonUniqueObjectException`. To resolve this issue, simply use the `Merge()` method instead of the `SaveOrUpdate()` method, as shown in Listing 5-34.

LISTING 5-34: Using the Merge() method to avoid a NonUniqueObjectException

```
public bool SaveInventory(Inventory inventory)
{
  try
  {
    using (ITransaction transaction = Session.BeginTransaction())
    {
      Inventory inventoryDetached = new Inventory();
      inventoryDetached.Id = inventory.Id;
      inventoryDetached.Builder = inventory.Builder;
      inventoryDetached.Model = inventory.Model;
      inventoryDetached.Cost = inventory.Cost;
      inventoryDetached.Price = inventory.Price;

      Session.Merge(inventory);
      transaction.Commit();
    }
    return true;
  }
  catch (Exception ex)
  {
    return false;
  }
}
```

Using Persist()

The `Persist()` method enables you to attach a transient object to a `Session`. At the same time, the object is not saved or updated to the database, nor is it granted an identifier until `Session.Flush()` is called. This may be useful in situations when you want to persist an object at the beginning of a business transaction but not save it until the end. This specific business transaction may take a large number of other actions, which, in turn, could change the original values of the unsaved persisted object. You therefore avoid an initial `INSERT` and then `UPDATE` of the object when the transaction is completed. Listing 5-35 shows how to use the `Persist()` method.

LISTING 5-35: Use the Persist() method with long-running transactions

```
using (ITransaction transaction = Session.BeginTransaction())
{
  Guitar transientGuitar = new Guitar();
  transientGuitar.Type = "ACOUSTIC ELECTRIC";
  Session.Persist(transientGuitar);
  //Do some other required activies for this specific transaction
}
  //Do some other transactions that modify persisted transient object
Session.Flush();
```

 NOTE *The code shown in Listing 5-35 exists only to demonstrate the behavior of the* `Persist()` *method. This method, while powerful, exists to address some unique cases that many typical programs don't experience.*

EXECUTING BATCH PROCESSES

Many activities require the insertion, updating, or deletion of a group of data. Using a `for` or `foreach` loop, as shown in Listing 5-36, is considered an anti-pattern. Additionally, when the `Session` is used to perform the batch update, insert, or delete of a large set of data, the entities are loaded into the identity map and second-level cache, if enabled. The code in Listing 5-36 can be added within the `Main()` method of the `Program.cs` file found in the `NHibernate.GuitarStore.Console` project.

LISTING 5-36: Batch update method using a stateful Session

```
Guid guitarType61 = new Guid("471c5b3f-19da-4fcb-8e9f-48dd17a00a3d");
using (ITransaction transaction = Session.BeginTransaction())
{
  //Performs an UPDATE per CHILD record
  IQuery queryUpdate = .Session
                    .CreateQuery("from Inventory where TypeId = :TypeId")
                    .SetGuid("TypeId", guitarType61);
  IList<Inventory> invUpdateList = queryUpdate.List<Inventory>();

  foreach (var item in invUpdateList)
```

```
  {
    item.Cost = (decimal)item.Cost * (decimal)1.15;
  }
  transaction.Commit();
}
```

The preceding method is considered an anti-pattern because it results in one UPDATE statement per item. The foreach loop could potentially attempt to process hundreds of thousands of updates. This method results is more memory utilization and slightly worse performance compared to, for example, using the IStatelessSession. To use the IStatelessSession, simply replace the Session with the OpenStatelessSession() method. Listing 5-37 demonstrates this approach. Note that even when using the IStatelessSession, an UPDATE per row is generated and executed on the database.

LISTING 5-37: A batched stateless update process

```
Guid guitarType61 = new Guid("471c5b3f-19da-4fcb-8e9f-48dd17a00a3d");

using (ITransaction transaction = StatelessSession.BeginTransaction())
{
  //Performs an UPDATE per CHILD record
  IQuery queryUpdate = StatelessSession
                      .CreateQuery("from Inventory where TypeId = :TypeId")
                      .SetGuid("TypeId", guitarType61);
  IList<Inventory> invUpdateList = queryUpdate.List<Inventory>();

  foreach (var item in invUpdateList)
  {
    item.Cost = (decimal)item.Cost * (decimal).85;
    StatelessSession.Update(item);
  }
  transaction.Commit();
}
```

NOTE When saving data, use the Insert() method in conjunction with the StatelessSession. The IStatelessSession interface does not have a method named Save() that is used with the ISession.

Another approach you can use to perform stateful batch insertions, updates, or deletions is to use the adonet.batch_size attribute. This attribute, as the name states, batches a configurable number of INSERT, UPDATE, or DELETE statements together for execution. By batching these statements together, fewer database round-trips are made for the batch process, therefore making it somewhat faster. There are several ways to implement this, including the following:

➤   Within the app.config file

➤   Strongly typed within the configuration

➤   Directly on the Session

To implement batching via the `app.config` file, add the code in Listing 5-38 to the program's `app.config` file within the `session-factory` element.

LISTING 5-38: Setting the batch size from the app.config file

```
<hibernate-configuration xmlns="urn:nhibernate-configuration-2.2">
 <session-factory
  <property name="adonet.batch_size">10</property>
 </session-factory>
</hibernate-configuration>
```

Then, simply execute the stateful batch process and record the performance improvement of the program.

To set the batch size from a strongly typed configuration, modify the `ConfigureNHibernate()` method found within the `NHibernateBase.cs` file of the `NHibernate.GuitarStore` project so that it resembles Listing 5-39.

LISTING 5-39: Setting the batch size from a strongly typed configuration

```
using NHibernate.Cfg.Loquacious;

public static Configuration ConfigureNHibernate(string assembly)
{
  Configuration = new Configuration();

  Configuration.DataBaseIntegration(dbi =>
  {
    dbi.Dialect<MsSql2008Dialect>();
    dbi.Driver<SqlClientDriver>();
    dbi.ConnectionProvider<DriverConnectionProvider>();
    dbi.IsolationLevel = IsolationLevel.ReadUncommitted;
    dbi.Timeout = 15;
    dbi.BatchSize = 10;
  });

  Configuration.AddAssembly(assembly);
  return Configuration;
}
```

Note that the batch configuration methods in Listing 5-38 and Listing 5-39 have a scope of the `SessionFactory`. The batch size setting is applied to all batches for all `Sessions`. If this is not what is needed, it is possible to set the batch size for a specific `Session`. Listing 5-40 shows how to set the batch size for a specific NHibernate `Session`.

LISTING 5-40: Setting batch size for a specific Session

```
Guid guitarType61 = new Guid("471c5b3f-19da-4fcb-8e9f-48dd17a00a3d");

using (ITransaction transaction = Session.BeginTransaction())
```

```
{
  //Performs an UPDATE per CHILD record
  IQuery queryUpdate = Session
              .CreateQuery("from Inventory where TypeId = :TypeId")
              .SetGuid("TypeId", guitarType61);
  IList<Inventory> invUpdateList = queryUpdate.List<Inventory>();

  Session.SetBatchSize(10);
  foreach (var item in invUpdateList)
  {
    item.Cost = (decimal)item.Cost * (decimal)1.15;
  }

  transaction.Commit();

}
```

Another alternative is to use the ExecuteUpdate() method. There are a number of classes within the NHibernate source where the ExecuteUpdate() method is implemented. For our purposes, the classes of special interest are SqlQueryImpl, QueryImpl, and SessionImpl, found within the NHibernate.Impl namespace. Listing 5-41 shows an example of using the ExecuteUpdate() method with the QueryImpl class.

LISTING 5-41: ExecuteUpdate() method example

```
using (ITransaction transaction = Session.BeginTransaction())
{
  //Performs a single UPDATE
  string hqlQuery =
          "update Inventory set Price = Price*1.15 where TypeId = :TypeId";

  IQuery queryUpdate = Session.CreateQuery(hqlQuery)
                              .SetGuid("TypeId", guitarType61);
  int UpdatedCount = queryUpdate.ExecuteUpdate();

  transaction.Commit();
}
```

As shown in the preceding example, this method results in the generation of a single update statement. This is much better than creating and executing an update statement per row. However, two very important topics need to be discussed in regard to using either the IStatelessSession interface or the ExecuteUpdate() method: versioning and their effect on a cached entity.

The method shown in Listing 5-41 will not update the VERSION column that was added to the INVENTORY table column. This means if a user is working with some detached data and the preceding batch update is executed via another process, the user will not receive a StaleObjectException and the data will be overwritten by the user (i.e., that data is being modified from two different sources). Modifying the HQL query as shown in Listing 5-42 will update the version number. Note the addition of the HQL keyword, versioned, before the Inventory reference in the HQL statement.

LISTING 5-42: HQL query to enforce versioning

```
string hqlQuery =
        "update versioned Inventory set Price = Price*1.15 where TypeId = :TypeId";
```

The issue regarding the effect of using either the `IStatelessSession` or the `ExecuteUpdate()` method on a cached entity is a little more complex. One of the reasons a programmer would want to implement the solution shown in Listing 5-36 is because by doing so, the data stored in memory — that is, the first- (identity map) or second-level cache — remains consistent with that stored on the database. This means that the object remains persistent. This is not the case when using the `IStatelessSession` and the `ExecuteUpdate()` methods, whereby neither the identity map nor the second-level cache, if implemented, are updated, and this can cause some data integrity issues.

You can handle this by confirming that objects being modified or used for reference are persistent. Using either the `Merge()`, `Get()`, or `Persist()` method will ensure that the objects remain in a valid state.

NOTE *If a program loads a large amount of persistent data into memory and uses it for the lifetime of the program, be aware that the data can become stale if another process performs an update of that data from another transaction.*

SUMMARY

This chapter covered many topics regarding the management and insertion of data. By gaining insight into the differences among persistent, transient, and detached states, and the impact these states have on the data's integrity, you are better able to implement superior technical solutions. Furthermore, it should be clear that the integrity and performance of the database are enriched with the implementation of concurrency rules and versioning, both of which have strong functional representation within NHibernate. With a broad understanding of NHibernate terminology and its capabilities, programmers can build, and architects can design, better data-driven solutions.

Using NHibernate with an ASP.NET MVC 3 Application

Once a company has created a database and the internal systems to control the data, it is not very difficult to use the data again with other functionality. The myGuitarStore database contains information about the types of guitars, the builder, the model, and the cost. Obviously, this information is something a potential customer would like to know before making a purchase. One of the best means of providing this information to a customer is via a website. Therefore, this chapter describes and creates a website that implements ASP.NET MVC 3 using NHibernate.

To create the website shown in Figure 6-1, you will perform the following activities:

1. Install ASP.NET MVC 3, which deposits the MVC 3 assemblies and registers them into the Global Assembly Cache (GAC).

2. Add an ASP.NET MVC project to the existing GuitarStore solution.

3. Configure NHibernate and the Session solution.

4. Configure the View and Controller.

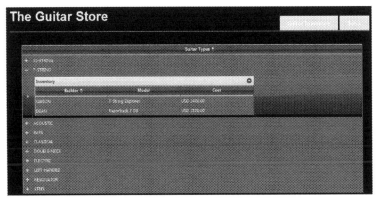

FIGURE 6-1

INSTALLING ASP.NET MVC 3

ASP.NET MVC 3 is not installed with Visual Studio 2010. Therefore, you need to download it from the Microsoft website at `www.asp.net/mvc/mvc3` and install it just as you would any other software package. The ASP.NET MVC 3 download used in this example is `AspNetMVC3ToolsUpdateSetup.exe`.

ADDING AN ASP.NET MVC 3 PROJECT TO THE GUITARSTORE SOLUTION

Open Microsoft Visual Web Developer 2010 Express and select New Project. Then select ASP.NET MVC 3 ⇨ Web Application, name it **GuitarStoreMVC**, and click OK. In the dialog that appears, select Internet Application, and in the View Engine drop-down, select ASPX. Click OK. Figure 6-2 shows the created project.

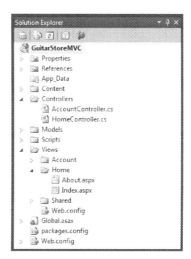

FIGURE 6-2

CONFIGURING NHIBERNATE

Several activities are required to configure NHibernate within an MVC project. In order to have an MVC project work with NHibernate and to use the `NHibernate.GuitarStore` library, you need to do the following:

1. Add references to the `NHibernate` and `NHibernate.GuitarStore` binaries.
2. Add `connectionString` to the `Web.config` file.
3. Add the NHibernate configuration setting to the `Global.asax.cs` file.
4. Configure the ASP.NET MVC 3 program to use a session-per-web-request solution.

Adding References to the Binaries

Begin by right-clicking the `Reference` folder and adding the NHibernate binaries, then add the `NHibernate.GuitarStore.dll`. Refer to Chapter 1, "Getting Started with NHibernate 3," for more details on which NHibernate binaries are used and where they are located.

Adding connectionString to the Web.config File

Open the `Web.config` file found in the root directory of the MVC project. The `Web.config` file is modified to contain the `connectionString` and configuration settings used by NHibernate to connect to the `myGuitarStore` database. Add the code in Listing 6-1 to the `Web.config` file.

LISTING 6-1: MVC 3 Web.config settings

```
<configSections>
    <section name="hibernate-configuration"
            type="NHibernate.Cfg.ConfigurationSectionHandler, NHibernate" />
</configSections>
<hibernate-configuration xmlns="urn:nhibernate-configuration-2.2">
    <session-factory>
      <property name="connection.connection_string_name">
                        GuitarStore</property>
      <property name="connection.provider">
                        NHibernate.Connection.DriverConnectionProvider</property>
    </session-factory>
</hibernate-configuration>
<connectionStrings>
    <add name="GuitarStore"
        connectionString="Data Source=(local);Initial Catalog=myGuitarStore;
        Integrated Security=True"/>
</connectionStrings>
```

 NOTE The `connectionString` provided in the preceding listing is an example only. You should modify parameters to meet your specific needs.

Next, open the `Global.asax.cs` file and add a static class-level `SessionFactory` property, as shown in Listing 6-2.

LISTING 6-2: Creating a static class-level SessionFactory

```
using NHibernate;

namespace GuitarStoreMVC
{
  public class MvcApplication : System.Web.HttpApplication
  {
    public static ISessionFactory SessionFactory { get; private set; }
  }
}
```

Then modify the `Application_Start()` method so that it resembles Listing 6-3.

LISTING 6-3: MVC 3 Application_Start() method

```
using NHibernate.Cfg;
using NHibernate.Cfg.Loquacious;
using NHibernate.Context;
using NHibernate.Dialect;
using NHibernate.Driver;
using NHibernate.GuitarStore;

protected void Application_Start()
{
    AreaRegistration.RegisterAllAreas();

    RegisterGlobalFilters(GlobalFilters.Filters);
    RegisterRoutes(RouteTable.Routes);

    var configure = new Configuration();
    configure.DataBaseIntegration(dbi =>
    {
        dbi.Dialect<MsSql2008Dialect>();
        dbi.Driver<SqlClientDriver>();
        dbi.Timeout = 10;
    });

    configure.CurrentSessionContext<WebSessionContext>();
    configure.AddAssembly("NHibernate.GuitarStore");

    SessionFactory = configure.BuildSessionFactory();

}
```

Notice that an additional setting, `CurrentSessionContext`, is applied to the `GuitarStore` WPF configuration discussed in Chapter 1. Several contexts can be used within web-based programs; the `CurrentSessionContext` class is being set to `WebSessionContext` in this `GuitarStoreMVC` example system. The `NHibernate.Context` classes provide methods to bind and unbind a `Session` to a context. The programmer, who is responsible for specifically defining the context of the `Session`, would then use the `GetCurrentSession()` method of the `SessionFactory` to retrieve the NHibernate `Session` used to perform transactions against the database. Table 6-1 describes the most common context classes.

TABLE 6-1: NHibernate Session Contexts

CONTEXT CLASS	DESCRIPTION
ManagedWebSessionContext	Works only with web programs. The `HttpContext` tracks the current `Session`. The programmer is responsible for binding and unbinding an `ISession` instance on this class.
WcfOperationSessionContext	Works only during the lifetime of an WCF operation.

CONTEXT CLASS	DESCRIPTION
WebSessionContext	Analogous to the ManagedWebSessionContext, but the ISession instance is bound and unbound using the CurrentContextSession class.
ThreadStaticSessionContext	Provides a current Session if more than a single SessionFactory is used.

The context and management of a Session varies according to the type of program being created. For example, recall the session-per-presenter solution used in the GuitarStore WPF program, where the context of the Session is explicitly bound to a WPF window instead of using the CurrentSessionContext setting. The GuitarStore WPF program called for that type of implementation, whereas this ASP.NET MVC program calls for a session-per-web-request solution within a WebSessionContext context.

CONFIGURING THE ASP.NET MVC PROGRAM TO USE A SESSION-PER-WEB-REQUEST

To implement this session-per-web-request Session solution, add an Application_BeginRequest() method and an Application_EndRequest() method to the Global.asax.cs file as shown in Listing 6-4.

LISTING 6-4: Application_BeginRequest() and Application_EndRequest() methods

```
protected void Application_BeginRequest(object sender, EventArgs e)
{
  var session = SessionFactory.OpenSession();
  CurrentSessionContext.Bind(session);
}

protected void Application_EndRequest(object sender, EventArgs e)
{
    var session = CurrentSessionContext.Unbind(SessionFactory);
    session.Dispose();
}
```

The Application_BeginRequest() method is called each time a request to an ASP.NET page is processed; the method opens a Session and then binds it to the current context. When the ASP.NET request is complete, the Application_EndRequest() method is called, which unbinds the Session from the current context and disposes of it, which makes it available for garbage collection.

CONFIGURING THE VIEW AND CONTROLLER

Now that NHibernate is installed and the session management solution is implemented, the code required to view and retrieve the data can be programmed. In this section, you perform the following:

1. Add a method named `ExecuteHQL<T>()` that accepts an HQL query and an `ISession` and returns a `IList<T>`.

2. Add a method named `GuitarList()` to the `Controller`.

3. Add a method named `ExecuteCriteria<T>()` that accepts an `ISession` and an `Id` search parameter and returns an `IList<T>`.

4. Add a method named `InventoryList()` to the `Controller`.

5. Modify the `View` to use the methods created in the `Controller` and present the data using `jqGrid`.

First, to continue with the separation of the NHibernate details from the implementation of the NHibernate query APIs, you need to create a new method within the `NHibernateInventory` class found in the `DataAccess` directory of the `NHibernate.GuitarStore` project. Add the method shown in Listing 6-5 to the `NHibernateInventory` class.

LISTING 6-5: Generic HQL method with a Session

```
public IList<T> ExecuteHQL<T>(string hqlQuery, ISession session)
{
  using (ITransaction transaction = session.BeginTransaction())
  {
    IQuery query = session.CreateQuery(hqlQuery);
    return query.List<T>();
  }
}
```

Next, configure the `Controller` by opening the `HomeController.cs` file located in the `Controllers` directory and add the `GuitarList()` method shown in Listing 6-6, which retrieves and populates the `jqGrid` with the `Guitar` data using NHibernate.

LISTING 6-6: The Controller GuitarList() method

```
using NHibernate;
using NHibernate.GuitarStore.Common;
using NHibernate.GuitarStore.DataAccess;

public ActionResult GuitarList(string sidx, string sord, int page, int rows)
{
  IList<Guitar> guitarList = null;

  try
  {
```

```
    NHibernateInventory nhi = new NHibernateInventory();

    var session = GuitarStoreMVC.MvcApplication.SessionFactory.GetCurrentSession();
    using (var transaction = session.BeginTransaction())
    {
      guitarList = nhi.ExecuteHQL<Guitar>("from Guitar order by Type", session);
    }
    var jsonData = new
    {
      rows = (
        from g in guitarList
        select new
        {
          id = g.Id,
          cell = new string[] { g.Type }
        }).ToArray()
    };
    return Json(jsonData, JsonRequestBehavior.AllowGet);
  }
  catch (Exception ex)
  {
    ViewBag.Message = ex.Message;
    return View();
  }
}
```

The `GetCurrentSession()` method of the `SessionFactory` is used to get the `Session` within the previously configured context described in Listing 6-3. Then the `Session` is used to begin, execute, and commit the transaction that retrieves the data from the GUITAR table. Finally, the result set is converted into a `Json` data type using LINQ and returned.

Next, add the `ExecuteCriteria<T>()` method, which accepts an `ISession` and an `Id` search parameter. The code is shown in Listing 6-7.

LISTING 6-7: Generic ICriteria method with a Session

```
public IList<T> ExecuteCriteria<T>(ISession session, Guid Id) where T : class
{
  using (ITransaction transaction = session.BeginTransaction())
  {
    try
    {
      ICriteria criteria = session.CreateCriteria<T>()
                            .Add(Restrictions.Eq("TypeId", Id));
      return criteria.List<T>();
    }
    catch (Exception ex)
    {
      transaction.Rollback();
      throw;
    }
  }
}
```

Next, add the `InventoryList()` method, which is executed when the `Guitar` list is expanded to the `HomeController.cs` file found in the `Controllers` directory, as shown in Listing 6-8.

LISTING 6-8: The Controller InventoryList() method

```
using NHibernate;
using NHibernate.GuitarStore.Common;
using NHibernate.GuitarStore.DataAccess;

public ActionResult InventoryList(string sidx, string sord, int page, int rows,
  Guid Id)
{
  IList<Inventory> inventoryList = null;

  try
  {
    NHibernateInventory nhi = new NHibernateInventory();

    var session = GuitarStoreMVC.MvcApplication.SessionFactory.GetCurrentSession();
    using (var transaction = session.BeginTransaction())
    {
      inventoryList = nhi.ExecuteCriteria<Inventory>(session, Id);
    }

    var jsonSubData = new
    {
      rows = (from i in inventoryList
              select new
              {
                id = i.Id.ToString(),
                cell = new string[] {
                i.Builder,
                i.Model,
                "$" + i.Cost.ToString()
              }
            }).ToArray()
    };

    return Json(jsonSubData, JsonRequestBehavior.AllowGet);
  }
  catch (Exception ex)
  {
    ViewBag.Message = ex.Message;
    return View();
  }
}
```

This method receives the `Id` of the guitar type that was expanded in the `jqGrid`. Again, the `GetCurrentSession()` method is called to get a `Session`, which is used together with the `Id` to retrieve the list of inventory for the requested guitar type.

Next, to begin the View configuration, open the Index.aspx file located in the Views\Home directory and add the GuitarList function, which displays the guitar information, as shown in Listing 6-9.

LISTING 6-9: GuitarList View function

```
<table id='GuitarList'></table><div id='GuitarList_pager'></div>
<script type='text/javascript'>
   jQuery(document).ready(function () {
       jQuery('#GuitarList').jqGrid({
           url: '/Home/GuitarList/',
           datatype: 'json',
           mtype: 'GET',
           colNames: ['Guitar Types'],
           colModel:
               [
                   { name: 'TYPE', index: 'TYPE', width: 60, align: 'left' },
               ],
           autowidth: true,
           height: 'auto',
           sortname: 'TYPE',
           sortorder: "ASC",
           viewrecords: true,
           multiselect: false,
           subGrid: true,
           subGridRowExpanded: showDetails
       })
     jQuery("#GuitarList").jqGrid('navGrid', '#GuitarList_pager',
           { add: false, edit: false, del: false, search: false })
   })
</script>
```

The preceding function uses jQuery to redirect the request to the GuitarList() method found in the Controller\HomeController.cs file. Listing 6-10 shows the function that displays the inventory based on which guitar type is expanded.

LISTING 6-10: InventoryList View function

```
<table id='InventoryList'></table><div id=''InventoryList'_pager'></div>
<script type='text/javascript'>
   function showSubGrid_InventoryList(subgrid_id, row_id, message, suffix) {
       var subgrid_table_id, pager_id;
       subgrid_table_id = subgrid_id + '_t';
       pager_id = 'p_' + subgrid_table_id;
       if (suffix) { subgrid_table_id += suffix; pager_id += suffix; }
       if (message) jQuery('#' + subgrid_id).append(message);
         jQuery('#' + subgrid_id).append('<table id=' + subgrid_table_id +
           ' class=scroll></table><div id=' + pager_id + ' class=scroll></div>');
         jQuery('#' + subgrid_table_id).jqGrid({
             url: '/Home/InventoryList/' + row_id,
```

continues

LISTING 6-10 *(continued)*

```
            datatype: 'json',
            colNames: ['Builder', 'Model', 'Cost'],
            colModel:
                [
                { name: 'Builder', index: 'BUILDER', width: 10, align: 'left' },
                { name: 'Model', index: 'MODEL', width: 10, align: 'left' },
                { name: 'Cost', index: 'COST', width: 10, align: 'left' },
                ],
            caption: 'Inventory',
            sortorder: "ASC",
            width: '550',
            height: 'auto'
        })
    }
</script>
```

Lastly, add the showDetails function, shown in Listing 6-11, which is called from the SubGridRowExpanded event to bind the GuitarList and InventoryList together.

LISTING 6-11: The showDetail function called from the subGridRowExpanded event

```
<script type="text/javascript">
    function showDetails(subgrid_id, row_id) {
        showSubGrid_InventoryList(subgrid_id, row_id, "", "InventoryList");
    }
</script>
```

> **NOTE** *The installation and configuration of* jqGrid *is not discussed here, but it only requires downloading the scripts and referencing them from within the ASP.NET files. The downloadable source code contains the* jqGrid *library and theme.*

SUMMARY

A database can be accessed from many sources and used in a number of different ways. NHibernate has the functionality to support ASP.NET, ASP.NET MVC 3, WCF, WPF, and other types of access. It is important to apply a context for the Session, whether it is a session-per-presenter, a session-per-web-request, or something else, so that the full capabilities of NHibernate can be realized.

INDEX